FAME REVOLUTION

Cover Design: Zachary L. Houghton
Interior Design & Layout: Zachary L. Houghton and Olivier Darbonville

Published by st. john's press
www.stjohnspress.com

For general information and special discounts on bulk purchases, please email info@stjohnspress.com or visit www.stjohnspress.com.

For more information and bulk sales, please email info@stjohnspress.com.

LIBRARY OF CONGRESS CATALOGING-IN-PUBLICATION DATA
Bryhn, Torund
Fame Revolution: New Era. New Strategy to Expand Your Circle of Influence, Wealth, and Impact
The Public Figure Series. Book One: Fame Revolution.

Library of Congress Control Number (LCCN): 2023924051
Paperback ISBN: 978-1-955027-09-0
Hardcover ISBN: 978-1-955027-12-0
E-book ISBN: 978-1-955027-06-9
Audiobook ISBN: 978-1-955027-14-4

First edition: February 2023

Printed and bound in the United States of America.

Ten percent of the proceeds from the sale of the book will go to the Inner Science Research Fund, a nonprofit 501(c)(3) dedicated to funding research on the biological and physiological effects of meditation on the human body, empowering individuals to heal and thrive, www.innerscienceresearch.org

The Public Figure Series.
Book One: Fame Revolution

FAME REVOLUTION

NEW ERA. NEW STRATEGY TO EXPAND YOUR CIRCLE OF INFLUENCE, WEALTH, AND IMPACT

By

TORUND BRYHN

st. john's
press

"In the future, everyone will be world-famous for 15 minutes."

—ANDY WARHOL
American visual artist, film director, producer, and leading figure in the pop art movement.[1]

"The Era of Mass Fame is upon us."

—CHRIS HAYES
American political commentator, television news anchor, activist, and author.[2]

"15 min of Fame is here. Practically everyone on the planet can be famous for real."

—FAB 5 FREDDY
American visual artist, filmmaker, and hip-hop pioneer.[3]

CONTENTS

PART TWO: HOW TO BECOME FAMOUS: THE PUBLIC FIGURE STRATEGY

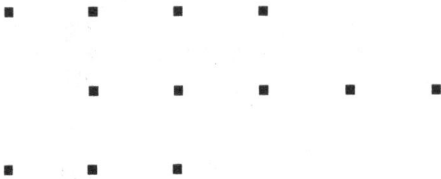

The Fame Revolution,
which paves the way for
the democratization of
fame, beckons you and your
company to be famous for
your work by incorporating
the Public Figure Strategy.
In this fame era, your
unique essence is the
greatest factor for success.

ENTER THE FAME REVOLUTION

> *"I want to go back to when I did not have to be a movie star!"*
>
> **—John Johnson,** CEO of a renewable energy company [1]

HAVE YOU FELT IT? Suddenly, you are expected to be in the spotlight. Meanwhile, your entire life up until now, you have been expected to follow the rules and stay comfortably and quietly behind the scenes.

Business as usual has changed.

The business world has gone personal. With social media and everything being digital, people want more than just products—they want people. Being in the spotlight is about being relatable, building trust, and having real conversations that click. It's a way to show the human side of your business.

For those who can relate, stepping into the public eye might feel as unfamiliar as walking on your hands. Our client, John, a prominent CEO of a new energy company, felt the pressure when an industry association requested a video of him—a written quote was no longer enough. Accustomed to quietly running global B2B companies for over two decades, John suddenly found himself front and center.

---

1 The name of the CEO we worked with has been kept anonymous at their request.

This client is experiencing what I have been observing for years. We are now in the midst of the Fame Revolution, where everyone needs to become famous for what they do.

Fame has been democratized. Before the Fame Revolution, achieving fame was for the few, the political leaders, actors, musicians, and artists with teams of professionals behind them, but the playing field has been leveled. Now, in the world of business, it is no longer enough to let your product speak for itself. Now, you have to be known.

John was uncomfortable with the changes and the new challenges he faced. Gone are the days of ample preparation time, a full production team, and a studio if and when he makes a television appearance. Now, videos are shot on smartphones, with makeshift backdrops, lighting, and limited support.

The loudest voices on social media and reality television might make it seem like everyone is interested in fame, but I can understand the desire to avoid it. Think of fame as a pair of incredibly stylish yet slightly uncomfortable shoes. Sure, they look fabulous and gain attention and compliments, but they can also give you blisters! Some folks would rather skip the fancy shoes and enjoy a quieter, more comfortable stroll through life. The problem with that is if your goal is to grow your business, educate your audience, and, in the best of all circumstances, make a real impact on the world, then you have to be seen and known. You have to put on your dancing shoes.

Traditional press releases and ad campaigns no longer suffice. The spotlight now demands selfies, blogs, and reels that showcase not just your product or service but who you are as a person. You might have encountered a situation where you felt pressured to step in front of the camera at a moment's notice to share your opinions or personal experiences, and it shows that you can no longer rely on crafted corporate communication. You are expected to be more free-flowing and authentic, which can sometimes be harder for those who are used to relying on formulaic business language or talking points.

When relying on dated corporate tactics, marketing your product or service can feel like a black hole, sucking up all your time, money, and resources. That's because in today's world, the aim is not quite right. So, what should we be aiming for in this new Fame Economy?

Surely, factors like supply and demand, budget size, location, and length of time in business will always play a role in a company's success. But with each new era and economic shift comes a fresh approach to connecting with customers, presenting oneself, and doing business. There was a time when ads would boast something as simple as "Soup is good food!" But as mindsets evolve, so must the ways in which business tries to reach them.

HOW DID THE FAME REVOLUTION COME ABOUT?

I noticed that the way of doing business shifted with the COVID-19 pandemic and saw that the strategies once only for the few are now necessary for everyone.

It has been a slow shift over the past fifteen years from Justin Bieber blowing up on YouTube all the way to the endless one-hit wonders on TikTok. However, I believe that the COVID-19 pandemic was the tipping point to the Fame Economy.

I noticed a revolution where fame is democratized. I saw that the strategies I have used in my career to help politicians, celebrities, and musicians become famous are now necessary and useful for business. The strategy for the few—movie stars, rock stars, politicians, and presidential candidates—is now needed for everyone.

What exactly changed with the COVID-19 pandemic?

The way we connect changed. In a world of COVID-19, where face-to-face interaction was often restricted, many of us gravitated toward the online world to fill the gap. I connected with my friends and family, collaborated with colleagues, and even spoke at a national conference, all from behind a computer screen. In many cases, this non-optional push to online connection forced so many people, me included, from behind the camera to in front of the camera. At first, it felt awkward, but we got used to it after a few tries. Even though the COVID-19 pandemic is over now, the normalization of video meetings has forever changed office culture, which has played a significant role in tipping us over to the Fame Economy.

The power of authenticity

We all want the authentic. As the influence of curated public personas began to wane, authenticity took center stage. Many of us experienced this firsthand during the pandemic when we showed up on camera with no makeup or casual clothes. We got to meet our colleagues' children and pets.

These days, showcasing your authentic life, while uncomfortable at first, will help you professionally, as your colleagues or customers will see you as a whole, interesting, relatable person and not just another cog in the machine. And everyone loves relatable!

The emerging trend I saw made me realize that we all need to gain some level of Fame. The same strategies used in Hollywood and Washington D.C. are now becoming useful for everyone.

Fame is no longer for the few. It is for everyone

There are many names to describe the famous. In entertainment, we have talent, artists, and actors. In politics, it's the candidate, senator, or congressman. In business, it often distills down to the title of CEO. To simplify it further, I assert that we should all view ourselves and our companies as public figures.

According to the *Merriam-Webster Dictionary*, a **Public Figure is a "well-known person."**[4] As you will see later in the book, fame is not about crazy fans hunting you down or sex, drugs, and rock 'n' roll. Fame has gotten a reputation challenge. Fame simply means to become known for what you do.

LET'S CUT TO THE CHASE: YOU ARE A PUBLIC FIGURE

The purpose of this book is to guide you, whether you're an individual, entrepreneur, CEO, corporate leader, influencer, or creative professional, through the transformative power of the Fame Revolution. By delving into the evolving landscape of fame, we aim to empower and equip you with the framework to understand that you are a Public Figure and need a Public Figure Strategy. By embracing the power of being a Public Figure, you will see opportunities you did not see before adopting a Public Figure Strategy, thereby maximizing your reach, amplifying your success, and enhancing your overall impact.

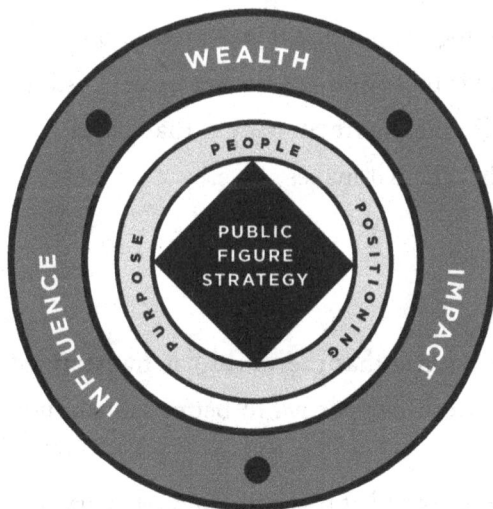

What is the Public Figure Strategy?

The Public Figure Strategy harnesses the collective power of people, purpose, and positioning to transform influence into impactful action.

The concept of a Public Figure Strategy is much like "yin and yang" with strategy as the glue that holds it all together. The Public Figure Strategy combines the human essence of an individual with the metrics-driven nature of business, product, or service.

I like to say:

PUBLIC FIGURE = PRODUCT + PERSON

. . . .

What sets the Public Figure approach apart from other approaches is its focus on understanding the balance between return on investment (ROI) on the balance sheet and nurturing relationships at every level. The Public Figure Strategy is a collaborative fusion of strategy, marketing, and communication with the understanding that being in the spotlight will provide a return on wealth, influence, and impact.

To be in the spotlight is not just about recognition; at its heart, it is an act of service that many times results in a lasting impact. Those who build a legacy with talent and service uplift and serve others. In so doing, they shine brighter and become famous for what they do in such a way that they will inspire and elevate others to gain recognition for their gifts.

Adopting a Public Figure Strategy is not about self-promotion. It's a nuanced shift that expands your visibility and ensures sustained business engagement. The benefit of the Public Figure Strategy is that you do not have to be everywhere. Instead, be where it makes sense.

WHO IS THIS BOOK FOR?

This book is perfect for you if . . .

- You have the gut feeling and a sense that the world has transformed and you're eager to explore a fresh perspective to better sail through life's choppy waters.
- You are curious about how we've arrived at this point and recognize the value of successfully gaining fame for your message to navigate work and life in this new era.
- You are someone who aims to be the best version of yourself and understands the rules of engagement in this economy have changed.

- You are ready to ditch mediocrity and do whatever it takes to thrive—whether it's your passion, story, idea, business venture, service, or product.
- You know that times have changed, and stepping into the spotlight is the quickest way to boost your bottom line.
- You're willing to take risks, stand in the arena, and share your unique gifts.

WHO IS THE BOOK NOT FOR?

This book might not be your cup of tea if . . .

- You are convinced that your achievements, products, or services will magically speak for themselves.
- You do not buy into the idea that individuals can make a real difference.
- You are solely focused on the client, believing that they are the sole source of your potential income, neglecting to see the potential of your circle of influence.
- You see that the facts, figures, and benefits are more important than authenticity when building credibility and expanding your business.
- You are convinced that storytelling is best reserved for bedtime and novels.
- You would rather rely on the good old ways and pass on change.
- You champion formal corporate communication styles.

The Fame Revolution, which paves the way for the democratization of fame, beckons you and your company to be famous for your work by incorporating the Public Figure Strategy. In this fame era, your unique essence is the greatest factor for success.

HOW TO READ THIS BOOK

The book is a compilation of three parts with different vantage points on the Fame Revolution. Each part serves various purposes for you, the reader.

First and foremost, it is not meant to be read in one sitting or sequentially. Some sections are designed to be read once, providing essential knowledge or insights, while others serve as reference points.

"PART ONE: Why Fame Revolution and Why You Are a Public Figure," presents my thesis on why we are in the Fame Revolution and provides an outline of how fame is no longer for the few but for the many. As such, everyone needs to **become famous for what they do** and embrace their new role as public figures. I outline what this means for you as an individual who is a business owner, CEO, or a leader in an organization.

From this point, you have two paths to choose from; if you're eager to explore the practical aspects of becoming a Public Figure, proceed to **"PART TWO: How to Become Famous: The Public Figure Strategy,"** where I outline strategies for public figures and set up operations around them.

Alternatively, if you're interested in a deeper understanding of the pathway to fame, go to **PART THREE: The Exploration of Fame**. In this part, I will show how fame is part of our DNA. In fact, to become famous is integral to our society and culture. It has been a fixation since the times of Ancient Greek philosophers. I will provide a better understanding of fame and what it takes to reach the highest levels mentally, emotionally, and even spiritually.

Intro to me (The author)

Who am I?

I almost forgot to introduce myself. My name is Torund Bryhn, and I am not famous...unless you know me from Kaffebrenneriet on Skovvelen 8 in Oslo, Scottsdale Living Hub, or my favorite café in Scottsdale, JoJo Coffeehouse. You might recognize me if you were part of Senator Hatch's team during the early 2000s or part of the European Association for Communication Directors (EACD) from 2018 - 2020. In certain parts of the energy sector, my name is synonymous with CCS-Safari. You see, I am known in certain circles. If you are not part of those groups, let me introduce myself...I am a Norwegian American who has worked with clients in various industries to help them become famous (known) for what they do. Don't be surprised if I reference my Norwegian roots a few times. Now, I'm taking all of my background in politics, environment, entertainment, and communications plus everything I've learned on my travels and endless unique experiences, connecting the dots and giving you the red thread that weaves through each industry and is the secret sauce for success.

If I'm honest, I would rather not be famous for what I do; I would rather not be 'out there' with high visibility. I have preferred to stay in the background for most of my life, but I can't stay there. Even I must step out and become famous for what I do. As you read on, you will discover what it means to become famous for what you do and how each of us must strategize ourselves as public figures. If an introvert like myself can do it, so can you.

PART 01

Why Fame Revolution and Why You Are a Public Figure

We live in the fame revolution, where it is no longer good enough to entertain and delight the customer but to stand in the limelight, take center stage to promote your product, and inform on an important issue. To be different. To be authentically you.

WHAT IS FAME AND WHY IT SHOULD MATTER TO YOU

In chapter one, we explore the foundations of the "Fame Revolution," offering an overview of the concepts of fame and their significance for your life.

I outline your newly held powers and the consequences of these powers, highlighting some of the key drivers of this transformation.

This chapter further discusses the profound ways in which social status is being redefined, emphasizing the personal relevance of fame to you, the reader.

By understanding the shift in how fame is perceived and its impact on our daily lives, you'll be equipped to identify the type of fame you seek and the considerable influence it wields.

And I touch on the best kind of fame, Luxury Fame.

YOU HAVE GOT THE POWER

> *"The most common way people give up their power is by thinking they do not have any."*
>
> **—Alice Walker,** American novelist, short story writer, poet, and social activist

"I'VE GOT THE POWER!" beat blasts while film icon Jim Carrey strides confidently through the streets of New York in the 2003 blockbuster movie *Bruce Almighty*. Penny Ford's powerful vocals proclaim power in the opening beats of "The Power" by Snap!. At the same time, Jim channels his inner magician by putting all his force and focus on his hands directed toward a fire hydrant. The invisible surge of energy and focus of Jim Carrey's hand causes the water to burst into an eruption of three streams blasting up into the air for what seems to be hundreds of yards.

Seeing his powers burst the fire hydrant, a triumphant Carrey's face shines with the satisfaction of scoring a Super Bowl touchdown. Like a football player who scores, he raises his hands in celebration.

But almost immediately, the realization comes over Jim Carrey; dread, as he looks at what his hands can do. Dread, fear, and amazement intertwines as he contemplates the implications: "I've got the power."

A PARADIGM SHIFT

We are in the midst of a remarkable paradigm shift, a Fame Revolution that turns conventional business practices upside down. Never before have so many people been seen by so many strangers. Today, we can claim our slice of fame, particularly on social media platforms.

Think of the rise of Instagram influencers. In April 2023, Instagram had over 2 billion active users monthly[5] and a staggering 500,000 influencers actively promoting brands and products[6]—not to mention, as of 2022, there are more than 51 million YouTube channels, and the number keeps growing; in 2021, it grew by 36 percent.[7] Even in LinkedIn, individuals strive to stand out, with LinkedIn users nearly doubling from 2017 to 2021.[8]

"Digital technology is so broad today as to encompass almost everything. No product is made today, no person moves today, and nothing is collected, analyzed, or communicated without some 'digital technology' being an integral part of it," states Louis Rossetto, founder, and former editor-in-chief of *Wired* magazine.[9]

> In the Fame Revolution, the good news is that you have got the power to reach the greatest heights all from a smartphone. The bad news is you have got the power and so does everyone else.

SMARTPHONES TRANSFORM

As of May 2023, <u>86 percent of the world's population owns smartphones.</u>[10]

Smartphones have revolutionized our lives. Recently, I was reminded how things have changed. I was ten minutes late to a meeting that I missed on my Google calendar and apologized to the potential client, and she stated, "Well, I rarely am late, thanks to my Day Runner."

I asked, "What is a Day Runner?"

She laughed and claimed that she had a better overview because she was putting all of her tasks and commitment into paper-based personal organizers and a time management system called Day Runner.

Day Runner and other planners like Franklin Covey Planner kept Americans organized until the personal computer and the Internet took over in the mid-1990s. By the 2000s, most planners went in the red, went bankrupt, or sold to private equity. The personal organizers of the 1990s are still available and are now a niche product to accommodate people like my client to be on track and on time with her life, business, and projects.

The world did so many things differently before we had these powerful little gadgets in our lives. Think about the sheer amount of *stuff* people had to carry around so they could listen to music or have family's and friends' contact information on hand. Stacks of newspapers and magazines could be found in any home. To catch up with old classmates, people went to a school reunion, not Facebook. Photos were shot with a camera and then film had to be taken to a shop to be developed and *printed*(!), which took a few days, and then you never knew if the photos would even turn out to be any good!

I became curious about how much more has changed with smartphones, so I asked ChatGPT, another new technology that is in the midst of transforming society.

| SIDENOTE | Smartphones |

1 **Alarm clock:** replaced traditional alarm clocks with built-in alarm and timer functionalities

2 **Banking tools:** transfers, payments, and balance checks

3 **Books:** e-books and audible books

4 **Calculator:** from basic to complex mathematical computations

5 **Calendar:** digital scheduling and reminders

6 **Camera:** high-quality photography and videography

7 **Compass:** digital compasses

8 **Design and graphic tools:** use various apps for graphic design, image editing, and creative artwork

9 **Dictionary/translator:** translate in real-time or define words

10   **Fax machine:** send and receive digital faxes

11   **Film: create** and **edit** moving pictures

12   **Flashlight:** built-in LED flash

13   **GPS device:** for navigation and location-based services

14   **Handheld gaming devices:** play games on the go

15   **Landline telephone:** voice calls and text messaging anytime and anywhere

16   **MP3 player:** replaced traditional music players for music and audio playback

17   **Music creation and production:** use apps to compose, mix, and produce music, simulating instruments, synthesizers, and soundboards

18   **Newsprint:** news and magazine apps

19   **Notepad:** digital notes or making lists

20   **PDA (personal digital assistant):** for organizing personal information, appointments, and notes

21   **Phonebook:** with contacts saved and easily searchable

22   **Physical maps:** replaced with digital maps and navigation apps

23   **Portable audio recorder**: for recording high-quality audio for things like podcasts

24   **Portable video player:** for watching movies and videos on the go

25   **Radio:** FM radio or apps that stream radio

26   **Remote control:** for controlling TVs, ACs, and other devices using infrared or Bluetooth

27   **Scanner:** using the camera and apps to digitize documents

28   **Stopwatch:** included in many clock apps

29   **Travel tickets:** e-tickets and boarding passes on apps

30   **Voice recorder:** for recording voice memos

31   **Watch:** for timekeeping and timers

32   **Weather forecast device:** with weather apps providing real-time updates[11]

At first, ChatGPT came up with thirty items and agreed to add two more upon my suggestion, that is, you can record and edit videos, so we ended up with thirty-two main things that have been replaced by the mobile phone. Thirty-two-plus businesses have had to change, accommodate, and transform to meet the digital era.

As a Generation Xer, the change has been a tremendous upheaval of life of ease and a new way of living. We are digital immigrants who went from paper to desktop computer to laptop, ditching our cameras to take photos on the phone, making video shorts, and even editing them on our smartphones. When it comes to music, we started with LPs, then had cassette tapes listening on our Walkman, to transforming all our tapes to CDs, only to discover a few years later, the MP3s and the power of downloading all the music we could for 'free' from Napster to now paying a monthly subscription to listen to all our music on Spotify.

When explaining the magnitude of this global transformation to Sage Toomey, my Gen-Z colleague, her response was, "Well, that just made your life easier."

No!

Hell, no!

While all of the things that have come to be eventually made parts of life more convenient, I am still a digital immigrant. I had to go through each of the developments and learn them, adapting each time to whatever technology overtook the last. I did not grow up at the speed of video games and hypertext. I didn't have a library in my pocket as a child. My Gen-Z colleague has been networked for her entire life!

All that having been said, smartphones are fantastic devices. They make it easier to connect with your loved ones, make your job easier, remember things for you, and even make you seem smarter, with all the answers right at your fingertips. I am excited to see what is yet to come.

When I saw for the first time that 86 percent of the world's population did not just have a regular mobile phone, but a smartphone, I was astounded and asked a few friends at a personal development workshop about their views. One of them said, "A homeless person will have nothing of value, but a smartphone." Everyone nodded in agreement, and a woman chimed in, recounting that in Uganda, local tour guides would have the latest smartphone, yet live in dilapidated houses. Their number one investment was having that phone.

Essentially, most of the world's citizens can be their own publishing house, with easy apps to design colorful posts and videos, creating an impression that can elicit millions of followers. In your own hands, you have a media company, a publishing company, and even a fully operational department in a corporation. You can close sales, write, and sign contracts, send invoices, and hold video meetings. Many influencers talk about how they operate an entire company from their pocket.

I know from my own life that I can run my business by taking a video call while walking in the park, faxing necessary documents, signing contracts, setting up calendar meetings, and waking up in the morning to the alarm on my Google Pixel 6.0 phone. I have an analog alarm clock, and when I am really nervous about getting up for travel or an overseas meeting with a client, I will put this on as backup. After COVID-19, with the ease and acceptance of video conferencing, travel has decreased, and I can now live full-time in the United States while having clients in Europe. I just get up at 5:00 a.m. to accommodate their schedule.

YOU ARE A MEDIA CONGLOMERATE

As I like to say, each individual has the power to be what I call a media conglomerate.

In the past, only big corporations with deep pockets and connections could create and distribute media content. However, in the age of smartphones, social media, and digital platforms, anyone can become a media conglomerate.

> Being a media conglomerate means being at the forefront of shaping narratives, influencing opinions, and driving conversations that impact society.

Traditionally, a media conglomerate has been a company that owns numerous companies involved in mass media enterprises, such as music, television, radio, publishing, motion pictures, theme parks, or the Internet. **In a nontraditional sense, however, a media conglomerate could be defined as any individual or organization that has built a significant media presence or influence across multiple platforms and channels.**

Why you are a media conglomerate?

You have the tools: With your smartphone, you possess a powerful media creation and distribution device. You can capture high-quality photos and videos, edit them with free or low-cost apps, and share them with the world on social media or video-sharing platforms like YouTube.

You have the platforms: Social media platforms such as Facebook, Instagram, and X provide massive audiences for your content. With just a few clicks, you can connect with followers, build a brand, and gain influence.

You have the control: Gone are the days of waiting for traditional media gatekeepers to provide you with a platform. You can create your own content, distribute it on your terms, and control your message and brand.

You have the potential: The rise of the Fame Revolution means anyone can become an influencer, content creator, or celebrity. You do not need a TV show or a book deal to build a following and make an impact.[12]

Using the term "media conglomerate" to describe your phone may sound over the top, but I'm using it to make you see that times have changed. Your potential is greater than ever. Today, you can create an empire on a shoestring budget and scale up without losing control or making massive investments.

Don't sell yourself short. You have the power to create, distribute, and influence media content just like a traditional media conglomerate. All you need is your smartphone, some creativity, and a little bit of hustle. The era of the Fame Revolution has arrived, and you can be a part of it.

In a world where "likes" and "follows" are currency, using technology to get your name out is the obvious tool for becoming known. It's the magic megaphone that lets your products, services, talents, and quirks reverberate through the digital cosmos, reaching corners you never thought possible. The digital stage awaits with its pixelated spotlight. So, prepare to surf the waves of algorithms and hashtags because, in this high-tech age, **fame isn't just knocking on your door—it is sending you a friend request!**

A MEDIA CONGLOMERATE UNFOLDS: MARIE FORLEO

"Everything is figureoutable."

When you think of the words "multimillionaire" and "media mogul," you might imagine someone like Oprah Winfrey or Rupert Murdoch. But have you heard of Marie Forleo?

Marie Forleo is the ultimate modern-day media maven who used all her resources to become a modern-day media conglomerate. She's an entrepreneur, author, and speaker who has built a significant media presence and personal brand. And she's done it all without owning a traditional media outlet.

Marie started her journey with a few jobs, including working on the trading floor of the New York Stock Exchange. In 2001, she established an online newsletter and gained subscribers and coaching clients from relationships she formed while bartending and instructing fitness and dance classes and, in 2008, wrote a book called *Make Every Man Want You*. The book was her break and she maximized this opportunity to launch an online coaching brand and quickly became a leading voice in entrepreneurship, personal development, and marketing[13].

Through her website, YouTube channel, podcast, and online courses, Marie has built a following of millions of fans. She's even created a number of successful business ventures, including B-School, an online business training program, and MarieTV, a web-based talk show focused on entrepreneurship and personal growth.

Marie calls herself a "multi-passionate entrepreneur," and it shows in her content. She incorporates her love for music, dance, spirituality, fitness, psychology, and even philanthropy into everything she does.

But what makes Marie truly exceptional is her commitment to authenticity and helping others. As she puts it, "The world needs that special gift that only you have." Through her personal brand and content creation, Marie has shown that you don't need to be a traditional media mogul to make a significant impact. You need a phone, Internet connection, and a great idea.

So, if you're looking for inspiration to start your own media empire, look no further than Marie Forleo. As she says, "The key to creating more wealth, happiness, and success in your life is to simply be more of who you truly are."

LIVING IN THE FAME REVOLUTION

We live in the Fame Revolution, where it is no longer good enough to simply entertain and delight the customer. You must also stand in the limelight, take center stage to promote your product, and inform on an important issue. To be different. To be authentically you.

The Fame Economy focuses on the person's talent and power to communicate on a human level the differentiation of the product, service, or company authentically and transparently. **The person, not the product or service, drives sales or expansion of the company or organization.**

The person takes center stage by informing, educating, and interacting on the differentiation of a company, product, or service. Recognizing that the person is the central vehicle to drive sales and success.

This is the economy Andy Warhol foresaw more than fifty years ago when he stated, "In the future, everyone will be world-famous for 15 minutes."

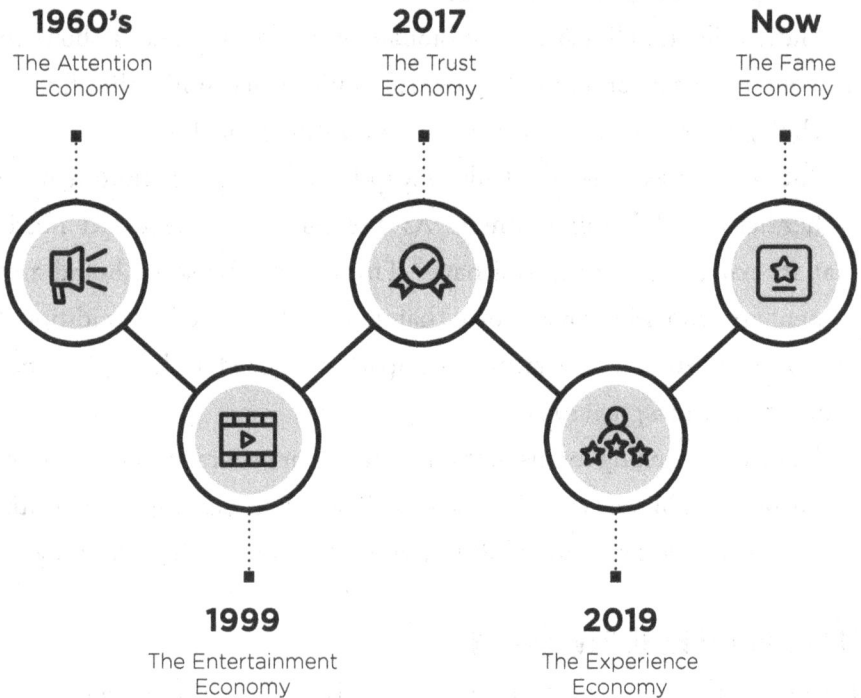

1960's
The Attention
Economy

2017
The Trust
Economy

Now
The Fame
Economy

1999
The Entertainment
Economy

2019
The Experience
Economy

SIDENOTE	**"Evolving through Economies: Decoding Our Era"**

Over the past twenty years, theorists have proposed various economic models to reflect shifting societal and business values. Rather than fixed blueprints, these frameworks help us adapt to our changing times.

The Attention Economy of the late 1960s, coined by Nobel Laureate Herbert A. Simon, championed the significance of capturing focus in an increasingly distracting world. But today, fleeting attention has given way to the quest for enduring influence.[14]

The Entertainment Economy, as coined by Michael J. Wolf in 1999, highlighted the ubiquity of entertainment in shaping consumer behavior. Entities, even traditional ones like Citibank, now integrate entertainment to enhance customer engagement.[15]

With social media, **the Thank You Economy** by Gary Vaynerchuk entered center stage in 2011, stating that the dynamics between businesses and customers have forever shifted and emphasizing authentic relationships, customer-centricity, and the importance of saying thank you to build a company culture, that also leads to substantial growth and engagement.

The Trust Economy, introduced by Philipp Kristian Diekhöner in 2017, emphasized the role of trust in business, with technologies like AI and blockchain amplifying its significance.[16]

Around the same period, **the Experience Economy**, articulated in 2019 by Joseph Pine II and James H. Gilmore emphasized crafting memorable, emotionally charged experiences to deepen customer loyalty.[17]

And I would assert that today we are in **the Fame Economy**. In this era, the ultimate currency is to be recognized for what you do, a culmination of various economies before it.

To truly achieve fame, one must capture attention like in the Attention Economy, spice it with elements of entertainment like the Entertainment Economy, connect and honor our relationships on all levels by saying Thank You, craft memorable experiences reminiscent of the Experience Economy. and foster trust as highlighted in the Trust Economy.

In essence, fame today requires a multifaceted approach, blending attention, entertainment, experience, trust, and gratitude.

YOU HAVE THE POWER, AND
SO DOES EVERYONE ELSE

66 | *"Today, average is officially over."*

—Thomas Friedman, three-time Pulitzer Prize–
winning journalist and author of *The World Is Flat*

"EVERYTHING'S CHANGED," declared the man beside me, leaning in over a coffee table, surrounded by five others. A mix of physiques—some with muscles popping from every angle, others lean but fit. Taking a closer peek, and tuning into their chatter, it became evident: they were law enforcement. A few donned workout gears, some in plainclothes, and one—probably a private investigator—sported handcuffs on his belt. Their shared frustration was unmistakable. They discussed the need to differentiate themselves from other units. Their tried-and-true methods of showcasing their skills and teaching others felt outdated. They believed in their team's excellence, yet it seemed their superiors weren't paying attention.

In today's world brimming with talent, just doing your job right is the baseline. Carla Harris, best-selling author and senior client advisor at investment banking company Morgan Stanley, puts it bluntly: "Merely ticking off your tasks doesn't guarantee upward mobility or, in some scenarios, even job security. Today's professional arena craves something extra: differentiation."

THE ESSENCE OF DIFFERENTIATION

Consider differentiation as the distinct imprint of your professional identity. Within the corporate sphere, it's the distinctive value, insight, or expertise you offer that differentiates you from the ensemble—be it an inventive approach to challenges, standout leadership, niche expertise, or a knack for knitting teams together. It's what sets you apart in a sea of equally dedicated professionals.

To become a respected figure in which people are willing to invest in, certain values must be delivered and your authority needs to be established. By positioning yourself as an expert in your industry, you will cultivate trust among your audience.

Having authority grants you greater influence over others' opinions and behaviors. When you are perceived as an authority in your field, your audience is more likely to heed your recommendations, such as trying new methods, products, or services. You become a reliable source of information and a trusted expert.

Just a few years ago, you could skate by as just another average Joe or Jane. But those days are gone. Now you're competing with the entire world.

But that also means you can work with the entire world. You can hire a virtual assistant in the Philippines, a designer in Serbia, and a writer in Australia. We live in a nearly borderless world, vying for attention with everything we do.

Thomas Friedman, the futurist, talked about the world becoming flat way back in 2005. But it wasn't until recently, with systems like Fiverr, 99designs, and Venmo, that we saw the world truly come together like one big global village. And then COVID-19 surprised us by confining us to our homes, and as a result, we all got familiar with videoconferencing. No more in-person meetings? No problem! Webinars in Australia, conferences in Norway, and client meetings from our living rooms became the new normal.

SO, WHAT EXACTLY HAS CHANGED?

We are competing with the world. With the Internet and the omnipresence of smartphones, you are now competing not only with your local town, state, and country but with the entire world.

We are competing for attention. Every two days now, we create as much information as we did from the dawn of civilization up until 2003, according to Eric Schmidt, the former CEO of Google.[18]

We are being transformed by technology. Today, we are witnessing a transformative shift that is redefining human interaction and visibility. The advent of cutting-edge technologies such as AI, robotics, and blockchain are radically reshaping various sectors, creating a seismic shift toward automation. *However, while these technologies reduce the need for human intervention in many tasks, at the same time, they elevate the importance of personal recognition and visibility.*

SOME THOUGHTS ABOUT AI, ROBOTICS, AND THE NEXT PHASE OF TECHNOLOGY

With AI-powered systems executing tasks in a few minutes that once took weeks, the human element is no longer defined by task execution. Instead, it's being redefined by unique contributions, creative thinking, and personal influence.

Moreover, the ubiquity of smartphones is propelling this revolution into overdrive. This allows almost everyone to have an open channel to the world at their fingertips. The smartphone revolution has facilitated the birth of an increasingly interconnected global village, providing unprecedented opportunities for individuals to build personal brands, share their ideas, and engage with a global audience. The widespread access to smartphones means that people are not only competing with those in their immediate vicinity but also with individuals across the globe, so standing out is more important than ever.

The emerging AI, robotics, and blockchain revolution require human proof. AI has the ability to write, edit, and design content, streamlining various tasks. Blockchain technology ensures transparency and integrity in the digital realm. Meanwhile, robots are revolutionizing industries, making operations more efficient. It's a fascinating time where machine technology is flooding platforms, blurring the lines between what is real and what is not, and also creating many potential problems.

Scott A. Martin, author of *Groundswell*, states on my podcast *Become Famous* that with AI saturating information channels, **there will be a heightened need for trust in the information we share.** This implies a greater emphasis on the human touch, validating our authenticity and building trust.

Reflecting on Martin's comment took me back to when my mentor, *The Wall Street Journal* best-selling author and renowned marketing strategist known for *The New Rules of Marketing & PR* and *Fanocracy* David Meerman Scott, reviewed my LinkedIn profile. When I contemplated omitting my work history, he advised against it.

He emphasized its value in demonstrating my accomplishments and, in essence, verifying my existence in a world increasingly influenced by AI. We might not know the full extent of AI's future impact, but one certainty is its potential to intensify competition. Those adept at harnessing its capabilities, like using prompts, will undoubtedly have a competitive edge.

Marc Cloosterman, founder of VIM Group and author of *Future Proof Your Brand*, believes that as competition evolves, the way we use social media might shift. He sees a future where closed, private groups become more popular to keep conversations human and free from AI interference. According to him, these groups could become a key strategy in managing AI's growing influence. While we're using AI's benefits now, it's clear that the future is unpredictable. But one thing is certain: we can use these tools wisely now, and those who don't might find themselves left behind.

The bottom line is that you are competing with the world for attention, navigating the changing landscape of technology. Either ride the looming wave of the Fame Revolution or risk being drowned by it.

WHAT IS FAME REVOLUTION
AND WHAT DOES FAME HAVE
TO DO WITH YOU?

> *"The gatekeepers don't control the gates, and the powers that be aren't as powerful."*
>
> —**G-Eazy,** an American Rapper

FOR THOSE OF YOU who don't know life prior to the Internet and social media, I offer you this perspective from Kalev Leetaru of Forbes.com:

> "In the era before social media, the path to fame was largely through elite gatekeepers that corralled would-be celebrities through activities like intellectual competitions, athletics, fashion, and similar pursuits.
>
> The rise of reality television added a new dimension, that of outrageous behavior and attention seeking, but even this was still mediated through broadcast decency laws and the desire of networks not to push the envelope too far.
>
> In the social media era, the role of these gatekeepers has been washed away, replaced with self-service fame in which anyone can leap from obscurity to global prominence on their own volition."[19]

The fame era is not just a passing trend, but a profound societal shift. With 4.9 billion people or more than half of the world's population using social media in 2023, the potential reach is phenomenal.[20] As we lean into this future, the value of personal visibility and recognition will only continue to grow. The revolution is here, and it's time for us to step into the spotlight.

WHAT DOES THE FAME REVOLUTION MEAN FOR YOU?

To thrive in the Fame Revolution, you must be front and center in promoting your company, product, or service, showcasing your personality, beliefs, and values. You need to embrace the Public Figure Strategy for you and your company.

It turns out that we are all stars in our own stories. It's more than being a movie star; it's being the hero of your story, understanding that everything you do matters in its own way. It is the millimeter mindset shift that can significantly impact you and your business. It's about transitioning from having your product or service as the face of your company to YOU becoming the face of your company, embracing that as the Public Figure leading the way, you are the star of the story. You are the main character.

Fame often starts when a person's talent, skill, achievement, or intriguing personality or story captures widespread attention. While fleeting attention may result from a one-hit-wonder event, **true fame is established when a person becomes widely known and recognized.** This can happen through a single viral event or years of dedicated investment. This is the kind of fame that comes with being a respected voice with knowledge and expertise.

What fame is not? Fame is <u>not celebrity,</u> and fame is <u>not being an influencer.</u>

It's essential to distinguish between celebrity, influencer, and fame. Author Jo Piazza, in her book *Celebrity Inc.*, defines **celebrity** as a commodity bought and sold by fans. **Influencers,** on the other hand, are paid by companies to promote products on social media. And **fame,** in its purest sense, is different from both celebrity and influencer, in that it focuses on visibility to a target audience on which a person has made a lasting impact.

Historically, fame was associated with glory and honor, and those who pursued it aimed to leave a mark on the world that would be remembered for generations. Historian Douglass Adair eloquently states, **"Fame has to be earned. Fame can never be a gift; it cannot be inherited; it must be won by a person who imposes their will, their ideas, for good or ill, upon history in such a way that they will always be remembered."**

Today, the pursuit of fame is no longer limited to a select few; social media, the Internet, and easily accessible publishing platforms have made it accessible to all.

Fame Revolution is changing the influencer industry as we know it. **"The influencer industry's core business is continually reassessing, redefining, and reevaluating authenticity,"** states Emily Hund, author of *The Influencer Industry*. With the breakdown of the financial crisis in 2008, the influencer industry grew exponentially. Traditional gatekeepers and experts waned, while regular folks with no degrees or expertise began to rise and shine by connecting with followers and selling products based on their experiences.

Influencer Levels

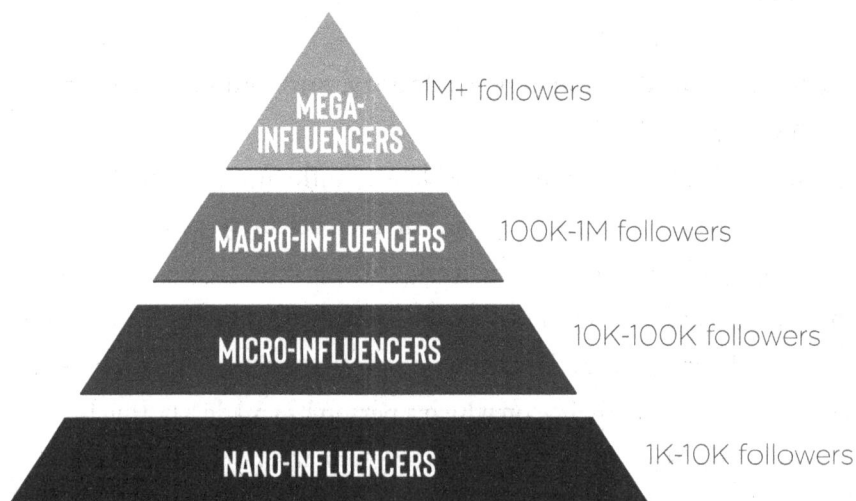

MEGA-INFLUENCERS — 1M+ followers

MACRO-INFLUENCERS — 100K-1M followers

MICRO-INFLUENCERS — 10K-100K followers

NANO-INFLUENCERS — 1K-10K followers

Emily Hund sees influencers becoming more formalized and possibly being viewed as entertainers, getting a SAG card (proof that you are a member of the world's largest labor union, the Screen Actors Guild; cards must be earned by performers, often through years of work), or forming their own association. At the same time, author Kelly Keenan of *Everyone Is an Influencer* sees the definition and meaning to continue to evolve.

Both are right. Some influencers such as the mega influencers might get more formalized as they can be viewed as celebrities being known everywhere, while the smaller influencers will not.

I recall being on TikTok, where one TikToker angrily exclaimed that everyone is an influencer. He is right. After the pandemic, it became evident that everyone can exert influence online, and an indication of this has been the proliferation of affiliate marketing.

Between 2018 and 2021, the affiliate industry has seen 47 percent growth, cementing itself as a go-to channel for many retailers. Regular folks with a few followers can sell products with their endorsement.

The idea that "everybody is an influencer" indicates that everyone should strive to become famous for what they do.

Influencer versus fame

In the landscape of fame, there's a fascinating distinction that has emerged: the line between being famous and being an influencer. Both are in the spotlight, but the paths they walk are quite different.

Being famous is about being known for your skills or talents—it could be your way with words, a knack for fixing cars, leading a nonprofit, skill in selling houses, or flair for creating standout conferences. Whatever your area of expertise, fame is that nod of recognition you get for doing it well.

Meanwhile, **influencers leverage their popularity of followers with sponsorships or affiliate marketing deals**—whether influencing with their fashion sense, enchanting with culinary skills, or inspiring with fitness dedication.

Emily Hund describes an influencer **as someone who is not an expert yet can sell a product or service without being deemed certified**, that is, selling health supplements based on the personal experience that they work. Essentially, the influencer's true skill is selling authenticity and personal experience.

On the other hand, fame comes to those who shine for their field-specific achievements. It can certainly result in profit, but the core of the recognition comes from a person's expertise. Influencers are chameleon-like, blending with current events and trends, coming forward to cash in on their visibility.

In the grand scheme of recognition, influencers have their time and place, but fame is a legacy of substance and expertise that withstands the test of time. Fame is not just about being seen—it's about being remembered.

YOU ARE THE ARBITER, AND SO IS EVERYONE ELSE

> *"Hail, Caesar, those who are about to die salute thee."*
>
> **—Suetonius**, a Roman biographer known for *'De vita Caesarum'* (About the Life of the Caesars), commonly known as *The Twelve Caesars*

So, YOU HAVE GOT THE POWER, and so does everyone else. This means that your greatest differentiator is you, and the gatekeepers as we have known them are a thing of the past.

YOU ARE LIKE CAESAR

"Friends, Romans, countrymen, lend me your ears!"

—Julius Caesar

The message and image masters of the past do not have the power they once did. You have the power as the receptor of the message, and like Caesar at the arena, you have a say in deciding whether those messages live or die. Caesar communicated his decision of whether a gladiator would die that day by turning his thumb up, down, or sideways. Your sovereign social media audience will decide the relevance, popularity, and longevity of your content by giving it a thumbs up, commenting, sharing, or just scrolling by.

The even greater challenge is that it is all in real-time; there is no time to prepare a proper response.

WHEN REAL-TIME CAME

It was just another day, but it was also the day that everything changed. The day the world went real-time. Before that day, we had to rely on newspapers, TV broadcasts, and other traditional media outlets to get our news and information. We could only hear about what had happened after it had happened, and often with a delay of hours or even days. But on July 15th, 2007, something new arrived: X. And with it, the power of real-time information sharing.[21]

Suddenly, anyone with a smartphone and an Internet connection could share their thoughts, opinions, and updates with the world in real time. And everyone else could see what was happening, as it happened.

Suddenly anyone could be the arbiter as there was no time for the gatekeeper to stop the opinion from being aired on X. It was exhilarating, exciting, and sometimes terrifying. We could see events unfolding as they occurred, from natural disasters and political protests to celebrity scandals and viral memes.

But with this power came new challenges. How could we know what was true and what was false? How could we avoid getting caught up in the frenzy of the moment, only to regret it later? The speed and scale of real-time information sharing can be overwhelming, and it can be difficult to keep up with the constant flow of updates and notifications. As Eric Schmidt, Google's former CEO, stated, **"The Internet is the first thing that humanity has built that humanity doesn't understand, the largest experiment in anarchy that we have ever had."**

Perfect real-time reaction

Some have been generous in using real-time to their advantage. Oreo and its marketing agency 360i seized the moment during the unexpected power outage at Super Bowl XLVII (47); they swiftly posted on X a solitary picture of an Oreo in the darkness, accompanied by the tagline, "You can still dunk in the dark." The event marked the significant emergence of real-time marketing on a grand scale. It was the perfect reaction, one that will remain etched in the public's memory for a long time.

THE GATEKEEPERS ARE STILL RELEVANT AND GROWING

In the digital era, news has not only maintained its relevance but has also seen a remarkable surge in viewership, with leading platforms like *The New York Times* (*NYT*) achieving a staggering 70 million unique monthly visitors, a testament to the enduring appetite for quality journalism. Reinforcing this notion, The Guardian Media Group has reported substantial growth, drawing 82 million unique browsers globally, of which 39 million are from the United States alone.

The median age of newsreaders is forty-two, with a gender split of 54 percent male and 46 percent female in the United States, indicating a mature audience still dominates traditional news consumption.[22] However, the landscape is rapidly changing, especially among younger audiences. A quarter of people under thirty are now turning to platforms like TikTok for their daily news fix.

Mainstream media and outlets like that still have influence but not as much as they used to be. They were the main arbiters of taste and news but are now sharing the stage with the main arbiter—the public.

Bow to the new arbiter: you

There is a new arbiter in town, and it is you and everyone else. It is no longer possible to put lipstick on a pig and have it pass muster. The public will ridicule it. Before, a CEO or company would have time to brush up on the image and have the media's support to control the message, but that is no longer possible.

Molly McPherson, author, crisis management and PR expert, TikTok's 'PR Lady,' and 2023 Adweek Creative Visionary Award Winner, states that cancel culture is the public not accepting foul behavior. She states on X, "The cancel culture is not an excuse. I repeat—this term is not an excuse, especially for abhorrent behavior. Replace **'I am a victim of a cancel culture'** with, **'This is a consequence of my own doing.'**"

Molly McPherson states that cancel culture is about taking ownership if you do something wrong. It can be that simple unless it has been a grave consequence.

Will Justin Timberlake be forgiven by the public for having used Britney Spears to further his career as asserted in Britney's memoir? She wrote that his breakout song as a solo artist, "Cry Me a River," was written about her having an affair when the reality is that Justin had the affair and broke up with her via text message.

Not sure.

If Justin went out and recanted and said sorry, he might be forgiven.

But, at the same time, does this scandal about Justin have the power it once had?

What is interesting is that I got the news about Justin on TikTok and told a friend of mine; as a fellow NSYNC fan, she surprisingly had not heard the news. She does not have a X or a TikTok account and even though it spilled over to the tabloids, it was competing with other news stories and did not have the impact it would have pre-pandemic.

THE STING OF CANCEL CULTURE IS WANING

In an instant, you can be the viral star of the day, and in an instant, you can be canceled. But the sting is not as widespread as it used to be. I was reminded of this when Matthew Perry from the television show *Friends* passed away. I was surprised at how sad I was and lamented to my team, but no one had heard the news or had even been interested. It is not like it used to be when we were glued to the 7:00 p.m. or 11:00 p.m. news, and we all gathered around the watercooler the following day to recount our reaction to the news or share our reactions to the latest episodes of *Cheers, Friends,* or *Seinfeld.* Today, sports remains one of the few cultural references with the power to unite people. The culture has been broken into thousands of pieces.

We are all judged

In the digital era, online rating systems have become an integral part of our lives, helping consumers make informed choices about their purchases and services. For brands, the importance of receiving high customer ratings is obvious, though it places considerable influence in the hands of consumers.

What I found surprising was being rated myself. I got a coupon and tried Dazzling Cleaners. The lady came and did a great job cleaning my home. When I inspected what she had done, I complimented her and gave her a 20-percent tip. She accepted the tip, and when she was about to leave, my judge concluded, "I have decided to give you a five-star rating."

I felt exposed and realized the power of hiring is a two-way street. The person who hires a service gets rated as much as the one providing it. Having a five-star rating will get you better service and demonstrates the intricacies of one side no longer having control.

Today's feedback is a two-way street, with businesses rating their customers. Platforms like Airbnb and Uber introduced us to "scoring" guests and passengers, making feedback into a mutual exchange. These ratings can have a significant impact on our daily lives. Drivers may refuse to pick you up, and hosts can deny your stay in their vacation home.

We are all arbiters in all areas of life, from shopping on Amazon to taking Lyft/Uber to liking, sharing, or commenting on Facebook posts— we can put our thumbs up or thumbs down. The difference from the time of Caesar is that while we are the arbiter like Caesar, someone else is Caesar judging us.

REFLECTIONS ON ADDITIONAL FAME REVOLUTION CHANGES
(for the digital immigrants)

> *"It was the best of times, it was the worst of times."*
>
> —**Charles Dickens,** British author who penned the beloved classics *Oliver Twist,* *A Christmas Carol, David Copperfield,* and *A Tale of Two Cities*

This section is for the digital immigrants brought up with rules, corporate hierarchy, and gatekeepers with expectations to be behind the scenes. If you are impatient and want to go to the next section, do so. This section is to provide a deeper context to what has changed.

PERSONALLY, I AM AMAZED at how much of society has changed since I was a kid, and vowed to myself not to be like my grandmother and say, "I remember when I was young . . ."

And more and more frequently, to my utter chagrin, I have become my grandmother and keep reminding my younger Millennial and Gen-Z colleagues of how it used to be.

There is a part of me that retells the past to remind myself how much has changed to give me grace.

And I am keeping this for you, the digital immigrant, to remind you how much has changed and how much we have done to adjust and to give grace.

No Rules

"There are no rules,"

—Sage Toomey, entrepreneur and TikTok influencer

When I met Sage at the Scottsdale Living Hub where I have my office, we ended up having long conversations about TikTok, entrepreneurship, and success. She is a Gen-Zer and empathically states that her compatriots are disenfranchised with society: the few who are deciding now to go to college do not want a nine-to-five job and want to own their time while making a living. And she is right—there are no rules in making money. And these members of Gen-Z who are breastfed on social media, know intuitively about fame, influence branding, and making a mark online—a new generation of self-made millionaires.

The pandemic brought a new era of work. The traditional progression of the corporate ladder has given way to a new way of life in our rapidly changing world. Success is no longer only achieved by relentless hard work and following the rules. Gig work, remote work, and an emphasis on flexibility are changing work and life. Being willing to embrace change and challenge conventional wisdom makes way for exploring new skills, experiences, and opportunities. Agility and open-mindedness are new paths toward success.

Side hustles are increasingly becoming the norm. And nearly two-thirds of Gen-Z has started, or plan to start, their own business and use social media to turn their side hustles into seven-figure empires.

Take for example a Tik Tok influencer like Stone Fredrikson. He started when he was ten years old, and now at age nineteen has a thriving six-figure income and teaches digital immigrants like me to make a living on TikTok. He runs two 150K+ accounts on TikTok and is obsessed with helping people grow, become successful, and learn about everything. At nineteen!

This is a perfect example of the Fame Economy. Stories like Stone's are the ways the world has been turned upside down.

The era of prescriptive norms has given way to authenticity and personal touch. Traditional rules have been upended. Instead of fitting into predefined roles, there's now an emphasis on individuality. The new narrative champions storytelling and brand ideals as the driving forces in our approach to marketing and engaging with clients or customers.

No rules for communicating at the office

The new remote office environment caused by the pandemic has revolutionized how we communicate in business at all levels. The business lexicon, like any living language, adapts, and the business jargon, just like any language, evolves to reflect the changing times and sentiments over time. Not so long ago, corporate communication was defined by its formal tone and prescriptive language. However, it is clear that the prescriptive corporate language is being replaced by a more casual/personal communication style. The ignitor for this change is not merely stylistic but is rooted in the very fabric of modern business dynamics.

We are more discerning. Whether you are an investor, employee, or consumer, you are more discerning than ever. **We all crave genuine engagement, looking beyond superficial promises. The formulaic, boilerplate corporate statements of the past no longer cut it.** In this age, organizations are quickly realizing the undeniable value of being real. We are scanners. We are inundated with an unprecedented volume of information, leading to a phenomenon aptly termed "information overwhelm." This saturation has prompted a shift in how we consume content. Just to give a few statistics:

- **The average American office worker now receives over 200 emails a day.**[23]
- **A majority of these emails, about 61.9 percent, are read on a smartphone.**[24]

- An audience typically gives sixty seconds of attention to a long-form document, 11.1 seconds to an email, 7.4 seconds to a resume, and roughly five seconds to a text.[25]

Given this reality, crafting messages that cater to such limited attention spans has become paramount. No longer are we patient readers; we are swift scanners. Short-form content, visuals, videos, and succinct text—especially optimized for mobile platforms—is now the gold standard.

We are all shaping the company narrative. The democratization of corporate communication has also been pivotal. Gone are the days when communication was a rigid, hierarchical structure, descending from the upper echelons of management. Modern businesses are championing the voices of their employees. Employees are not just clocking in hours. They're shaping the narrative, telling stories, and making brands come alive.

Diversity in communication? Non-negotiable. We are not a one-size-fits-all world. We're talking to a global audience with diverse perspectives and voices and the corporate voice is reflecting that.

Transparency has become non-negotiable. The digital realm acts as a perpetual magnifying glass, where every slip is readily visible to the global audience. The shift isn't just about being transparent but is about crafting a meaningful dialogue with authenticity at the center.

What's the bottom line?

As businesses, we've got to dig deep. It is not just about numbers anymore. Stakeholders want to know what we stand for and what we're all about. It's less about fiscal performance and more about intent, purpose, and commitment.

> *A stakeholder is someone who cares about or is affected by a company or Public Figure, such as investors, employees, customers, suppliers, communities, governments, or trade groups.*

NEED TO MANAGE ON AND OFF(LINE)

"You are an analog girl, living in a digital world."
—**Neil Gaiman,** English author

We are one persona with two parts: digital and physical
We are digital, where we unfold on screens through social media. It is where we connect, share, like, tweet, and create our digital footprints.

We have our physical life—the tangible, the face-to-face interactions, the real-world experiences.

Both these lives, digital and physical, are interconnected yet distinct, shaping our identities and how we perceive and interact with the world around us. Recognizing and navigating both these identities is crucial in this modern era.

I was confronted with the need for digital persona during my job hunt in 2008. A career coach insisted on the importance of establishing a robust LinkedIn presence and building a network of over 500 connections. Until then, I used to hand-deliver my resume, printed on high-quality paper, and this personal touch would often result in job offers. Now, to get a job, I was reduced to a number and a name on the screen.

The challenge was how to differentiate myself in the online world. After a while, I got the hang of it and actively utilized LinkedIn as a vehicle for various companies to build their online presence. Eventually, my highly detailed profile caught the attention of a recruiter at Tesla, who was looking for someone to lead a division of 350 people in Scandinavia. Even though I was turned down after the second interview due to my lack of experience managing such a large team, the fact that my LinkedIn profile alone had attracted Tesla's attention was a victory.

The power of the on and off (line) community

After the pandemic, we might think that everything is happening online. Not so. Half of Americans still prefer to shop in person but have accepted that sometimes it is easier to shop online. E-commerce sales increased 25 percent during the COVID-19 pandemic. Currently, 57 percent of global consumer spending is online and 41 percent of the Americans shop online at least once per week. As of January 6, 2023, 90 percent of the shoppers believe they can find better deals online than in a store.[26]

Stranded in Utah due to the COVID-19 pandemic, Zoom became my lifeline to stay connected with family, friends, and community in Norway. It also allowed me to expand my business and I got used to getting up early to serve my clients in Europe. After spending two years in the southwest with most of my interactions online and knowing I wanted to settle in Arizona, I decided to engage locally and become not just a digital civic citizen, so I took up an office at the Scottsdale Living hub. The experience of connecting with people in person was a powerful reminder that I had overlooked. Although I have traveled and met many people during and after the COVID-19 era, the power of personal connection cannot be overestimated.

An excellent example of the integration of the physical and the digital is Scottsdale Living, founded by Gen-Xer John Doering, businessowner of a real-estate agency, 4SaleArizona. John truly grasps the dynamic power of an integrated online–offline strategy. Amid the COVID-19 pandemic, his online Facebook group flourished, growing to 47,000 members with one of the most engaged groups on Facebook. Originally conceived to generate leads, the initiative blossomed into something far greater. Today, the group has several subgroups, including a paid business group with 2,100 members.

John's success is deeply rooted in collaboration, fostering profound relationships and a commitment to active service. At the heart of his strategy lies a dynamic Facebook group, which acts as a pivotal communication and interaction point. Beyond the digital, John has established a physical hub, allowing members to meet and further deepen their connections. Through various events—spanning both digital and in-person platforms—he ensures a diverse range of opportunities for everyone: from learning and sharing to educating and staying informed. This multifaceted approach ensures that the community is connected and actively engaged in meaningful actions that make a real difference online and offline.

IF FAME IS FOR EVERYONE, WHAT ABOUT FAME INFLATION?

"Everybody can be great because everybody can serve."

—Martin Luther King, Jr., civil rights leader, and recipient of the Nobel Peace Prize in 1964 for his nonviolent campaign against racism

IS THERE A DANGER OF FAME INFLATION? Yes, if you define fame as a hierarchal pursuit where only a few can make it. As economist Sherwin Rosen implies in his theory of the superstar model, there is a risk of fame inflation, similar to grade inflation. When fame becomes too readily available, it can be debased and lose its meaning.[27]

But is there only one top spot to achieve? Pursuing omnipresence, where everyone knows your name, may not be necessary or desirable if you want to maintain a private life. Marcus "Bellringer" Bell, American music producer, influencer, and entrepreneur, defines **fame as "visibility to a particular target audience."**

Marcus is quite familiar with fame, with about 89,900 followers on X garnering 20 million impressions a month. In Marcus's lifetime, he has marketed, promoted, produced, remixed, written for, mentored, and developed some of the world's biggest superstars and brands, including Nicki Minaj, Katy Perry, Snoop Dogg, Timbaland, Sony Music, Warner Bros., Arista Records, EMI, and Universal Music.

"Fame can be as small as securing visibility to a customer, or even visibility to a love interest," Marcus explains. "Fame sets you apart to draw attention from certain levels or sectors. Fame could be achieving visibility from business-to-business (B2B), business-to-customer (B2C),

or person-to-person (P2P)."

Dr. Jordan B. Peterson, a renowned psychologist and the author of best-selling books such as *12 Rules for Life* and *Beyond Order,* which have sold millions of copies worldwide, adds, "There are definite tiers of fame. There are celebrities known locally and then there are celebrities known internationally, and then there are celebrities like the Queen that is known everywhere in the world. Among famous people, the Queen is hyper famous."[28]

Tyler Cowen, another economist, emphasizes in his book *What Price Fame?* that **"fame is a positive sum game"[29] where everyone can benefit, and there's room for everyone to succeed.**

> Fame is a positive sum game because
> fans expand the Fame circle.

Fans expand the fame circle, and the publicity of top stars trickles down, benefiting less popular performers and decentralizing the fame rewards.

Look at awards like the Grammys and competitions like the Olympics; they keep creating new categories in which to become famous.

True fame is not just about having a large number of followers or views but also about having a significant impact and being widely respected in a certain circle.

> Fame is achieved by becoming known within
> your circle, whether it's at a local, regional,
> national, or industry level, and the ultimate goal
> is to showcase your unique talents within your
> community and create the desired impact.

THE GOAL IS LUXURY FAME

> *"The best Fame is a writer's Fame: It's enough to get a table at a good restaurant, but not enough that you get interrupted when you eat."*
>
> **—Fran Lebowitz,** American author, public speaker, and occasional actor

I FIRST HEARD THE TERM "Luxury Fame" while I was writing this book. I was privileged to meet two famous individuals—Nassim Nicholas Taleb and Felipe Gomez—at the Oslo Business Forum in 2022.

The international multi-bestseller Nassim Nicholas Taleb, with 800,000+ followers on X, is a renowned speaker and the author of *The Black Swan: The Impact of the Highly Improbable*. This book is considered by the *Sunday Times of London* as one of the twelve most influential books since World War II.

When I asked him at what point he knew that he was famous, to my surprise, Nassim responded, "I am not famous."

He reasoned that this was the case because no one had recognized him in the four days he'd recently been vacationing at a resort.

At the same conference, I met Felipe Gomez, considered one of the most requested and inspiring keynote speakers in the world by using music as a metaphor for life and leadership. When I asked him the same question, I got a similar response, so I rephrased the question and asked when the first magic moment was that his gifts were seen by others.

Felipe glowed then and immediately said that it was when he gave his first speech, which was for a smaller audience in his hometown of Bogotá,

Columbia. I could tell he went back in time as he spoke, reliving the moment of joy he felt when he first shared his love for using music to teach about leadership.

I was perplexed by both men's responses, and Sofia Haraldsson, the senior consultant at Transcendent Group, Scandinavia's leading employee consulting firm, came up with the best explanation. **"Nassim and Felipe have acquired Luxury Fame status,"** she said and continued to explain that a person has achieved Luxury Fame when they are famous within a niche market but can be anonymous when they want to be.

Luxury Fame is being recognized within your niche market while still being able to remain anonymous when you want to.

I believe most of us would prefer to have Luxury Fame. It gives the best of both worlds, where you can be known in your circle but remain private otherwise. I also find it fascinating that as people become well-known, they don't always believe it. We all have an inferiority complex with ourselves and don't recognize that we are as great as we are.

My mentor, David Meerman Scott, has achieved Luxury Fame, a testament to his expertise and recognition in the field. David is a regular speaker at Tony Robbins's Business Mastery conference, an event hosted by Robbins, who is renowned as a transformative life and business strategist, best-selling author, and philanthropist. His ability to attract a global audience and his impact on millions through his empowerment programs make his conference a prestigious platform. At these events, David becomes a celebrity, drawing attention and admiration from attendees eager to gain insights from his experiences.

David provided a similar perspective on the difference between fame and Luxury Fame: "In my mind, leadership and fame are very different. I see fame or being famous as being more mainstream. . . . For example, in my case, I'm not famous in that sense. No one recognizes me when I walk down the street, and most people don't know my name. However, if I went to a marketing conference, many people would recognize me, and many would know my name, so I don't consider myself famous. And I don't think people say I'm famous." And that's exactly how he likes it.

But achieving Luxury Fame isn't just about being recognized—it's about positively impacting your field and contributing to the greater good.

Most of the time, Luxury Fame is achieved through thought leadership.

This is the premise of this book, that you can be famous in your industry or niche and not necessarily become a household name or be mobbed at the grocery store. Being a Public Figure involves having a high level of visibility and influence in the public eye—as an individual—even if that is just within your niche.

The Public Figure is not driven by sensationalism, fleeting trends, and the desire for instant gratification. Public figures are highly regarded and respected within their respective industries or communities and are considered experts or authorities in their chosen pursuits. As we have moved into a time when fame is for everyone, we can't hide behind the curtains forever. To find the next level of success, we need to reframe our thinking to become Public Figures.

FAME = BEING RECOGNIZED FOR YOUR ACHIEVEMENT

A TOP PUBLIC FIGURE RECEIVES 80% MORE OPPORTUNITIES

> *"Opportunities blossom in the garden of distinction, where each achievement sows seeds for unforeseen possibilities and growth."*
>
> **—Unknown**

WITH AVERAGE BEING OFF THE TABLE, Tony Robbins, the renowned life and business strategist and best-selling author, wisely noted that even striving to be above average isn't enough in today's competitive landscape.

Settling for great?

That's a strategy destined to fail.

To genuinely differentiate yourself, aim to be exceptional, meaning, in the top 4 percent of your field. It's worth noting that you don't have to hit the very top 1 percent to gain the advantages associated with elite performance.

In the current Fame Revolution, where standing out is crucial, being good or great simply doesn't cut it. The bar has been raised.

Let's draw an analogy from the academic world. While both "B" and "A" grades signify notable accomplishments, it's the straight "A" students—the ones in the top 4 percent—who typically receive greater recognition, scholarships, and opportunities. The "B" student is above average, but in a world vying for attention and recognition, it's those with straight A's who stand out and are remembered.

> In the quest for excellence, aim not just to rise but to soar. Landing in the top 4 percent isn't just about prestige—it's where opportunity meets visibility and distinction becomes the norm.

Likewise, consider the Olympics. While every athlete at the games is undeniably exceptional, it's the top three—the medalists—who capture the world's attention and admiration. In many events, the difference between a medalist and a non-medalist can be mere milliseconds or points. But that slim margin makes all the difference.

The emphasis here isn't on being the absolute best but rather on the importance of striving to be within the top echelons, like the top 4 percent. In the Fame Revolution, this is the bracket that captures the limelight, receives the most opportunities, and ultimately, achieves the broadest impact.

In my experience with industry leaders, it's clear: the top 4 percent secure about 80 percent of the opportunities. Why?

They're not just good at what they do; they're also well-known in their sectors. Because of that, they are the first people who come to mind when an opportunity comes up.

BENEFITS OF FAME

"Legacy is greater than currency."

—Gary Vaynerchuk, American entrepreneur, best-selling author, and social media influencer, is the Chairman of VaynerX and CEO of VaynerMedia

Gary Vaynerchuk, commonly known as Gary Vee, is a prime example of how fame can lead to incredible, multifaceted success. He started his career working in his family's liquor store, but he always knew he was meant for bigger things.

In the early 2000s, Gary saw the potential of the Internet and began creating online content, first through a wine video blog called Wine Library TV and later through his personal brand on social media. His ability to create engaging content and connect with his audience led to his rise as a thought leader in the world of digital marketing.

As Gary's fame grew, so did his influence and income. He founded VaynerMedia, a digital marketing agency that has worked with major brands like PepsiCo, General Electric, and Johnson & Johnson. Gary has also authored several books, including *Crush It!: Why Now Is the Time to Cash In on Your Passion* and *The Thank You Economy*, which have helped many aspiring entrepreneurs learn from his experience and success.

Today, Gary is one of the most well-known and respected public figures in the marketing industry, and his fame has allowed him to build a massive following on social media. He has over 12 million followers across various platforms, where he continues to share his insights and motivate others to pursue their dreams.

Through his hard work, passion, and dedication to his craft, Gary has shown how Luxury Fame can lead to incredible success. He is Internet famous and has inspired countless people to pursue their passions, build their personal brands, and leverage their names to create a better life for themselves and others.

"I have Internet fame. Real fame is more intense."

—Gary Vaynerchuk

Becoming famous opens the door to a multitude of opportunities, extending beyond just career prospects. This newfound recognition often leads to diverse avenues for growth.

THE GREATEST DIFFERENCE IS YOU

"The best gifts are the ones you give."

—Unknown

WHERE DOES THAT LEAVE US in the Fame Revolution? It leaves with our gift. Our differentiator. For painter Vincent Van Gogh, this was his paintings; for you, it's probably something entirely different. In this world where technology seems to take our jobs, our livelihoods, and what we know, *we still matter.* Our action reverberates.

As actress Lena Olin stated in the movie *Havana*, **"A butterfly can flutter its wings over a flower in China and cause a hurricane in the Caribbean. So the action we take is even more important."**

We are all heroes moving forward in this life. We have just forgotten the heroic powers that lie within our hearts.

Mathematician and meteorologist, Edward Norton Lorenz, the father of Chaos theory and the Butterfly Effect theory, demonstrated that one butterfly flapping its wings could impact the movement of a tornado weeks later.[30]

In fact, we matter even more than the Butterfly Effect theory states. Author and professor Karen O'Brien, in her book *You Matter More than You Think,* shows through recent research within quantum social change that society is built upon fractal patterns, just like nature and mathematics. Social scientists demonstrate that human interactions are part of nature and mathematics, and, in fact, our actions create many kinds of fractal patterns.[31]

The significance of this research is that it shows how powerful you are.

- One action by you can influence the fractal system **horizontally, including your peers, family, and friends.**

- One action by you can influence the fractal system **vertically, including the whole hierarchy of your company, government, and society.**

Every conversation and every interaction by you have the potential to be significant. Karen O'Brien states, "From the perspective of quantum fractals, every person who takes action based on universal values such as equity, dignity, compassion, and integrity affects all scales. Connecting to others from an {I/we} space transcends separations and fragmentation."[32]

We matter.

You matter.

Your mission matters.

When we take our role as a Public Figure seriously, we change the patterns of our lives that can have ripple effects beyond our imagination.

The only way your gifts will shine is if you allow them to shine.

May you embrace the role of stepping into the limelight and being the Public Figure.

As the world is evolving and fame is becoming democratized, it's an exceptional time to be alive, offering us a unique opportunity to let our talents shine.

I believe that using our gifts is our duty.

"From everyone who has been given much, much will be demanded; and from the one who has been entrusted with much, much more will be asked."

—Luke 12:48 (NKJV)

Have you ever heard the story of the *Parable of the Talents*? A talent in this story was a large amount of money. It's a story told by Jesus in the Bible that illustrates the importance of using our unique gifts and talents to the best of our ability. In the parable, a master entrusts his property and money to his servants while he is away. He entrusts each of the three servants with a different amount of money, which he expects them to use wisely and make it grow. The amount was given according to their abilities. The first two servants invest their money and double the amount, while the third servant buried his money and returned it without any gain. When the master returns, he promotes the first two servants and banishes the third because he did not use the treasures wisely.

WHAT CAN WE LEARN FROM THIS STORY?

1 First, a common application is that we all have unique abilities and resources that we should use to the best of our ability. Just like the servants in the story given different amounts of "money" based on their abilities, in real life, we all have different talents and resources that we can use to make a difference in the world. It is our duty to share them with others.

2 Second, we are responsible for using our talents productively. The first two servants invested their money and earned a profit, while the third servant wasted his opportunity. We each have a responsibility to use our talents and resources productively and not waste them.

3 Third, we will be held accountable for how we use our talents. The master in the story returns and settles accounts with his servants, rewarding the first two and punishing the third. Similarly, we will be held accountable for how we use our talents and resources in life.

So, what does this mean for us today?

In a world where fame and recognition are becoming increasingly democratized, it's more important than ever to showcase our talents and make them known. We all have something unique to offer, and by using our talents wisely and productively, we can make a difference in the world.

Remember, those who use their talents wisely will be rewarded, while those who waste their talents will suffer the consequences. Let's take a lesson from the Parable of the Talents and use our unique gifts to make a positive impact in the world. Strut your stuff, own your brand, and let the world appreciate the powerhouse that is you.

SO, HOW DO YOU STAND OUT AND USE YOUR GIFTS TO MAKE AN IMPACT?

By bringing more of YOU to the table.

There are people who NEED and WANT someone with your talents, someone with your unique personality.

That's how you leverage your differentiator, by leveraging YOU.

BECAUSE AT THE END OF THE DAY, YOUR GREATEST DIFFERENTIATOR IS YOU.

Embracing the idea of being a Public Figure is a profound millimeter shift in mindset that makes the biggest difference in understanding and managing the Fame Revolution.

CHAPTER TWO

THE PUBLIC FIGURE IS THE FAME SOLUTION

We have established from the last chapter that we are in the Fame Revolution.

Fame has been democratized.

You have the power to be a media conglomerate and so does everyone else.

We concluded that to win is to cultivate your differentiator. And the solution is ... drum roll ...

To be a Public Figure.

This chapter, I will share why you are a Public Figure.

Yes, even if you are an employee or a CEO, you are a Public Figure.

A company is also a Public Figure.

I will share what it means for the Public Figure to thrive.

YOU ARE A PUBLIC FIGURE

> *"I don't really have a comprehension of being a Public Figure."*
>
> **—John Malkovich,** American actor nominated for two Oscars

YOU ARE PROBABLY THINKING, "But, I'm not a Public Figure."

I am here to tell you that you are a Public Figure.

When I was young, before the internet, we did not have the same possibilities to share our message as we have today. We could not just bring our story to the people. There were gatekeepers—journalists and TV editors with their pens and cameras giving us the story of the day. Today, we all have a camera, a video, and publishing capabilities so *we* can tell the story of the day with our smartphones. With the push of a button, our story goes out into the world—sometimes it is seen by many and sometimes by few. Still, the potential to reach millions exists with each post we share.

The biggest travesty is that we don't all think of ourselves as public figures

In the Fame Revolution, we are each starring in a blockbuster of our own making, where every interaction turns us into the lead of our unique story. In today's digital world, the concept of being a Public Figure has taken on an entirely new dimension. The average person sharing their life online can inspire, influence, and impact others profoundly.

THE PUBLIC FIGURE IS THE FAME SOLUTION | **75**

How Internet Fame Redefines Identity

"In the same way that electricity went from a luxury enjoyed by the American élite to something just about everyone had, so, too, has fame, or at least being known by strangers, gone from a novelty to a core human experience.

The Western intellectual tradition spent millennia maintaining a conceptual boundary between public and private—embedding it in law and politics, norms, and etiquette, theorizing and reinscribing it. With the help of a few tech firms, we basically tore it down in about a decade.

That's not to say the experience of being known, paid attention to, commented on by strangers, is in any sense universal. It's still foreign to most people, online and off. But now the possibility of it haunts online life, which increasingly is just life. The previous limiting conditions on what's private and what's public, on who can know you, have been lifted." [33]

—A reflection by Chris Hayes, published in the *New Yorker*, September 24, 2021

Have you ever wondered how celebrities, politicians, and public figures become famous? As someone who has worked in both Washington D.C. and the entertainment industry, I can tell you that it takes more than just talent or hard work to become a household name. To adopt the "Public Figure" mindset it takes a learnable and essential approach to making your gifts known and creating the impact you desire.

. . . .

A PUBLIC FIGURE IS THE MERGING OF WHO YOU ARE WITH WHAT YOU OFFER

. . . .

WHAT EXACTLY IS A PUBLIC FIGURE?

The key to being a Public Figure lies in forging a synergy between a data-driven approach, which quantifies our impact, and the art of storytelling, which qualitatively connects with our audience. It's not just about the stats or the stories alone: it is about how the analytics of our reach can inform and enhance the stories we tell. This balanced alliance is what will equip us to stand out in the crowded space of potential public figures.

The best way to illustrate this is by looking to the masters. And who does it better than Hollywood and Washington, D.C.? You might want to cringe and tune out as if Hollywood and D.C. do not apply to you, but please read on.

We can learn quite a bit from Hollywood and Washington, D.C. Aside from their talents and powers of persuasion, they know how to succeed in the public eye. They also know how and why to embrace being a Public Figure.

Public figures in **Hollywood and the entertainment industry** refer to talent, encompassing actors, recording artists, and directors. In contrast, **the political sphere of Washington, D.C.,** extends to include politicians, ranging from senators and members of Congress to individuals as high-ranking as the president of the United States.

LOOK TO HOLLYWOOD AND WASHINGTON D.C.

❝❝ *"Washington and Hollywood spring from the same DNA"*

—Jack Valenti, former president of the Motion Picture Association of America

As I REFLECT ON MY CAREER, I remember my time working briefly at SONY BMG, where I was the assistant to the senior vice president of digital sales and marketing. I was fascinated by how the artists at SONY were positioned and marketed, and I saw the same strategies used in politics and nonprofits when I worked in Washington, D.C. We can learn a lot from how Hollywood and Washington, D.C., manage public figures such as movie stars, rock stars, politicians, and presidential candidates.

In Washington, D.C., the goal is to sell a message through a person, organization, or issue and get it out through campaigns, events, press conferences, summits, workshops, and congressional hearings. The objective is to sell the message to the target audience, whether it is the inner circle of D.C. or all of America through CNN or the Sunday morning talk shows, the "must-watch" events for Washington, D.C., policymakers, lobbyists, and media professionals where policymakers clarify their stances on pressing issues. The programs set the tone for the agenda of the coming week and offer an opportunity to test new policy ideas and influence public opinion.

Having worked in politics and dabbled in the entertainment industry, I can attest to the similarities between these two worlds. When I worked in D.C., we used to refer to the town as "Hollywood for the Uglies," because we utilized many of the same strategies as Hollywood to manage public figures and promote our causes but without the same level of glitz and glamour.

Whenever Hollywood celebrities visited D.C. for the Washington Correspondents' Dinner or a senate hearing, we, the staffers, delighted in how we could speak the same language as our Hollywood counterparts regarding handling public figures and promoting issues to the public.

I'll never forget my time working as Senator Orrin Hatch's photographer. I was privileged to meet icons like U2's Bono, Muhammad Ali, and actress Linda Evans from the hit show *Dynasty*, who all stopped by to visit the senator. I was up close, taking photos for the senator's website and newsletter.

Many senators have even appeared in Hollywood movies. In Steven Soderbergh's Oscar-winning movie *Traffic*, senators Orrin Hatch, Barbara Boxer, Charles Grassley, Harry Reid, and Don Nickles, along with former Massachusetts governor William Weld, appeared in brief cameos in a scene set during a Washington, D.C. cocktail party. And in true Hollywood fashion, we were even invited by Jack Valenti, the president of the Motion Picture Association of America, to a private movie premiere.

Despite the differences in these fields, both industries are masterful in managing public figures and promoting their causes. Hollywood creates entertainment, while Washington, D.C., focuses on politics and public policy. By learning from their strategies, we can navigate the world of fame and use it to achieve our goals.

What do they do?

Both Hollywood and D.C. intuitively utilize the Public Figure Strategy by operating with the Public Figure at its epicenter. **Public Figure is not just a person but a product. It is the personhood that drives the bottom line and influence**. For example, the movie star with their stardom will

PERSON

PRODUCT

"PUBLIC FIGURE"

help ensure high movie ticket sales, while the politician with their campaign promise is selling a promise to win the election and get two to four more years using their influence to create legislation impacting society. Both industries see that the person is what drives their operations.

So what? What distinguishes a Public Figure from being a CEO or Business owner

Hollywood and D.C. have mastered blending the personal touch with smart strategy and sharp business acumen. While a CEO and business owner know intuitively that their statements and action can drive the business, rarely do they think of themselves as a product that is part of the business strategy. It is this nuance that is so critical to accept in the Fame Revolution: that we are more than persons but also products that can drive the bottom line with our viewpoints, actions, and statements.

Public Figure merges what you offer with who you are

When I think about the yin and yang, it strikes me how much it resembles the life of a Public Figure. In Chinese philosophy, the yin and yang concept describes forces that are opposite yet interconnected and mutually reinforcing, as symbolized by the dot in each, representing the seed of its opposite. They are not completely opposed but exist in a dynamic balance relative to each other.

- **The "person" side, or yin, is not just about who you are at your core but also about how you engage with your community, the stories you share, and the relationships you build.** It's the heart and soul of your public identity, encompassing the meaningful interactions, the personal touch in your communications, and the genuine connections you forge. It's where your unique narrative and individuality shine through, creating a bond with your audience that goes beyond mere recognition. For instance, each star or politician has a story, emotions, and complexities with genuine connections and heartfelt moments that audiences and voters feel.

- **On the other side is the "product," the yang, which represents the measurable, market-driven side of your public persona.** This side is defined by hard data like audience metrics, sales figures, and market influence. It's an objective measure of your reach and impact in the public sphere. For instance, in Hollywood, an actor's market value can dictate a movie's budget or if the movie is even made. In politics, a candidate's appeal can translate directly into votes, funding, and grassroots support.

For a Public Figure, achieving an integrated balance between these two aspects—the personal, relationship-building side and the tangible, market-oriented side—is crucial. It's about maintaining personal authenticity while also capitalizing on your market value.

Millimeter shift

Embracing the idea of being a Public Figure is a profound millimeter shift in mindset that makes the biggest difference in understanding and managing the Fame Revolution.

I was reminded of the shift when I spoke with one of my beta readers, Ingvil Gaasland, a senior fellow at the Nexus Council. The idea of everyone being a Public Figure completely resonated with her, and she stated, "I now understand why my daughter intuitively manages her public persona and scrutinizes all of her posts. She knows she is a product where she is meticulously crafting her public profile and marketing and sharing only information that will communicate a certain message."

Ingvil recognized how, over the years, the clear distinction between being a private citizen and a Public Figure has increasingly been blurred and shared that one of the companies she consults is being pressured by the employees to have an opinion on a political matter, "just like a politician." Even companies need to be public figures!

"What grieves me is that my daughter will never have the privilege of having a completely private life offline."

I agreed and added that social media has created a global village similar to a small village of 300 people where everyone knows everything about you, where everyone knows your business, so you have to be really careful about how you act and what you say.

Think of Public Figure as yin and yang

With all your unique flair, combined with your product or service, you are your own ticket to becoming a Public Figure.

It is about recognizing the full spectrum—your authentic self on one end and your value proposition on the other.

The shift I am talking about is embracing the yin and yang with intention.

It's not just about selling a product or marketing yourself—it's about intertwining the two so tightly that they become a single, powerful brand narrative. That's your strategy to stand out in this Fame Revolution.

We cannot ignore the trade-offs that come with the Fame Revolution. While those of us who are digital immigrants may sometimes grieve for a past understanding of privacy and connection, there are also undeniable gains in this new era.

- We have lost the gift of being completely anonymous and thriving and traded for visibility to gain influence.
- We have lost our privacy and traded for the convenience of online

interactions, selling products, and sharing our viewpoint online.

- We have lost the clear boundary from private to public lives and traded for having a platform on social media to voice our opinions, advocate, and issue or sell our products and services.

YES, FAME CAN SUCK

> *"Fame is a bee.*
> *It has a song—*
> *It has a sting—*
> *Ah, too, it has a wing."*
>
> **—Emily Dickinson,**[34] one of the leading
> nineteenth-century American poets

THE ADVANTAGES OF fame are evident, but even in the times of John Milton and Emily Dickinson, it was clear that fame can also bring serious problems. I had to include just a few notes about the downside of fame.

We have all heard rumors and seen public breakups, breakdowns, and career-killing missteps. Fame makes people more vulnerable, not less. Fame opens people up to limitless judgment from throngs of people who can make any hurtful comments they want from behind the safety of their computer screens. Fame can be fickle because people are fickle.

In many cases, privacy is over. Your life becomes an open book, and you belong to the world. You have an image to maintain, and that image will come under scrutiny, especially as you increase your clout and your personal standing.

"I think everybody should get rich and famous and do everything they ever dreamed of so they can see that it's not the answer."

—Jim Carrey, Canadian-American actor and comedian

I agree with Jim Carrey in the sense that fame is not the answer if you are pursuing it as a solution to pain or insecurity. But I love to help make people famous for doing great things, as they can then model what important accomplishment looks like. When being well-known comes from highlighting your true value, I find it more exciting and compelling than anything else.

"Fame is . . . That last infirmity of noble mind."

—**John Milton,** Paradise Lost, 1637

THE PUBLIC-PRIVATE DILEMMA

> *"Fame is very agreeable, but the bad thing is that it goes on 24 hours a day."*

—**Gabriel García Márquez,** Colombian novelist and one of the greatest writers of the twentieth century, who was awarded the Nobel Prize for Literature in 1982

WHEN INGVIL GAASLAND highlighted the dilemma of trading off our private lives to be a Public Figure, I contacted Loveleen R. Brenna, an Indian Norwegian best-selling author and founder and CEO of SEEMA AS, a world-leading consultancy on diversity management. Loveleen R. Brenna has been a pivotal figure in advancing diversity leadership on a global scale. She played a key role in developing of the first international standard (ISO) on diversity leadership, marking a significant milestone in this field. Her efforts have not only been recognized internationally but also have had a profound impact on Norwegian society. As a vocal advocate for leadership, diversity, inclusion, and feminism, Loveleen's influence extends beyond organizational boundaries. Her collaboration with Standard Norway and the International Organization for Standardization (ISO) led to the creation of the first international certification on Diversity Management, a testament to her dedication and expertise in this area.

With nearly thirty years in the public eye and nine books to her name, she wrote *The Parable of the Dog and the Peacock*, a book I had the privilege of helping translate and edit. This book celebrates the value of diverse talents, illustrating a friendly and enlightening process where a workforce of dogs learns to accommodate a peacock. It focuses on the journey of making room for the peacock's unique abilities and the lessons learned along the way. **The key takeaway is that a company becomes more valuable and profitable when it fully embraces and utilizes the diverse skills and perspectives that each "feather" of the peacock brings to the table.** In our interview, Loveleen agreed that we all need to be public figures, similar to the peacocks in her parable.

In the interview, we unpacked various thoughts around the public–private dilemma in the Fame Revolution.

CORPORATE AND PUBLIC FIGURE

When asked about the concept that we are all public figures, Loveleen stated that the peacock, symbolizing individuals, should be free to display its splendor, knowledge, and insight.

She agreed that we all need to adopt a Public Figure mindset. She added that the **future belongs to the leader who can capitalize on the unique capabilities of their employees and match their unique talents with the company's values.**

"We need to recognize the unique and different skills, experiences, and backgrounds of each person to unleash innovation. However, balancing individual's gifts with a common set of values is crucial in forming a harmonious organizational culture. **The balance between individual brilliance and collective values is a crucial skill for future leaders**," Loveleen states and continues, "To foster this kind of corporate culture requires an environment of psychological safety, where people feel secure enough to express their insights, knowledge, and perspectives."

Loveleen sees that the greatest risk in the future will be the temptation "to clip the peacock's wings to make it fit into a narrow corporate culture." And she concludes, **"The future gold is creating a company culture that can foster a safe platform for individuals to express themselves freely."**

LOSS OF PERSONAL FREEDOM AND GAIN OF INFLUENCE

When I probed about the concern about the loss of privacy, Loveleen acknowledged the mental pressure of standing out and balancing what should be private versus public. But she sees more of an upside to being a Public Figure.

Loveleen stated, "We, Generation X, did not curate our private and public lives" and emphasizes, "But we did not have the influence or the power that today's youth possess."

"With fame comes great power and responsibility."
—**Loveleen**

She further stated that today's Norwegian youth have the privilege of standing out, presenting their ideas, and fully sharing their gifts but acknowledges that they also have greater responsibility.

I agreed with Loveleen that the youth have more power and influence, but the question that lingers is, "How do you curate your life and share authentically?"

"Privately, I have shared my developmental journey and life challenges without disclosing the intimate details of my crises," she said. "I focus on bringing out personal experiences that do not unfold my entire story."

She added that this approach has helped build trust and credibility "because I share my experiences from the vantage point of what I have learned." She does not see this as being inauthentic but rather being respectful to all parties.

Initially, she kept her private life under wraps and shared liberally her professional life as an author and expert on diversity management.

"I didn't publicly reveal my marriage until 2011, despite being married since 2002. In a society where minorities are emerging, it's essential that women are recognized for their professional achievements, not who they are married to."

In later years, Loveleen has opened more of her private life to the public but only what she feels comfortable with.

I think the lesson here is to stay in your comfort zone. It's perfectly reasonable to humanize yourself by sharing parts of your life, but do it with care.

"The art of handling the future and being famous lies in how much I choose to share and what I decide to share, in order to be relevant to those who listen to me."

—Loveleen

RELUCTANCE TO FAME

> *"You are much more interesting to people than you give credit for, and yet you are trying to act, trying to fit into and be what other people want you to be. You can't begin to change yourself in any meaningful way until you confront who you really are."*

—**Robert Greene,** international best-selling author on strategy, power, and seduction

WE'VE TALKED ABOUT how and why fame is necessary, but what if you don't *want* to become famous?

"No! I don't like public speaking! I hate photos of myself! I wouldn't be caught dead on video, and having a social media persona sounds horrible!"

Really?

Thoughts like these are not uncommon. But being caught in the middle of wanting to see your business and career rise to the next level and preferring to hide behind the curtains may not get you the success you desire or perhaps even the basic income required to support your family. More importantly, you may have a mission to improve some aspect of society. How will you accomplish what you want without being known? Overcoming your reluctance to fame can mean the difference between success and failure.

I acknowledge:

Not everyone is a performer.

Not everyone likes the spotlight.

Not everyone wants to be a household name.

Some even feel morally wrong about the word "fame."

Wherever you fall, it's okay . . . but if you want more, you may need to rethink some of this.

NOT BEING FAMOUS AFFECTS YOUR SUCCESS

Many find their careers stifled because nobody knows them or sees their personality. They feel a bit lost as to how to overcome this reluctance. They are terrified at the prospect of becoming famous. It's natural to feel these emotions, and honestly, it's okay! If this is you, read on!

What you may want: a good life with financial success, all while making an impact on the world.

What you don't want: your face plastered all over the internet with all attention on you rather than your cause or mission.

The word "fame" conjures up thoughts of being followed around the grocery store by paparazzi and other invasions of privacy. But let me say it again, I am not talking about celebrity fame. I'm talking about Luxury Fame or *Fame for a reason*; where you leverage your influence to make the world a better place.

THE FAME REVOLUTION IS A DOUBLE-EDGED SWORD

While I love that personalities are coming to the forefront, there are some people who really don't want to be there but who are almost forced to expose their uniqueness to the world out of necessity. Notably, personalities on the introverted spectrum are more prone to this reluctance about fame. They would rather have a spokesperson or their product itself speak for them. It provides a level of safety to hide behind the scenes. But this does their success a disservice.

DOES THE INTERNET REDUCE THIS RELUCTANCE TO PURSUE FAME?

When dealing with the Internet, there are no actual face-to-face interactions, so it should be easier, right? Well, yes and no. While some people become much bolder behind the screen, others are afraid of what response or lack of response they will receive. Whether it's an opinion they want to share, a comment they want to post, or a photo of themselves, for some, it can feel like similar pressures as in an in-person situation.

Sometimes we don't like photos of ourselves because we look different than we think we look. You see yourself in a mirror every day, and based on that, you have a perception of how you look. There, however, are moving and have depth. Photos and videos have much less depth, and your proportions vary depending on what lens is used, how good the lighting is, and a host of other variables. Compare that frozen-in-time representation of yourself to a live reflection in a mirror.

There are many other factors, but this example demonstrates how there are some built-in, understandable reasons we may not want to be seen on camera. Take a look at these two photos of Abraham Lincoln; one seems off, does it not?

Left: Iconic portrait   Right: Mirror reflection

The photo on the left is the infamous portrait of President Abraham Lincoln. The other is how he would have seen himself in the mirror. He probably would have thought something looked "funny" about his face in the photo, just as many of us do, but this is just a self-perception. Self-image is a small yet significant reason why many feel reluctant to go public with their Public Figure brand. They are just not comfortable with how they appear in photos of themselves and the more familiar reflection they're used to seeing in a mirror.[35]

THE INDUSTRIALIZATION OF AUTHENTICITY

"Authenticity is the quality that makes one person more influential than another, even if they have similar metrics. A sense of authenticity sells products."

—**Emily Hund,**[36] blogger and author of *The Influencer Industry*

IN MY EXPERIENCE ATTENDING a local mastermind, a significant but unspoken question hovered: "Do we support charities merely for financial gain?" Our conversation, though somewhat indirect, delved into how backing charities can be a strategic move for retaining and acquiring clients. This approach carries a dual purpose: to aid a worthy cause while also cementing long-term client relationships.

This raises a critical point about authenticity, especially for public figures and businesses. Is supporting charities for business advantage truly sincere?

I have seen many companies that support charities, but their support seems disingenuous with the real intent being to advance their business interests. Some would call it a "B.S. detector," but whatever you call it, we all can sense when someone is being authentic or not.

The question then becomes: is being authentic the same as being truthful?

We often believe we can spot the difference. At the mastermind, one participant shared her strategy of supporting her clients' charities, considering it a savvy business move. Despite having their own charity, she and her husband view this as a beneficial business decision. She's a person of integrity, yet her actions underscore the intricate balance public figures must maintain between business savvy and ethical considerations. This matter displays the heart of being a Public Figure. It can be murky. You are intertwined with business and relational questions and must continually check yourself. *Am I being genuine? Do I understand the complexities of this decision?*

As Emily Hund, a social media analyst, suggests, authenticity doesn't always align with truthfulness. We've all felt let down upon realizing that a seemingly sincere Public Figure is quite the opposite. Consider influencers on TikTok sharing life lessons amidst makeup tutorials – it's a curated form of authenticity.

IN THE FAME REVOLUTION, AUTHENTICITY SELLS

Emily Hund is right when she says authenticity has been industrialized and has become transactional. She states, **"My findings confirm that those who learn to construct and exploit the ever-shifting language and aesthetic of 'realness' online hold immense commercial, political, and ideological influence, but they also show how fraught, contingent, and transactional authenticity has become."**[37] She adds, "Authenticity is what has allowed some people to make money and gain genuine satisfaction from their working making content for social media. But it is also what enabled some to become cults of personality, spreaders of misinformation, propagators of disingenuous lifestyle ideals or worse."[38]

An example of the dark side is influencer and self-help couple Rachel and Dave Hollis selling the myth of the perfect marriage to the public and dispensing advice for wedded bliss. They had scores of followers, but the image fell apart when they divorced, and Dave Hollis later died of an accidental overdose of cocaine, ethanol, and fentanyl.

Yes, the dark side of the Fame Revolution can bring power, opportunity, and perhaps, great temptation. A new way is needed to navigate this new world.

When I was a kid, we lived in a small town of 3,500 people in Norway, and everyone knew everyone else. Being confined to living in our small village meant had to be on our best behavior because word got around town fast and everyone knew your business. We are now living in a global village where being mindful of what we say and do and having a pure intent is the best course of action. It is important to know the rules and understand how to practice authenticity.

The most authentic person can be the best liar and many who are the most honest are also the most nervous to be out in the spotlight. Now is the time to understand new skills, and new operations and new strategies are needed to thrive.

AUTHENTICITY AND THE WORKFORCE

Carla Harris, best-selling author, and senior client advisor at investment banking company Morgan Stanley, emphasizes the critical role of authenticity in today's Fame Revolution and its impact on career progression. In this era where personal branding and public perception are key factors in professional success, embracing one's authentic self becomes a non-negotiable aspect of climbing the corporate ladder.

Harris highlights that being your genuine self is not only a desirable trait but also a powerful tool for building trust and credibility in the eyes of colleagues, clients, and superiors. In an environment where individual reputation carries significant weight, showcasing your unique talents, interests, and passions becomes essential for personal differentiation and standing out in a crowded field.

CARLA'S STORY

During the early stages of Carla Harris's career, she kept her investment banking persona separate from her passion for gospel singing. However, when her colleagues discovered her talent and asked her to perform,

Harris faced a pivotal decision. She chose to integrate her two passions, which turned out to be a game-changer for her career. Being known as a gospel singer not only sparked intriguing conversations but also added a unique dimension to her personal brand, opening doors to new opportunities.[39]

This story serves as a compelling reminder of the value of sharing personal interests and passions in professional settings. Carla Harris's wisdom reminds us that authenticity is not just a personal preference but a strategic necessity. By remaining true to ourselves, we establish an authentic and powerful presence in the Fame Revolution, setting the stage for meaningful professional connections, opportunities, and ultimately, success in our chosen endeavors.

"Your authenticity is your distinct competitive advantage.
There's nobody who can be you like you.
You can be the best version of yourself or
the worst version of yourself,
but there's nobody who can be you like you."
—**Carla Harris**

Authenticity lies at the core of success in this new era. In the corporate world, it is no longer enough to rely on corporate-speak. Authenticity and genuine connection have become essential ingredients for achieving success.

As Tony Robbins wisely said, "We cannot be average in what we love."

Embracing authenticity is marked by vulnerability and openness. It's as much about acknowledging your flaws as it is about showcasing your strengths. Entrepreneurs often start businesses by solving a problem in their own lives. Their passion for the solution becomes a powerful narrative that resonates with their audience. Loving what you do is the cornerstone of this authenticity.

Don't try to be all things to all people. The idea of an infallible leader is outdated. Admitting your weaknesses fosters a connection with others, demonstrating an authenticity that people can relate to. Moreover, seeking assistance empowers those around you, allowing them to step into their own leadership roles.

Authenticity isn't just a quality, it's a commitment to real, meaningful connections. There is no "cookie cutter" example. Every Public Figure brings a unique combination of attributes to the table. Be yourself.

HOW DO YOU ENSURE THAT YOUR REALNESS IS AUTHENTIC TO THE WIDER CIRCLE?

Sometimes, when we plan to share our authentic selves, nerves can get in the way and hinder our ability to communicate effectively. I have found that practice is the best way to ensure that what is on the inside is conveyed on the outside. The best, simple hack is to do video live for at least twenty-one days. It is transformative and has changed many of our clients as they become better presenters and leaders; some have even gotten promotions.

There is something magical about live video, and it changed my life. It helped me practice my authenticity and express what's on my heart more smoothly, without nervous twitches or awkward pauses.

Being on live video is scary because mistakes cannot be corrected. Live video captures everything. When I took the Live Video Mastery challenge where I did live videos for sixty days with Michelle Sorro, a former host on ExtraTV, podcaster of top-ranked podcast *Fire and Soul*, and transformation mentor, I went from someone who was often rated as a "good" conference speaker to consistently receiving "excellent" ratings after Michelle's challenge. Additionally, the practice of live video was instrumental in helping me tackle my tendencies toward perfectionism and imposter syndrome.

I now conduct private live video training with my clients through a twenty-one-day challenge, during which I pose a question for them to answer daily; as the days pass, I see the transformation. It reminds me of another training session I had with a group of Norwegian political leaders. One leader on the first day of training read from a sheet of paper about why chocolate ice cream was his favorite ice cream. By day fifteen, he had gained enough confidence to spontaneously invite the minister to join him on a live video!

The act of training on live videos before going full throttle out on social media sets up a comfort level that is quite powerful and helps in conveying your authenticity. I like to say that it merges what is on the inside with what is on the outside and helps you become real.

EMPLOYEES ARE PUBLIC FIGURES TOO

❝ *"Why fit in when you were born to stand out."*

—Dr. Suess, American's children author and cartoonist

WE THINK WE ARE SAFE from the spotlight because we are employees. Not so. Now, you are expected to be authentic in the workforce, be unique, and become known for what you do.

Carla Harris stated in her speech at the Oslo Business Forum 2022, "Even if you have to wear a 'uniform' to work, it is important that you bring all of you to work every day. Even in the uniform that I wear, I bring all of Carla Harris to the office every day. Has it cost me money, time, or both? It may have."

Carla's got a point. Office politics can be a maze, and it is all about finding your path. Who says you cannot talk about your weekend hiking trip at the water cooler? It is all part of who you are. The big takeaway? Know your voice and use it well. It can make you invaluable in the corporate landscape.[40]

LESSON FROM "NORWAY ROB"

In fact, stories of regular people becoming famous have become increasingly common. With the power of social media and digital platforms, individuals from all walks of life can capture attention and admiration. Take the example of "Norway Rob," a bus driver who has amassed over 2.1 million TikTok followers as of September 2023 by sharing entertaining videos of his unconventional routines where he dances and sings when taking a break, earning him the title of the "Justin Bieber of Bus Drivers."[41] Similarly,

Sean McCarren, a UPS driver, has gained a massive following by sharing pictures of the dogs he encounters on his delivery route, transforming him into a viral sensation with 1.6 million followers.[42]

However, there can be consequences to being yourself too much. It is about finding the right balance. In fact, in April 2023, the bus company that employs Norway Rob requested that he no longer post videos while wearing the bus uniform due to complaints they received. So, while Carla encourages standing out, there are stipulations on how to do so. If we could rewind time and have Norway Rob ask the bus company for clear guidelines, he might have continued spreading positivity on their behalf. Fame, especially when it comes overnight, brings intense scrutiny. When representing a company you do not own, having mutually agreed-upon guidelines for acceptable behavior is a practice of good governance.[43]

These stories serve as a reminder that fame is not limited to a select few. You, too, can put yourself out there and showcase what makes you special.

In a world where competition grows fiercer, it's essential to discover your niche and stand out from the crowd and yet do it in a way not to get canceled. This is a balancing act we cover in the chapter "Safeguarding Your Fame."

Ingvil Gaasland shared her insights, saying, **"The realization that I could bring my whole self to work was a revelation. It's true, I am more than just an employee; I am a mother, a daughter, a runner, a reader, a farmer, a tech enthusiast, and so much more. Embracing all these aspects of who I am has been liberating."**

CEOs ARE EXPECTED TO STAND OUT

> *"Communication is the most important skill any leader can possess."*
>
> —**Sir Richard Branson,** British business magnate, founder of Virgin Group, and commercial astronaut

PRODUCTS AND SERVICES ARE VITAL, but there is another ingredient driving success: the public image of the CEO. In the Fame Revolution, each product or service is not merely seeking to entertain or deliver value but also leverage the fame and persona of the company's leadership as a major selling point. **Today's winning businesses have pinpointed that while products and services are foundational, the CEO's public persona is the key driving factor of success.**

Sara Blakely, the founder and CEO of the American intimate apparel company, Spanx, stands as a testament to the power of a CEO being a Public Figure. Not only did she pioneer her way to become one of the first female billionaires with Spanx, but the company's valuation has soared past $1 billion. Impressively, she retains full ownership, operates without any debt, and, since its humble beginnings in 2000 up to 2022, has not spent a single dollar on traditional advertising. Instead, Blakely astutely leveraged her public persona to drive the company's growth and expansion. She epitomizes the modern CEO, seamlessly merging leadership with public advocacy.[44]

The CEO is not just a decision-maker anymore; they're the face, and often the primary sales driver and now expected even more than ever to lead on issues that have nothing to do with the business.

I was surprised to learn that according to the Edelman Trust Barometer (an international measure of citizen's trust in government, business, media, and nongovernmental organizations),[45] respondents expect CEOs to take a public stand on societal issues. The survey indicates the following expectations for CEOs to address:

- Treatment of employees: 89%
- Climate change: 82%
- Discrimination: 80%
- Wealth gap: 77%
- Immigration: 72% [46]

Today's most successful businesses have realized that the product or service is secondary and that sales are driven just as much by the face of the company, i.e., the personality of the CEO. However, there are exceptions where the company has crafted a distinct brand personality, similar to that of a charismatic CEO, resulting in a strong following. Examples of this include coffee chains like Starbucks and Dutch Bros.

We could argue that the reason why CEOs' salaries have exploded in the past decade is because we are in a Fame Revolution where the leader and their persona drive the success of the company. I like to compare CEOs to trading professional football players. Why?

Consider the staggering shift in CEOs' salaries. Since 1978, CEO compensation has surged by 940 percent. In stark contrast, the typical worker's pay rose just 12 percent.[47]

Is it fair to compare CEOs with elite athletes?

Critics argue that while spotting a sports star's talent is straightforward, measuring a CEO's worth is less clear-cut. I disagree because the underlying principle is all about potential. Much like sports teams, corporate boards are betting big on potential—not just on a CEO's current capabilities but their future potential to drive change, innovation, and profit. CEOs are not just operational leaders, they've become intrinsic to the company's valuation and bottom line.

More than ever, the CEO's identity is intertwined with their company. They've transitioned from shadowy figures pulling strings behind the scenes to front-and-center public figures. In the same vein that sports scouts constantly search for the next big player, corporate sectors are headhunting for CEOs who can change the game. The times have changed, and the CEO's role has been redefined—they are not just leading their companies but are now central to their public perception and success.

THE PUBLIC WANTS CEOS TO BE FRONT AND CENTER

The Edelman Trust Barometer shares that the public expects a CEO to be a Public Figure. An impressive 81 percent of the consumers assert that it's not enough for a CEO to lead; they must also be visibly engaged and active in the public domain. Furthermore, in a testament to the importance of leadership credibility and authenticity, 69 percent of the employees now express greater trust in their CEO compared to other authoritative figures. [48]

These dynamics underscore a shift in workplace values and the premium placed on leadership transparency.

Notably, the financial implications are significant: 60 percent of the key decision-makers are prepared to pay more for products or services when they perceive genuine depth and core virtues in the brand's leadership. This data shows a profound change in how leadership impacts the bottom line and corporate reputation.[49]

How much does a CEO have to stand out and be in the public eye?

Grant Cardone, one of the world's leading financial influencers, leverages social media to sell his training programs and real estate investments. The multiple *New York Times* best-selling author, known for *The 10X Rule* book, states, "You need to be omnipresent," meaning everywhere all at once, because "attention drives money."

But being omnipresent is a full-time job. And not everyone was born to be a movie star with a twenty-four-hour publicity machine and all the responsibility that comes with it. But how do you share what's important and create a meaningful connection that drives sales and impact without getting lost in the noise?

While omnipresence has its merits, strategic visibility—being at the right place at the right time—can be equally powerful.

BOX VERSUS DROPBOX

Take, for instance, the contrasting cases of Dropbox and Box, both cloud-based platforms for file storage and document collaboration. From an investment angle, both companies are rated with a grade of B in earnings estimate revisions by the American Association of Individual Investors. However, their communication styles significantly differ.

Dropbox CEO Drew Houston maintains a low media profile but is highly engaged within their industry sector, while Box CEO Aaron Levie is more engaged in the limelight and on social media.

How do they compare?

Box CEO Aaron Levie is extroverted, charismatic, and engaged in social discussions. He has impressively gathered 2.4 million X followers. While he is vocal about the latest in AI and delves into various subjects, he infrequently talks about Box or its earnings. Aaron's rise in the public eye was marked by his appearances from TechCrunch to high-profile customer events, even earning him a profile by Adam Bryant, one of the world's leading experts on leadership. It is significant that Aaron, not Drew, caught Adam Bryant's attention, emphasizing Aaron's prominence outside of the Silicon Valley circle of influence.[50] His iconic X account blew up with new followers. His charisma and connection to customers allowed Box to stand out as a product and made him stand out as a CEO.

Dropbox CEO Drew Houston maintains a relatively low profile. Drew Houston epitomizes the quintessential CEO, directing his focus toward company-specific communications and industry discussions. He lets the product speak for itself. Though he has a smaller follower base with 224K on X (compared to Aaron's 2.4 million X followers), Drew has amassed immense respect within the industry. This recognition leads to invitations to speak on numerous platforms and be featured in prominent publications like Forbes and CNBC. Drew's proactive approach ensures that stakeholders stay updated about Dropbox's milestones, quarterly earnings, and key industry events.

> *Being a Public Figure is not about getting attention first and standing out; it is understanding the nuance of where and how to stand out.*

You want to stand out where it counts for your vision, goals, and business. Aaron Levie got out in front of people, speaking publicly, guest blogging, and putting on events. He is known as being one of the funniest guys in tech.

But this does not mean you have to be in front of CNBC sharing the latest quarterly numbers; you can be like Drew Houston, who is using Luxury Fame to his advantage—he doesn't need to be known everywhere. He is working to be known in the sectors that count for his bottom line.

So, who emerges as the clear winner between Aaron Levie from Box and Drew Houston from Dropbox?

Both, in their unique ways. It's all about understanding where and how one wants to be recognized.

THOUGHT LEADERSHIP
NEEDS A FAME REVAMP

"Part of the role of a thought leader is not to necessarily have all the answers—I certainly don't—but it's to be able to ask the right questions and the privilege of being able to lead the conversation."

—**Michael Hyatt,** New York Times Bestselling Author, founder and chairman of Full Focus, one of *INC Magazine's* Best Workplaces for 5 years.

THOUGHT LEADERSHIP has been the vehicle for organizations and leaders to utilize experts to differentiate from other organizations and leaders.

The main goal of thought leadership is to become recognized as an expert and be used as a go-to resource in your field.

Peggy Brønn, professor emerita at BI Norwegian Business School's Department of Communication and Culture, says that many industries, particularly B2B industries, use thought leadership to legitimize themselves and be seen as the leaders in their industries.

When the term "thought leadership" comes up, it's easy to think of images of C-suite executives and massive corporations sharing their white papers on their latest technology or business method to drum up more clients. While corporations have certainly staked their claim in the realm of thought leadership, it's not exclusive territory. The essence of being a thought leader isn't about your title or the scale of your operations but about sharing innovative ideas and offering new perspectives, relevance, and value, irrespective of the size of your enterprise.

In 1994, the year before Amazon went live and Yahoo! was founded, Joel Kurtzman, founder and first editor of *strategy+business*, coined the term "thought leadership." This concept was thrust into the business world and has since become a mainstay with B2B companies. CEOs, executives, and other leaders are all clamoring to get their white papers, webinars, books, ideas, and speeches out to the marketplace.

Kurtzman defined a thought leader as "recognized by peers, customers and industry experts as someone who deeply understands the business they are in, the needs of their customers and the broader marketplace in which they operate." The concept of thought leadership was ignited by the 24/7 news cycle and the new monster that was the Internet, and it evolved to meet the demands of the insatiable appetite for news and information. Thought leadership has become a crucial tool for companies and individuals to showcase their expertise, share innovative ideas, and gain influence in their industry.

WHY THOUGHT LEADERSHIP NEEDS A REVAMP IN THE FAME REVOLUTION?

But thought leadership alone is not enough to make a lasting impact. Here's why.

First, there are too many mediocre thought leaders

The biggest challenge coming out of the COVID-19 pandemic has been the proliferation of mediocre thought leadership.

In the 2021 Edelman LinkedIn Impact Study, 71 percent of the decision-makers said that less than half of the thought leadership content they consumed gave them valuable insights. But there is a craving for forward-thinking educational pieces. The same survey stated, "More than half (51%) of C-suite executives say they spend more time-consuming thought leadership content than before the pandemic began."[51]

Second, the content is too corporate

Thought leadership tends to be trapped in corporate-speak and is more of a sales brochure. When it is churned through editing and rewrites by the corporate machine, it can lose the leader's voice. One of the major findings in the Edelman survey was that leaders longed for the casual and informal voice of an author to be attached to a piece. Also noted was that the voice would be better received if it were "authoritative and provocative yet human in tone and even fun."

Third, the content is salesy and stifled

As the saying goes, you can put lipstick on a pig, but it is still a pig. Superficial actions do not sell. Humans can smell a sales pitch at twenty paces.

"Thought leadership should be experiential, leading the reader/viewer/user on a journey toward surprised enlightenment."

—John R. Brandt, strategist and blogger, in a LinkedIn post

The Edelman LinkedIn 2021 survey stated, "87% of buyers say that thought leadership content can be both intellectually rigorous and fun to consume at the same time."

THOUGHT LEADERSHIP AND FAME

In the Fame Revolution, thought leadership has become even more critical, providing a platform for individuals and organizations to stand out and share their expertise. But for thought leadership to be effective, it should be revamped and replace corporate-speak with a human tone of voice, allow the employees to have a byline, and add some stardust of entertainment and engagement. When we look at the Public Figure model, thought leadership should add more of the personal to the equation.

Emphasize the person side of the Public Figure

In an era dominated by fleeting attention spans, the mere concept of a "company" can sometimes feel impersonal. Our minds are naturally drawn to the familiar, which explains the surging interest in storytelling.

Consider these statistics: 92% of consumers prefer brands that frame their ads as stories, 55% are more likely to remember a narrative over a straightforward list of facts, and, even more compelling, 68% admit that a brand's story influences their purchasing decisions.[52]

We all know of Apple as the great storyteller that captures our imagination. For the past few years, more and more books and courses are advising on story. The reason is that stories capture all parts of our brain— the right side and left side—and they are memorable.

"Story is the greatest weapon we have to combat noise because it organizes information in such a way that people are compelled to listen," states Donald Miller, multiple *New York Times* best-selling, including *StoryBrand*.

While there's an abundance of stories in the market, there's an even more powerful narrative tool—the human element. People are more than mere statistics. They're dynamic beings, each with their unique story. This explains the rising significance of CEOs in branding. Think of them as the rock stars in the corporate narrative; a CEO personifies a company's journey. And if they're skilled storytellers, it enhances their impact. They form that crucial link, connecting the brand to the consumer.

In essence, people resonate with people. Create a story others find worth listening to, and the best way to tell it is to deliver it yourself.

The thought leader spokesperson: the connector to the company

The role of a spokesperson, particularly for a thought leader within a company, is to bridge the connection between the audience and the corporate brand. While conventional wisdom advocates for personifying the company to make it relatable, there's a limit to how "human" a company can feel. Yes, a company can embody certain values, have a vision and mission, and elicit emotional resonance. However, leveraging a CEO or another key figure as a spokesperson for the company can improve the company's reach and relatability.

Employees as influencers and connectors

When I discussed the concept of nurturing thought leaders within a group of business owners, they were reluctant. They didn't envision themselves as spokespersons.

When I proposed investing in employees to fulfill this role, they posed a familiar challenge: **Why invest in employees when they might eventually leave?**

The investment in employees in such a manner might seem risky. Yet, data supports this approach. Studies indicate that employees are more loyal when they feel valued and recognized. In fact, 94 percent of the workers surveyed have stated they'd remain with a company longer if their employers showed a commitment to their professional growth[53]

In today's Fame Revolution, relying solely on the company's brand might be insufficient. Consider the enduring popularity of the Virgin Group founded by Sir Richard Branson, which today controls more than 400 companies in various fields. Much of its appeal can be attributed to founder Richard Branson's personal connection with his audience. Similarly, empowering employees to be the face and voice of a company can foster a deeper, more genuine connection with its customers.

One small business owner complained to me, "I end up investing all this money in resources for someone else to be a spokesperson and then they leave, and I have to train someone else."

This is why I say, have many employees be public figures and share their expertise as well as have the brand be connected to the CEO. Nevertheless, what I told this business owner was that the best would be if he took the role of being the main Public Figure of his company.

Companies need thought leadership to build their business

Thought leadership can be a powerful tool for companies and brands to establish themselves as experts and influencers in their industry. However, it's important to ensure that the content is insightful, engaging, authentic, and entertaining to truly make an impact.

As David Meerman Scott states, "True thought leadership is about sharing knowledge, inspiring others, and developing a fandom based on your expertise."

BUSINESS ES ARE PUBLIC FIGURES TOO

> ❝❞ *"Business is a matter of human service."*
>
> **—Milton S. Hershey,** founder of the Hershey Chocolate
> Corporation; he was instrumental in popularizing chocolate
> candy throughout much of the world

"BUSINESSES ARE PUBLIC FIGURES," Ingvil Gaasland, senior fellow at the Nexus Council, remarked, shedding light on the expectation for companies to behave and communicate more like a person than a distant, product-centric company. Now, employees, the public, and the media expect companies to have a stance on critical social issues. A survey concluded that over four in five (82%) members of Gen-Z believed that companies should take a stand on social issues, followed by 69 percent of Millennials.[54]

Companies today need a flexible strategy that connects with their profits, public image, and overall vision, while also understanding and meeting customer needs to reflect their values.

Businesses, large and small, and entrepreneurs or leaders wanting to increase their bottom line need to create a living and breathing strategy document that provides the room to change the product or service at a moment's notice. The Person + Product framework, illustrated in our image that details the characteristics of both elements, serves as a guide to ensure a balance between the person and the product. This balance is key to positioning yourself effectively, facilitating a swifter journey toward your goal. I recommend revisiting this framework regularly, especially during challenging times, to align it with your strategy and vision.

PERSON-CENTRIC BRANDING

Seeing the people side of branding is what renowned author and former CMO of Procter & Gamble, Jim Stengel, saw and revolutionized by creating a human-centric branding approach by looking beyond mere numbers and finding the purpose with each company.

Jim delved deep into the essence of products like Pampers, identifying their unique personalities. This marked a significant cultural shift in brand development, emphasizing the idea that ideals can be pivotal growth drivers. In his book *Grow*, Stengel asserts, "The counterintuitive fact is that doing the right thing *in* your business is doing the right thing *for* your business."[55]

His transformative influence on P&G centered on intertwining personal elements with corporate culture and was exemplified by the Stengel 50. He eloquently puts it, **"A brand ideal is a business's essential reason for being, the higher order benefit it brings to the world."** And continues to state that **"A brand ideal of improving people's lives is the only sustainable way to recruit, unite, and inspire all the stakeholders a business interacts with, from employees to customers."** Jim saw the importance of balancing the product and the person.

• •

COMPANIES ARE PUBLIC FIGURES TOO

• •

The Power of the Stengel 50

Jim Stengel was at the vanguard of the Fame Revolution, viewing companies more as individuals than faceless entities. He breathed life into brands of familiar names like Pampers, Max Factor, and Cover Girl. A notable instance was with Max Factor, which had been facing annual losses exceeding $20 million. Jim revisited the brand's origins and its commitment to infusing Hollywood's romance and glamour into everyday life for women. This recentering quickly bore fruit: within a year, Max Factor broke even and began to see growth. Such strategies significantly propelled these brands. Under Jim's guidance as the chief marketing officer of Procter & Gamble from 2001 to 2008, the company's sales soared, doubling, while earnings surged five times.

Jim aimed to demonstrate that incorporating this personal touch was beneficial for business. Collaborating with research firm Millward Brown Optimor, he initiated a decade-long growth study. They selected brands with the highest customer bonding scores from Millward Brown's vast database. When comparing these brands, dubbed the "Stengel 50," to the Standard & Poor, they observed a 400 percent return on investment. These purpose-driven companies, rooted in brand purpose, ideals, and authenticity, grew at a rate three times faster than their competitors. **Over a decade, the Stengel 50 expanded by 393 percent, in stark contrast to the S&P 500's decline of 7 percent.**

ENTERTAINMENT'S LASTING IMPACT

Part of being human is to be entertaining, and who says a bank can't rock and roll?

The first time I saw the products becoming personable was in 1998 when I saw Citibank's campaign featuring Elton John dancing to "Saturday

Night's Alright for Fighting" beside an ATM. Their daring slogan, "Who Says a Bank Can't Rock & Roll?" both horrified and exhilarated. For me, this creative template signaled a seismic shift away from the traditional corporate and prescriptive norms that had dominated for so long. The advertisement was a watershed moment indicating that the corporate world was evolving toward a more personable, entertaining, and engaging mode of communication.

Michael Wolf insightfully noted in *The Entertainment Economy*, "While content might not always be inherently entertaining, when presented in a compelling way, it's that which captures the audience's imagination." In his book, he elaborated on the Citibank campaign, underscoring that entertainment wasn't just a fleeting trend but had lasting power to make companies more profitable.[56]

To be entertaining is a call for storytelling and to reach the heart of humanity.

"What sticks to the brain has to go through the heart."
—**Paul Polman,** former CEO of Unilever

Such pioneering moments signaled the beginning of a transition from conventional corporate paradigms to more personable, authentic interactions.

As this transformation has unfolded, today we see newly established companies like Integro Bank taking it a step further and breaking the mold of traditional banking. They see the importance of the person. As the CEO Thomas J Inserra stated at a reception I was attending, they are not merely offering financial transactions but building a community of best practices. By hosting lecture series and offering comprehensive support tools, they are going beyond typical banking practices. The event offered an engaging session packed with investment insights for small businesses, all set against a backdrop of delightful food, cocktails, and networking opportunities. This pioneering approach—shifting away from the traditional banking model and truly connecting with their clientele—seems poised to be their formula for success.

Integro's success signifies that even sectors as traditionally rigid as banking need to embrace the fact that they, too, are public figures in the Fame Revolution.

HOW CAN A COMPANY BE A PUBLIC FIGURE?

There are two ways a company can be a Public Figure:

First, revisit the company's origin and purpose

Jim Stengel has shown how successful companies can be when we go back to the company's founding and embody the person who founded the company. During my tenure as VP of strategic communications at AGR Petroleum Services, a subsidiary of AGR Group, I had lunch with Sverre Skogen, CEO of AGR Group, renowned as the world's largest independent oil services company. I wondered what the initials AGR stood for, because I could not find an explanation anywhere in the various company documents. The current brand of AGR was smooth and very professional, but at the same time, it seemed to me that it lacked heart. It was doing all the right things, but something was missing.

"AGR stands for Always Great Results," Sverre said.

While it sounded like a good answer, it did not seem genuine.

When I traveled around to different continents to conduct interviews on the rebranding with key employees, I discovered in an interview with one of the employees, who had been there from the beginning, that AGR stood for the first initials of the founders, Arve, Geir, and Reidar. These were three guys from a small town outside of Bergen who were young and ambitious and from humble beginnings. They had found a lucrative business model cleaning oil rigs and were now making millions. Wanting to grow, the founders had decided to buy an engineering company. This purchase brought together two very different company cultures with different types of people: on one side were the more educated and sophisticated engineers, and on the other was the blue-collar company having made millions on their lucrative business model.

Ambitions were high. The company leaders set their sights on becoming the world's largest sophisticated and international oil services company. The down-to-earth and honest company, breaking ground with practical innovation, did not fit that image. The employee who shared the real definition behind AGR stated, "It seemed like the founders were embarrassed by their past when they should have been proud."

Fast forward a few months, and I was at a rhetoric course hosted by RetoRingdal with leading Norwegian communications directors in Italy by the beautiful Lake Como. The atmosphere was laid-back, the usual corporate façades were set aside, and there was a genuine openness in the conversation. After I gave a presentation in front of the group, my peers challenged me. "What does AGR stand for?" they wanted to know.

I parroted the CEO, "AGR stands for Always Great Results."

The whole room laughed and called out, "BS!"

"Torund, seriously, what does AGR stand for?" they insisted.

All eyes were on me, and I sheepishly said, "It stands for the founder's names, Arve, Geir, and Reidar."

The group burst out in a round of applause. "We love it! Torund, you need to tell the true story."

With the leadership's permission, the founders became the central part of the company's rebranding under the banner of "pioneering achievements," telling the story of the founders breaking ground and how their innovative and out-of-the-box thinking was part of the company's DNA. We wrote a company history book highlighting and honoring those three young men and had a cartoonist draw them, a portrait we framed and gave to each of the founders as a "thank you." We had a round of local media honoring the three of them. The following year was one of AGR's most successful and profitable years.

The greatest success comes from being real and embodying the person, even for a big corporation. Tap into the personal traits of the company and look to the founder for guidance.

It is about tapping into the human aspect of the company. You don't necessarily need to draw from the founder alone; instead, it's often about embracing the collective vision of the group that came together to establish the company.

Shaping Products into Personalities

Some companies excel at infusing their brand with a human touch. This approach is particularly effective for products you can eat, drink, or wear, as they help express personal identity. Consider the cases of Dutch Bros versus Starbucks or Coke versus Pepsi. Asking whether someone prefers Coke or Pepsi can reveal a lot about them. These brands don't rely on a CEO or celebrity; their products define their image. Other successful brands in this strategy include Taco Bell, IKEA, Mercedes-Benz, and KIA Soul.[57] Each brand has tapped into their personal differentiator.

Second, adopt Murray's connector brand strategy

Robert Murray is a leading international brand strategist from the United Kingdom. When I saw his connector brand strategy, I realized that he put words and images to what I have done intuitively. Because we are in the

THE CONNECTOR BRAND STRATEGY

Company XYZ

CEO or spokeperson

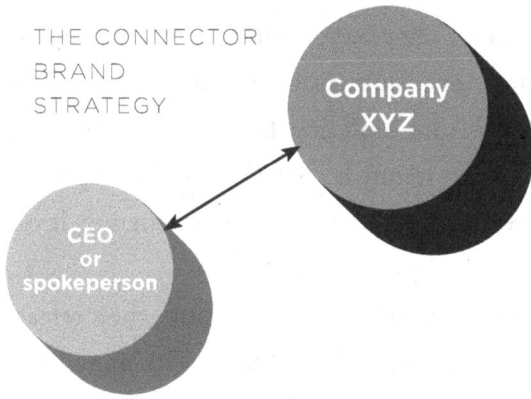

Fame Revolution, we are now overloaded with information, imagery, and videos. The key is to conserve brain calories and our brain usage and step away from just numbers and text by anchoring products and services with a person, i.e., the human elements. A person is a story. A person is interesting. A person brings life to the brand.

More about the brain consumption of information:

In "Building a StoryBrand," author Donald Miller explores how our brains handle information: they act as efficient editors, constantly filtering the endless stream of data. Intriguingly, the brain, which makes up only 2 percent of our body weight, consumes 20 percent of our body's energy.[58]

This selective process is more than mere sorting; it's a survival mechanism. When faced with trivialities, our brains smartly switch to daydreaming mode. It's not just idle wandering. it's a strategic energy conservation move, reserving power for moments that really count—those split-second, life-altering decisions.

So, when you catch yourself zoning out during a less-than-exciting conversation, remember this is your brain in its element, conserving energy for the crucial things in life. It's a small, yet fascinating aspect of our biology, reminding us that our brains are hardwired to focus on what's truly important, filtering out the unnecessary to save energy for what really matters.

The connector brand strategy is to connect CEOs and employees to be ambassadors to the company brand. They serve as the face of the company, attracting and encouraging clients or customers to discover more about the company. Look to Steve Jobs and Apple and how he expanded the brand with this personality. What I have found is that this can be expanded beyond the CEO and have several leaders out there at different levels speaking and being ambassadors to the company.

My favorite example comes from Intel when in 2009, they release the ad "Our Rock Stars Aren't Like Your Rock Stars." This innovative ad featured Ajay Bhatt, the co-inventor of USB, as a tech hero. It was a refreshing change from typical tech advertisements, highlighting the creative minds behind the inventions. Ajay Bhatt's newfound popularity led to appearances on The Tonight Show with Conan O'Brien and a feature in *GQ India's* July 2010 issue as one of the "The 50 Most Influential Global Indians." Beyond this, Bhatt helped humanize the brand, showcasing the real people and their contributions behind Intel's technologies. This approach elevated Intel's marketing strategy and resonated strongly with the audience, making the ad more relatable and impactful. Ajay Bhatt served as an exemplary ambassador for Intel, representing the company on various media platforms, including CNN, until his retirement in 2016, thus leaving a lasting imprint on the company's public image and branding efforts.

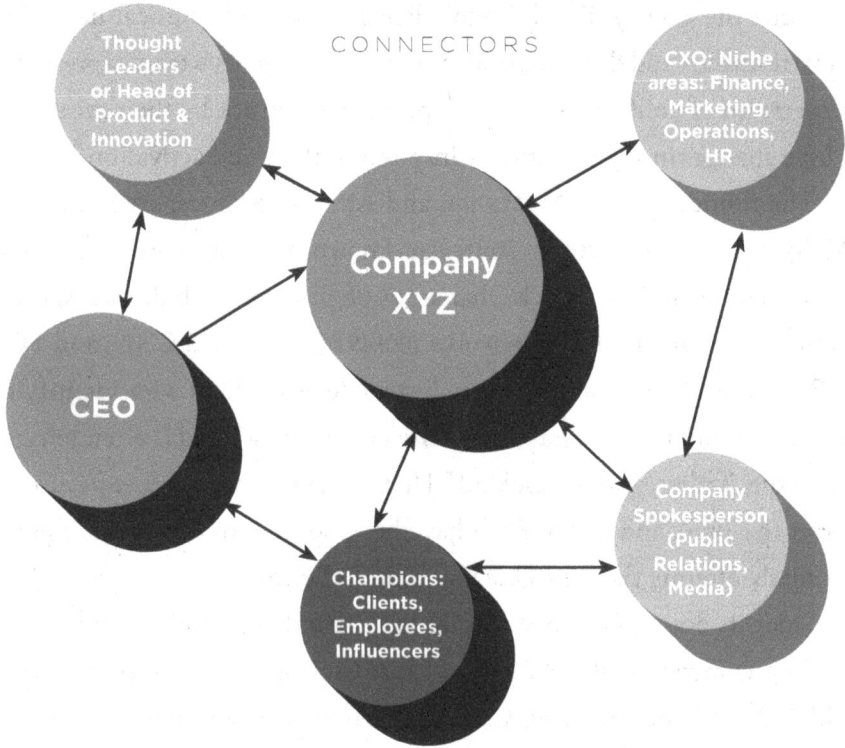

Thought Leaders or Head of Product & Innovation

CONNECTORS

CXO: Niche areas: Finance, Marketing, Operations, HR

Company XYZ

CEO

Company Spokesperson (Public Relations, Media)

Champions: Clients, Employees, Influencers

THE RISE OF THE PUBLIC FIGURE AGENCIES

From my observations, the most successful, groundbreaking agencies established in the last 15 years are intuitively using the Public Figure framework. These agencies, or strategic advisory firms, provide comprehensive support from strategy and planning to execution. From my vantage point, they manage their business clients with a Public Figure Strategy in mind; understanding the intricacies of relationships is similar to guiding a principal actor in a movie release or a political candidate through a campaign.

Purple leads the way

I remember when Purple Strategies first emerged onto the scene in 2008 in Washington, D.C. It was a breath of fresh air, especially their decision to name the agency 'Purple,' symbolizing a blend of political neutrality, bipartisanship, and deep political expertise. The agency's team represented a spectrum of political views. I was particularly struck by their mission to "drive change through politically inspired strategy and activation."

The founders, Steve McMahon and Alex Castellanos, are impressive. McMahon, a Democratic strategist known for his work on several campaigns, including Barack Obama's 2008 presidential bid, is a respected political commentator on networks like NBC, MSNBC, CNN, and FOX NEWS. Castellanos, on the Republican side, is credited with identifying the "soccer mom" demographic's political importance and is often referred to as the "father of the attack ad." He frequently shares his expertise on Meet the Press and CNN. Both have become well-known media figures, regularly offering their insights to a wide audience.

Since its origin, Purple Strategies has expanded globally, working with leading companies like B.P., Coca-Cola, McDonald's, Caterpillar, Bayer, PhRMA, and the American Chemistry Council. Their growth showcases their appeal and effectiveness across various industries.

The best PR agency in 2023

The best PR agency in America, chosen by the *Observer* in 2023, was BerlinRosen, founded by Jonathan Rosen and Valerie Berlin, both with backgrounds in politics. They began in New York, and on their website, they restate their original goal: "It all started in 2005 with a simple idea – build a communications firm that operates with the speed and intensity of a political campaign. That vision has taken us from a two-person startup to a team of 400+ professionals in New York, D.C, Los Angeles, and Amsterdam, working with the world's top companies, organizations, and leaders."

The rise of a Public Figure agency: First House

Bjørn Richard Johansen played a pivotal role in mitigating the 2008

Iceland economic crisis, serving as the head of the crisis management unit at the request of Iceland's Prime Minister. Following this significant experience, he established First House in Oslo, Norway, in the fall of 2009.

First House was founded on a deep understanding of the political landscape surrounding various industries and companies, including insights into the value drivers of their clients, shareholder value, crisis management, and political campaigning. First House's business model hugely succeeded in growing and enhancing their client's business success, influence, wealth, understanding of the political landscape, and impact, so much so that it ignited national attention.

One notable instance was the 2013 publication of the best-selling novel *Fyrsten* by the successful Norwegian author Henrik Langeland. The story in *Fyrsten* is a satire on First House and its key figures, setting them as a backdrop. The title "Fyrsten" resembles Niccolò Machiavelli's renowned 1513 treatise, *The Prince*. Like Machiavelli's work, which delves into acquiring power and governance, *Fyrsten* explores similar themes in its narrative. The release of *Fyrsten*, following Langeland's earlier success with *Wonderboy*, became a cultural phenomenon. Every leader in Norway felt compelled to read it, contributing significantly to First House's rise to legendary status within a mere three years of its founding.

The foundational strategy for Bjørn Richard Johansen has been to rapidly integrate public figures from the government and media as associates or partners. As a result of his recruitment strategy, the firm boasts a roster of prominent former politicians and political advisors. The firm has also been a desirable destination for retired media celebrities and anchors seeking new avenues.

First House's innovative approach, which I call the "Public Figure Framework," quickly set a new standard in the Norwegian industry. This strategy, focusing on leveraging the expertise and networks of public figures, was soon copied by competitors such as Zynk, Kruse-Larsen, Try

Advisors, Corporate Communications, and others.

Ingvil Gaasland, a senior fellow at the Nexus Council, summarizes the industry's landscape: "There seems to be a communications consultant on every corner helping craft messages, branding, and public image." Her statement underscores the growing influence and effectiveness of the Public Figure framework's widespread influence in Norway and its significance in shaping public perception, business, and policy.

When I contacted Bjørn Richard for fact-checking of this book, he shared his involvement in expanding a new agency called Paritee, a rapidly growing initiative in the international market. Currently, he serves as a strategic advisor to Paritee's board. He holds the position of commercial director at the advisory firm to one of Scandinavia's largest agencies, Geelmuyden Kiese, which was recently invested in by Paritee. With offices in Norway, Sweden, and Denmark, this firm aims to establish itself as a unique, high-end international advisory firm and recently made a significant move by acquiring Brands2Life, which boasts 200 employees in London, UK, and additional offices in New York, Minneapolis, and San Francisco. This acquisition is a major addition to the 140 employees in the Nordics that Geelmuyden Kiese had already integrated just 1.5 years prior. Paritee is positioned to become a prominent player in the ownership of agencies in the international market in the coming years.

Bjørn Richard Johansen stated, "It's all about people, strategy, and execution. I keep Sun Tzu's *The Art of War* on my desk to constantly remind me of the importance of leadership, analysis, strategy, and teamwork. I also regain inspiration when I read Walter Isaacson's biography about Steve Jobs or see his address to the Stanford students in 2005 on YouTube. The books and video mentioned are like an encyclopedia in strategy and tactics for me and I can read and see parts of it over and over again. Like Steve Jobs quoted the farewell message placed on the back cover of the 1974 edition of *The Whole Earth Catalog*, I advise everyone by saying: 'Stay hungry. Stay foolish.'"

The success of these agencies, founded on the principles of politics + entertainment, can be distilled into a framework that can help anyone achieve greater success by learning how to embody a Public Figure mindset and understanding that the person is now the driving force of campaigns. These agencies have achieved exponential success by consolidating services under one umbrella and personalizing their approach.

Taking cues from Hollywood and Washington D.C. can help anyone achieve success and influence in today's world. The framework used by these successful agencies can serve as a guide to help individuals and businesses achieve their goals and make a difference in the world.

PERSON

PERSONAL STORY IMPACT:

The resonance and influence of the brand's story.

Criteria:
- Story recall rate among surveyed audience
- Mentions of brand story in reviews or feedback
- Reach and engagement of storytelling content
- Audience retention ratetes

PUBLIC FEEDBACK:

Input from those closely aligned with the brand.

Criteria:
- Employee Net Promoter Score (eNPS)
- Partner satisfaction surveys
- Investor confidence metric
- Mainstream media mentions

EMOTIONAL ENGAGEMENT:

How often and deeply audiences react emotionally to brand campaigns

Criteria:
- Number of positive testimonials
- Engagement rate on emotional content (likes, comments, shares)
- Audience retention rates

SOCIAL ENGAGEMENT METRICS:

Digital presence and impact measures.

Criteria:
- Growth rate of followers across platforms
- Average engagement rate per post
- Virality factor (how often content is shared)

PRODUCT

MARKET VALUE:

The perceived worth of the product within its target market.

Criteria:
- Competitive pricing analysis
- Customer perceived value surveys
- Position in market compared to competitors

PRODUCT DIFFERENTIATION:

How the product distinguishes itself in its category.

Criteria:
- Features/benefits not offered by competitors
- Unique selling proposition strength
- Paent or IP uniqueness

SALES VOLUME:

Quantifiable sales metrics.

Criteria:
- Number of units sold monthly/quarterly
- Revenue growth rate
- Market share percentage

VISIBILITY OPTIMIZATION:

Where the product stands in its market journey.

Criteria:
- Sales trend (increasing, stable, declining)
- Innovations or updates frequency
- Sales engagement with customers

THE BALANCE BETWEEN PERSON + PRODUCT

"Yin and Yang are the source of power and the beginning of everything in creation."

—**Huang Di** (黄帝), The Yellow Emperor, legendary ruler (about 2717 BC–2599 BC) and forefather of Chinese civilization, culture, and medicine

TO EFFECTIVELY INTEGRATE the dual aspects of being both a person and a product, we have developed a sheet that serves as a tool to maintain a balanced approach between these two sides.

We aim to achieve a balance between:

- Personal story impact and market value.
- Social media engagement and sales volume.
- Emotional engagement and product differentiation.
- Public feedback and visibility optimization (SEO).

TWO TALES OF A PUBLIC FIGURE

"There are risks to action. But they are far less than the long-range risks of comfortable inaction."

—**John F. Kennedy,** the thirty-fifth president of the United States from 1961 until his assassination in 1963

What to do and not to do as a Public Figure is sometimes best illustrated in the two contrasting stories of two painters.

Short-term thinking and short-term windfall

The first time I was enthralled with being a promoter of great works was when I was invited for an evening to meet a local Norwegian artist, T.K.[2] I fell in love with her style, similar to Salvador Dalí's, but with more poignancy that called to the truth in my heart. I took all my savings and bought two paintings from her and told her that when I got back to college in the United States, I would see if I could get a gallery owner to showcase her work. Whenever I could, I talked about T.K.'s work, especially when I would go to galleries and art shows in Chicago and New York. After enough pitches, a gallery, famous at the time, committed to showing the paintings in Los Angeles and Acapulco and commissioned twelve paintings for a gallery show dedicated to T.K.

Just the commitment to the paintings being shown at a famous gallery in the United States and Mexico increased their value a hundredfold in Norway, so instead of giving me the twelve paintings for the gallery, T.K. instead gave me four paintings as payment for my services (paintings which I calculated to be worth $40,000 to $45,000 at the time). The artist decided to settle for the short-term benefit of selling and producing her paintings instead of the long-term investment in her brand and having her work displayed in the United States.

I held on to the paintings for twenty years, thinking their worth would increase. Unfortunately, when I went to "cash in," believing they would have doubled in value, I found out that the paintings were worth nil, zero, nothing. T.K. was not even registered as a painter in the Norwegian register of leading painters.

---

2 Out of respect for the artist, the pseudonym 'T.K.' has been employed.

HOW COULD THIS BE WHEN THE PAINTER HAD ONCE BEEN THE TOAST OF THE TOWN?

The answer to that question was twofold: The wrong focus and a lack of understanding that the real power of fame is in leaving a legacy—the painter focused for twenty years on painting and not investing in building a name. She thought that her works would speak for themselves.

> No matter how great your work is, if you do not take the time to tell the story behind your work, others will not appreciate what you're doing.

The power of a long-term investment

Contrast this with the world-famous painter Vincent Van Gogh. Like my painter client, Vincent did not invest in building a name, but Vincent was lucky and had a sister-in-law who intuitively knew the importance of doing just that. Jo (Jo van Gogh-Bonger) stood alone in 1890 after her husband Theo, brother to Van Gogh, passed away six months after Vincent's suicide.

She was alone with more than two hundred unwanted paintings, a small child, and a promise made to her husband to continue to promote his brother's paintings—even though Van Gogh had only sold one painting and the market value of his work was dismal.

Jo was resourceful and wanted to honor her husband's passionate dying wish to build Vincent Van Gogh's name and legacy. So she set up a fame strategy and executed her plan. She met and talked with collectors, museums, and critics, and got them to review Van Gogh's work, show off the paintings, and host events to create support for her cause.

Critics started to praise Van Gogh's work. Museums bought the paintings for the public to see. Art collectors bought the works to hang in their homes.

Jo transferred her passion for Van Gogh's paintings to her son, and this passion has gone through generations to promote Van Gogh's paintings to the world.

WHAT WOULD HAVE BEEN THE FATE OF VAN GOGH'S ART WITHOUT THE STRATEGIC INVESTMENT OF JO?

The art and the artist would likely have been forgotten entirely. Currently, Vincent Van Gogh is a foundation and museum dedicated to ensuring that his name is on top of mind and at the forefront in the art world.

. . . .

BUILDING A NAME AND STAYING FAMOUS TAKES STRATEGIC INVESTMENT

. . . .

What does it take to be like a Public Figure like Van Gogh?

Van Gogh would not be as known without Jo Van Gogh. Jo showed how to create a Public Figure Strategy by promoting the paintings and Van Gogh as the Public Figure.

FIRST, ALWAYS LOOK BEYOND YOUR CLIENT. To succeed in the Fame Revolution, you need to view yourself from a 360-degree perspective. How do all of your connections from your family, friends, associates, local government, business, media, and industry sectors perceive you? What are the ramifications of what you say? Because at one point, what you say or do might go viral, and you will be known beyond your clients and friends. Everyone will know you. I always advise my clients not to say or write anything that you would not want on the front page of a newspaper. Your action on the personal front can implicate or support your career or business.

What do I mean by "look beyond your client"?

In an extreme example, I will take you back to the 2001 film *Legally Blonde*. Southern California sorority girl and fashion merchandising student Elle Woods is dumped by her boyfriend when he tells her she is not serious enough for him as he plans to go on to Harvard Law School. Elle believes she can win him back if she can follow the same plan, so she studies for months and scores high on the Law School Admissions Test (LSAT). Along with her application, she also sends an unorthodox video essay montage to the admissions board, making a compelling case for why she should be admitted. The video was a power move, with Elle showing herself as a unique applicant. Combined with her 4.0 GPA and high LSAT scores, it got her accepted to Harvard Law.

Yes, this scene from a movie may be a bit silly, but it dovetails into a real-life example.

In September 2023, the newspaper group Gannett announced hiring a "Taylor Swift reporter." [59] According to the job posting, the media company was seeking "an energetic writer, photographer and social media pro" to cover Swift and her cultural impact for *USA Today* and *The Tennessean*, a Nashville-based news outlet. Of course, thousands of people rushed to throw their hats in the ring, among them, freelance photojournalist Lexi Thompson.[60]

Thompson knew she would have to make an impression if she was to stand a chance, so she borrowed a page from the book of Elle Woods, filming a video application that paid homage to the taped essay in *Legally Blonde*. Thompson didn't have the exact background the hiring managers requested, but she decided to try to stand out anyway.

Ultimately, the title of "Taylor Swift reporter" went to Bryan West, a 35-year-old journalist. [61] He is a superfan of Swift but also has a journalistic background: a student from Northwestern, winning awards, and working in newsrooms nationwide. Like Elle Woods, who had the LSAT scores and the perfect GPA, West was a standout and qualified.

However, Lexi Thompson got media attention for her video application, which drew clients to her photography business. She found a way to stand out and to become memorable.

In fact, research backs up that being yourself pays off. Francesca Gino, Laura Huang of Harvard Business School, and Ovul Sezer of the University of Carolina at Chapel Hill conducted a study that measured the best course of action when meeting someone we do not know. Do you cater to the other person or stay true to yourself? Most of the participants thought that adapting to other's experiences would be more effective. Yet the evidence showed the contrary that those who stayed true to their authentic selves were more than three times as likely to succeed. Our first inclination might be wanting to adapt to the person, but being true to who you are is the best course of action.[62]

Looking beyond your client means capitalizing on your differentiator. You don't have to cater to clients. Be unapologetically you because you have your own stories, experiences, and perspectives to bring to the table. Please don't follow the herd; it's boring and not as effective.

SECOND, BEING A PUBLIC FIGURE MEANS YOU ARE A PUBLIC SERVANT. In his book, *Thank You Economy*, Gary Vaynerchuk states that we need to imbed thank you in all that we do. Express and demonstrate gratefulness to those we work for and those who work for us. A Public Figure understands the importance of having interests outside the main business, that is, founding or contributing to a charity or nonprofit organization, serving the community, and investing in personal hobbies and interests. Personal interests are often remembered more than what a person does for a living because it showcases uniqueness and connects with the client or the target audience.

THIRD, AUTHENTIC CONNECTION IS THE CURRENCY OF THE FAME REVOLUTION. The person who is authentic and transparent wins. How you connect matters. I advise people to practice authenticity.

Have you ever seen a friend who is talkative and fun when you hang out at home, but they clam up and get fidgety and nervous when they are asked to speak publicly or be on stage? This is where practice comes in. Those awkward moments can even come off like arrogance, so getting comfortable and knowing which personal stories you want to share will help you ward off the trolls and the cancellers.

FOURTH, YOU ARE THE PRODUCT. How is your personal brand perceived? How are you marketing yourself? What do you offer? What do you want to say? Know the ins and outs of social media. Learn to do live videos, share stories, and do reels/shorts. Come up with a process to manage the creation and sharing of information. Learn how to do light editing. Keep up to date. Be professional.

FIFTH, BE YOU. This is the most important rule. Be brave because the greatest competitive advantage is capitalizing on being yourself with all your quirkiness. It might be more of a challenge for the digital immigrant who was taught not to stand out and to follow society or corporate culture and rules. (If you must prioritize, the fifth rule cancels out numbers one and two on the list.)

SIXTH, HAVE A SUPPORT TEAM.

A Public Figure recognizes that a team of supporters is needed to manage both the person and the product successfully.

Having a team you can trust is indispensable in helping you stay on track, bounce off ideas, and navigate the right answers when Internet trolls come your way. Keep in mind that it is **not a matter of if someone** will come after you, **but rather when.** Success often relies on the makeup of your team. As stated in the Old Testament, Proverbs 1:22 (English Standard Version), "Without counsel plans fail, but with many advisers they succeed."

SEVENTH, HAVE A STRATEGY AND PLAN. Going out on social media without a plan and just impulsively telling your story for the story's sake is a waste of time. A solid product or Public Figure doesn't just happen;

it is a well-thought-out strategic plan. As former CEO of Disney, Michael Eisner, states, "A brand is the product of a thousand small gestures."

Art, cruise ships, and fame

I was delighted to discover that my office landlord, John Doering, the leader of Scottsdale Living, is an art aficionado. Early in his career, he was part of the rising success of Park West Gallery, a gallery in the Midwest that changed the art industry by making high-end art available on cruise lines through art auctions. The infusion of art auctions into the cruise experience enriched passengers' journeys, offering them an opportunity to immerse and invest in the world of art, including historical artists such as Renoir, Picasso, and Rembrandt, as well as contemporary artists such as Peter Max, and Mark Kostabi. By democratizing access to high-end art, Park West Gallery has grown into one of the world's largest art galleries, boasting an estimated annual revenue of $300 million today.[63]

John was part of the journey. While he gives the owner credit for exceptional business acumen, he attributes the fame-building of the artists to distribution and states, "Value is driven by distribution." He explains that the unique thing that Park West Gallery did was to create an international distribution network to show art globally and help artists such as Kre8 and Peter Max to have a platform to build their brands and value and become famous beyond the cruise ships.

What can we learn from Park West Gallery?

New platforms create new opportunities. Like Park West Gallery democratized high-end art with a new platform, the Fame Revolution provides new ways to be known for what you do. And while it is not a traditional route for art galleries to showcase on cruise ships, they achieved significant profit and prominence.

PART 02

How to Become Famous: The Public Figure Strategy

You do not have to be
everywhere all the time. I
recommend adopting a strategy
similar to movie stars and
political campaigns. As you
might have noticed, movie stars
are not always in the limelight;
they ramp up their appearances
in the media, typically around
six to eight weeks before and
after a film premiere or in the
news during the concert tour.

CHAPTER THREE

HOW TO BECOME FAMOUS: PEOPLE

People are the energy of life, the building block of any business, and the ingenuity that creates impact. It is easy to focus on the numbers and yet—people make the numbers happen.

Becoming famous and stepping into the role of a Public Figure means recognizing that it takes a village to shine in the spotlight. Consider the film credits at the end of a movie: they highlight all the individuals who work behind the scenes, supporting the stars. The same holds true for influencers who appear effortlessly on camera, and internet business leaders marketing their courses online—there's always a team behind them.

In this chapter, we explore the various aspects of people, because they are the ones who make the world go around.

Understanding the team behind the camera is critical to ensuring that the lights, camera, and action all align perfectly with your persona. It's also about understanding the strategists who shape the way you are perceived and help you navigate potential pitfalls, including public missteps. Knowledge of your peers, leaders, and network, and knowing how to connect and strategize with authenticity, are essential in getting your unique talents and gifts recognized. It all revolves around people and your interactions with them.

ASK GEN-Z: TAYLOR'S WAY

> *"The ability to ask questions is the greatest resource in learning the truth."*

—**Carl Jung,** a Swiss psychiatrist and psychoanalyst who founded analytical psychology

I WANTED TO SHARE how we operate as a team and provide a greater context that we can all learn from, so I asked Sage, our GenZ colleague, if she would like to take the assignment to translate how we operate with an example of a business operation.

Neither Sage nor my other colleague Zachary Houghton, who is on the cusp of the Millennial generation and Generation Z, have ever experienced the corporate world and the behemoth of departments that can foster silos and limited thinking. They had never heard of silos in this context. When I talk to them about my experiences in the corporate world, they look at me as if I am from Mars. When I talked to my voicewriter, Lisa Duncan, she could vaguely relate because she worked a six-month contract for Boeing several years ago. I am surrounded by people who have not worked in the corporate culture with rules of conduct and the challenges of silos. What a relief.

What is a silo? In the business world, silos refer to individual departments or industries that do not collaborate or communicate.

SAGE TOOK ON THE CHALLENGE

I should have seen it coming when Sage returned with an analysis of Taylor Swift's organization. I laughed at first, but after I heard Sage explain the intricate and intelligent operations, I saw that Sage was demonstrating through Taylor that this is the perfect example of Public Figure operations in the Fame Revolution.

Sage is a diehard Swiftie who has attended several Eras tour concerts and can sing every tune. Her sister is even more of a devoted fan, and Sage claims her sister is like an encyclopedia of all things Taylor Swift.

Please note that Sage's analysis of Taylor's role in Public Figure operations is purely speculative, as it is based on external observations rather than internal knowledge of the situation. Despite this, our model indicates that Taylor displays a notable proficiency in these operations. I will let Sage explain it to you in the next section.

SAGE'S ANALYSIS ON THE PUBLIC
FIGURE OPERATIONS: TAYLOR'S WAY

> *"I try to prepare for everything beyond the extent of preparation."*
>
> —**Taylor Swift,** American singer-songwriter

HOW CAN WE WRITE A BOOK about fame without mentioning Taylor Swift, who is arguably the most prominent Public Figure in the world today?

With countless industry records broken in the year 2023 alone, including the most number one albums by a woman in history, and the most attended concert by a female artist in the United States, surely there is something we can learn from her.

While Taylor is certainly an incredibly talented artist and songwriter, I believe that the reason for her unmatched success is her impeccable strategy. Furthermore, while Taylor herself may be a mastermind, she requires an entire team of support to accomplish these impressive feats. Taylor doesn't work without her team.

So, who are these team members and what is the framework for their strategy?

Well, much of her team's identity is kept private for security reasons; however, we do know that her right-hand woman or, as I like to call her, the "co-mastermind" is Tree Paine, her publicist. Tree joined forces with Taylor in 2014, from which point, Taylor's career has exploded while many other pop stars of her caliber have floundered or plateaued. Based on this,

I would say Tree's capability to strategize and manage Taylor's team and reputation is largely responsible for where she is today.

How does this apply to you?

Well . . . you are the mastermind, right? At least you should start seeing yourself that way, or, at the very least, that you are the talent. Tree and Taylor illustrate the importance of a strong team and how that alone can make or break your business. A "co-mastermind" can have many different titles. Chief of staff is probably the most fitting across sectors; however, in entertainment, the title commonly used is "publicist." Tree is what Torund calls the chief of staff of the Public Figure operations. Tree is Taylor's right-hand woman.[64]

Who else is on Taylor's team?

You may be thinking, "Doesn't she need a personal assistant?" Erica Worden has held this position since very early on in Taylor's career. She has been referred to as a "personal assistant and road manager." Erica accompanies Taylor to events and also supports her in her personal life. I think we can assume that she manages and acts as somewhat of a gatekeeper to Taylor's schedule. This is also an incredibly important role. To have a successful operation, you must also find your "Erica," someone you can trust with both professional and personal matters to assist with your schedule and day-to-day life.[65]

These three people, the mastermind, the chief of staff, and scheduler make up the core team. The mastermind's job is to well . . . mastermind . . . and to maintain the public image. Assisting the mastermind in every way to accomplish her goals is the purpose of both the chief of staff and the scheduler positions.

Now that we have the core team, who else is there?

Well, there is an infinite number of positions and people who could be employed by Taylor's company (13 Management LLC). However, I surmise that there must be a core group of team leaders or "niche experts" who then trickle down the vision from the core team to the execution teams. For example, The Eras Tour's creative director and production designer is Ethan Tobman. Ethan likely has direct access to the core team, regularly bouncing ideas off of Tree or Taylor, while his execution team likely does not. Due to this niche expert's direct access to the masterminds, their vision is brought to life.

But Taylor Swift could not keep the attention of her fans at the intimate level that she does without all the effective collaboration of the niche team leads. There are obvious examples like the choreographers and the set designers working closely together, but I want to focus on a much more interesting collaboration across teams, the Easter eggs.

THE EASTER EGG OPERATIONS

The Easter egg is Taylor's way of communicating with her fans. "I love to communicate through Easter eggs," she said in *Entertainment Weekly*. "I think the best messages are the cryptic ones . . ."[66]

For those of you who may be unfamiliar, an Easter egg is a hidden surprise or extra feature or message that is included in something such as a computer game, a piece of software, or a film, for the person using or watching it to find and enjoy. The cryptic messages keep her fans engaged, and Taylor's team actively hides hints within music videos, and allegedly other forms of communication, to hint at things such as upcoming album releases, or other things within the Taylor universe. There are many hints in the "Karma" music video that the next album to be released would be *1989 (Taylor's Version)*, which turned out to be true. (Text on the pedestal of a statue translates from Roman numerals to 1989, and a clock in the coffee cups says the exact time of the album release.)

"It's sort of a tradition that we started a very long time ago," the singer said to Jimmy Fallon in 2021 about the origins of her Easter eggs. "I think the first time that I started dropping sort of cryptic clues in my music was when I was 14 or 15, putting together my first album."

Swift continued, "I wanted to do something that incentivized fans to read the lyrics because my lyrics are what I'm most proud of out of everything that I do . . . When I was a kid, I used to read through CD booklets and just read the teeny, tiny print and obsess over it."[67]

Let's track all the different team members who likely had to work together to pull this off.

FIRST, THE CORE TEAM HAD TO DECIDE WHICH ALBUM THEY WOULD LIKE TO RELEASE NEXT, not just based on personal desire but also feedback from the niche team leaders. Taylor has an adjacent fan group called "Taylor Nation." Their exact role in gathering feedback is not clear but for simplicity's sake, let's say the head of this group functions as the niche role of "fan outreach lead."

SECOND, I BELIEVE THE FAN OUTREACH LEAD would likely help the core team decide which album to release next, based on the demand from the fans.

THIRD, THE CORE TEAM WILL MOST LIKELY TALK TO EXPERTS WITHIN THE TEAM ABOUT RECORDING AND PRODUCING THE MUSIC. They will be able to give an accurate timeline of album release. When this is established, the core team will likely collaborate with any other strategy experts within the team, including but not limited to mainstream media and social media experts, to start teasing the album release. They can't tease so much that the audience loses interest but must create a master plan to ensure that the fan base will continue to be engaged.

When the master plan of the Easter egg is established, the strategists and core team will work with the other team members to plant Easter eggs. Taylor's friends and other outside collaborators also sometimes help with

Easter eggs. Depending on the Easter egg, different members of the visual design team will need to be involved.[68]

In the above example, I imagine that costume designers, set designers, and video editors had to be involved. At what point the actual ideas for the videos are created is a mystery, but it could be at any point and by any team member during this process. This effective collaboration of every team and team leads during the process of teasing an album release is just a small example of the necessity of a strong team with solid teamwork for success.[69]

The ingredient for the Easter egg is the collaboration at each level. It starts with Taylor and Tree and expands out to the wider network, ensuring feedback from Taylor Nation to ensure it entices and delights the fans. The secret to Taylor's collaboration is that each link has a voice and with enough solid arguments is able to influence the goal of the Easter egg.[70]

There are many things we can learn from Taylor Swift as the quintessential Public Figure of our era, much of which is covered in this book. Her ability to manage her public persona while continually breaking records would not be what it is without the strong team behind her. Using this framework and creating your own team is essential for success in the Fame Revolution.

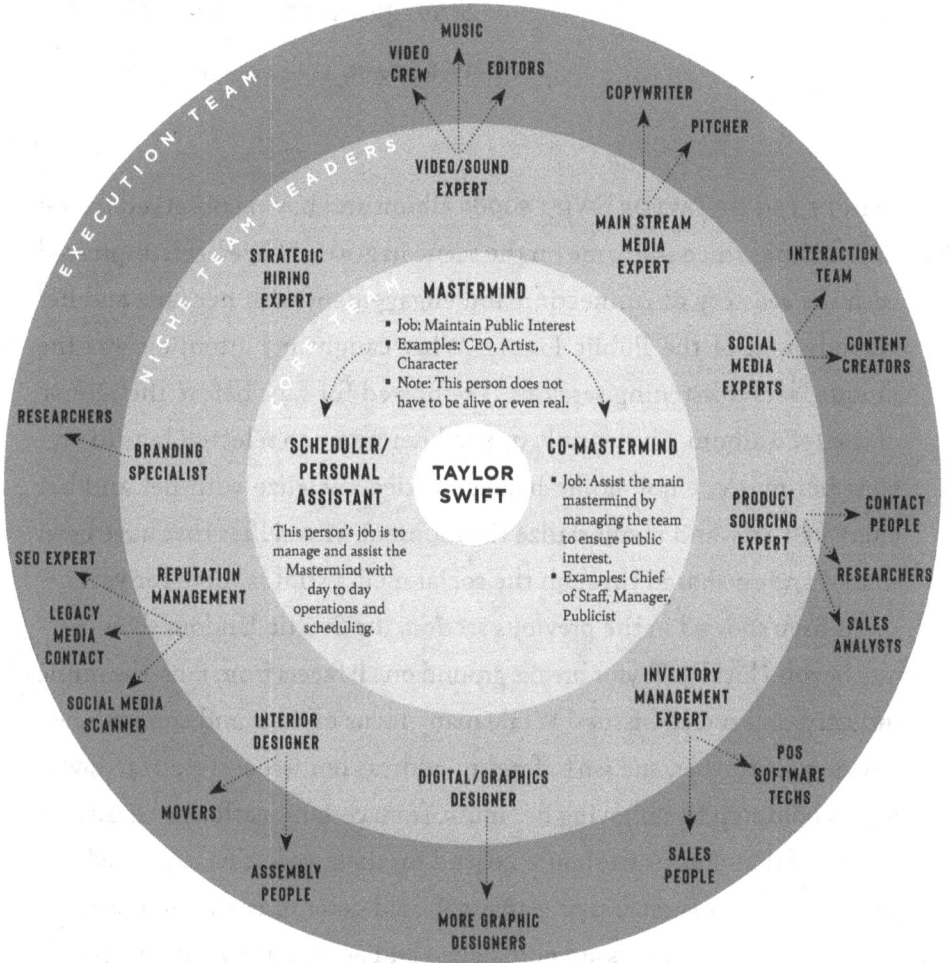

EXECUTION TEAM

NICHE TEAM LEADERS

CORE TEAM

MUSIC

VIDEO
CREW

EDITORS

COPYWRITER

PITCHER

VIDEO/SOUND
EXPERT

MAIN STREAM
MEDIA
EXPERT

INTERACTION
TEAM

STRATEGIC
HIRING
EXPERT

MASTERMIND

- Job: Maintain Public Interest
- Examples: CEO, Artist, Character
- Note: This person does not have to be alive or even real.

SOCIAL
MEDIA
EXPERTS

CONTENT
CREATORS

RESEARCHERS

BRANDING
SPECIALIST

**SCHEDULER/
PERSONAL
ASSISTANT**

This person's job is to manage and assist the Mastermind with day to day operations and scheduling.

**TAYLOR
SWIFT**

CO-MASTERMIND

- Job: Assist the main mastermind by managing the team to ensure public interest.
- Examples: Chief of Staff, Manager, Publicist

PRODUCT
SOURCING
EXPERT

CONTACT
PEOPLE

SEO EXPERT

REPUTATION
MANAGEMENT

RESEARCHERS

LEGACY
MEDIA
CONTACT

SALES
ANALYSTS

SOCIAL MEDIA
SCANNER

INTERIOR
DESIGNER

INVENTORY
MANAGEMENT
EXPERT

POS
SOFTWARE
TECHS

MOVERS

DIGITAL/GRAPHICS
DESIGNER

ASSEMBLY
PEOPLE

SALES
PEOPLE

MORE GRAPHIC
DESIGNERS

REFLECTING ON SAGE'S ANALYSIS

> *"Strategy sets the scene for the tale."*
>
> —**Taylor Swift,** American singer-songwriter

BEING A FAN OF TAYLOR SWIFT'S *1989* album and having observed her on the sidelines since she came on the scene in 2006, I have been impressed with her mastery of connection and engagement with her fans and her embodiment of the Public Figure. What caught my attention was the unique "secret listening sessions" she hosted for fans before the release of the *1989* album. She warmly opened her home to selected fans to preview her music, enjoy home-baked cookies, socialize with her and her cherished cats, and memorialize the moment with selfies that have been shared and re-shared through the social media stratosphere for years.

As Sage showed in the previous section, the Swiftie fandom shows loyalty beyond loyalty. Taylor breaks ground on all facets from fans, the music industry, and societal issues. While many focus on fans and concert sales, Taylor goes further, she isn't afraid to address hot issues. In 2014, Taylor took a bold step by removing her music from certain platforms because of her belief that musicians should be paid for their work. She expressed this in *The Wall Street Journal*, saying artists should determine album prices.

Taylor's achievements are unmatched and according to online research group QuestionPro, it was estimated that the US leg of the Eras tour will generate $5 billion in economic impact, "more than the gross domestic product of 50 countries."[71] Breaking down the numbers, on average, every $100 spent on live performances generates an estimated $300 in local spending on things like hotels, food, and transportation. What is interesting is that Taylor's "Swiftie" fandom spends between $1,300 and $1,500 per show to have the right outfits, costumes, and merchandise[72] beyond what is spent on travel and dining. Swifties want to mark the event and make it more than just enjoying Taylor's music.

Taylor's actions make her a modern public figure. In late 2023, she was named *TIME magazine's* Person of the Year for the second time. She first received this honor in 2017 when she was recognized as one of the "Silence Breakers" who inspired women to speak out about sexual misconduct. A true public figure leads the way, innovating and transforming their industry. Her operations demonstrate a shift in work practices that should be considered outside the music industry.

WHAT CAN WE LEARN FROM TAYLOR SWIFT'S OPERATIONS

1. Breaking down silos

Taylor's method eliminates traditional departmental boundaries, favoring a structure of specialized niches. This approach prevents the creation of silos, encouraging a more integrated and collaborative working environment.

In both Washington D.C. and the entertainment industry, Sage's analytical insight into Taylor's operations intuitively reflects the Public Figure way. Taylor's core team, mastermind and co-mastermind, work together and have set up a framework to prevent silos. The Public Figure way promotes leadership and information-sharing across the entire organization and is founded on collaboration. Trust and transparency form the company culture, fueling flexibility of breaking away from strict roles, and enables teams to adapt and share ideas freely, fueling creativity and innovation. Organizations that embrace the Public Figure way find themselves as agile, resilient, and ready for success. If there is anything I recommend you implement from Taylor, it is finding a way to break silos and create a system of collaboration that works for you.

2. Maximizing the person's talent

By focusing on individual strengths over rigid roles, the Public Figure way optimizes the distinct talents of every team member. For example, when I worked in the corporate environment after D.C., I was part of the events department. Yet, I had a strong media network and could have helped secure national news stories for the company. The media relations person welcomed my skill, but I was not permitted to help as this was not in my department. Instead of bowing to the rigid department rules and roles, the Public Figure way would have made room for me to utilize both talents and, in the end, benefit the company.

Maximizing the skills of a person is particularly important in small businesses where versatility is key. The Public Figure way emphasizes people and the value that each contributes to the outcome. Every team member comes with a different vantage point and can help with the outcome by sharing their unique perspective to drive the company forward. In my personal experience, I've found that administrative assistants and interns, often overlooked in initial discussions, frequently offer some of the most insightful perspectives. For me, they have proven to be invaluable advisors. Their fresh viewpoints and attention to detail can provide unique insights instrumental in decision-making. The Public Figure way recognizes that diverse viewpoints are essential for comprehensive problem-solving and innovation while also making team members feel valued and satisfied in their work.

3. The Campaign model

Nathan Hubbard, a longtime music, and ticketing executive who co-hosts a podcast called *Every Single Album*, says of Taylor Swift, "She is the best CEO and chief marketing officer in the history of music." [73]

The Eras Tour recaps Taylor's 17-year career in 3.5 hours with ten distinct scene changes and 16 different outfits that change according to each city, with 151 shows across five continents. How many hours did it take to plan and envision this tour? I can only imagine, but let's explore a possible scenario:

Taylor might have gotten the initial idea in the shower, I know that this is where many of my great ideas originate, and then she might have asked Mom and Dad over the dinner table, "What do you think about a tour where I sing all my songs and call it The Eras Tour?" Dad might have liked the idea and added, "Not just a tour, but let's maximize the opportunity and make a documentary." Mom would be excited to be part of planning out all of the outfits Taylor would be wearing to represent each album. After getting thumbs up from Mom and Dad, Taylor would most likely share her idea with Tree, her co-mastermind. Together with her core Team, they would set the initial strategy and invite her Niche Team leaders to develop the plan.

Creating a successful tour takes time, effort, strategic thinking, attention to detail, and luck – things can go wrong on the tour, but with hard work and strategic planning, luck is usually on your side. Taylor would have big thinkers on her team, but also the bean counters, the lawyers, the set, tech, costume designers, the promoters, and logistics masters, just to name a few, to ensure this could be pulled off. This process is all before the tour has even started!

What makes a campaign?

A campaign does not last forever. It has a beginning and an end. It is oriented toward one main event called the tentpole.

The term 'tentpole' is metaphorically derived from the central supporting pole of a tent, which keeps the structure upright and stable. This main event – be it a kick-off, an opening night, movie premiere, or another significant moment – serves as the focal point of the campaign. Smaller events, activities, and promotions are strategically designed to lead up to and support this key moment, much like how the canvas of a tent is supported and held up by its central pole.

A campaign goes through different seasons, mirroring the cycle of winter, spring, summer, and fall, where the tentpole event, as you might guess, aligns with the summer season, the hottest and longest days of the year. The summer is the campaign's peak, where activities are the most intense and impactful. It is the time to maximize the engagement and is the fruit of months and even years of planning.

> *A campaign is a planned effort to achieve a specific goal, often marked by public engagement, strategic planning, and a set timeframe, used in areas like politics, business, social issues, and the military.*

The seasons of the campaign:

| Planning and strategizing | Logistics and management | Execution and grunt work | Harvest time (reaping the rewards) |

And then, back into winter!

For example, with a presidential campaign, the shot that starts the campaign is the announcement that a candidate will run for office. This announcement will usually be staged as a press conference one to two years before election day. Election day is the tentpole event in politics. In contrast, in the movie industry, the tentpole event is often the release of a major film that the studios rely on to generate the most box office revenue. This movie will often be strategically released on Memorial Day or Christmas Day to maximize its potential for moviegoers. It all depends upon the target audience. Different audiences, different strategies.

The campaign season starts with the announcement to run for office, retreats into the winter season, planning the campaign, setting the message strategy, gearing up, and recruiting key endorsements; spring is a time for growth and spreading the candidate's message for the high intensity of the summer campaign until the major day of the election. In a political campaign, you either win or lose; in the movies, it depends on how much money you make at the box office. Many studios will release their tentpole on Memorial Day as it is the beginning of the summer and will create more opportunities for students out of school to go to the movies. Sometimes, a movie will flop in the US but do well when released internationally. No matter, after the main tentpole event, the summer transitions into the fall. Fall is the time to gather all the data and insights generated by the campaign and analyze its performance discerningly, comparing your achievements to the goals you set during the planning phase. You might create a celebration with stakeholders to commemorate the endeavor's success. It's also a great time to honor your team's hard work properly and discuss what worked and what didn't. By the end of fall, you've had a great run and are ready to return to planning mode (winter).

The Campaign Overview: Here is a sample of the seasons

❄ WINTER: PLANNING

- Brainstorm ideas and set campaign goals.
- Research your target audience and gather data.
- Develop the campaign strategy and messaging.
- Create a detailed plan outlining the campaign's components.

🌱 SPRING: LOGISTICS AND MANAGEMENT

- Execute detailed planning, finalize budgets, and allocate resources.
- Develop a timeline and assign responsibilities to team members.
- Design and produce campaign materials.
- Coordinate with partners or collaborators.
- Set up tracking and measurement systems.

☀ SUMMER: EXECUTION

- Launch the campaign according to the plan.
- Monitor and manage all aspects of the campaign.
- Engage with the target audience through various channels.
- Continuously assess progress and make necessary adjustments.
- Address any issues or challenges that arise.

🍁 FALL: REVIEW AND SHARE

- Gather and analyze data on the campaign's performance.
- Evaluate the campaign's success against the goals set in the planning phase.
- Celebrate achievements and share results with stakeholders.
- Gather feedback from participants and the audience.
- Document lessons learned for future campaigns.

Alex gathers the fruits of his work

Alex Hormozi, founder and CEO of Acquisition.com, executed a remarkable launch for his book *$100M Leads: How to Get Strangers to Want to Buy Your Stuff*. In doing so, he quadrupled the Guinness World Record for a business event, pulling in an astonishing 188,000 registrations with 85,000 attendees. Even considering that nearly half the audience opted for the replay stream, this feat surpassed the existing record four times. Quite the achievement and certainly cause for celebration.

But it took work of winter and spring to pull off his summer achievement, as Alex states in an Instagram post a few days after pulling off this amazing feat:

"Even with half our forces having to stream the replay - we 4x'd the Guinness World Record for a business event. The work paid off."

Here is an overview of the work it took:

- 67,000 Words
- 2000 Hours
- 270 Pages
- 106 Drawings
- 62 Pro Tips
- 25 Chapters
- 8 Tweets
- 5 Sections
- 2 Years
- 1 Cookbook for making money

A campaign isn't strictly defined by the span of a year. For Alex, it involved two years of meticulous preparation. Think of the "campaign season" as an indicator that we operate in cycles, each demanding different skills and capabilities from us and our team. The duration and intensity of your campaign hinges on your objectives. In your off-season, a moderate approach could be posting once a week across your active platforms, tailoring content for each. However, as you approach the heart of a campaign, this might escalate to producing as many as 80 pieces of content per month.[74]

The benefit of a campaign

You do not have to be everywhere all the time. I recommend adopting a strategy similar to movie stars and political campaigns. As you might have noticed, movie stars are not always in the limelight; they ramp up their appearances in the media, typically around six to eight weeks before and after a film premiere or in the news during the concert tour. Similarly, even though presidential campaigns seem ever-extending, candidates aren't always "on." They have their peak moments and their quieter periods.

Similarly, Taylor Swift seems to be everywhere with the Eras Tour but will tread back into the shadows planning her next tour and album release.

Take the example of singer Adele: between each of her albums, she takes a hiatus, yet her career thrives. After her debut with "19," fans eagerly waited three years for her sophomore album and another four for her third. However, with "30," the anticipation stretched for over six years.[75]

From my own experiences with campaigns, I've recognized a rhythm, a cadence if you will, that feels inherently human, well, at least, it resonates with my personality. The truth is, we aren't built to be 'on' all the time; it's neither sustainable nor authentic. But with a well-timed blitz, and by establishing a consistent cadence between campaigns, we can maintain the momentum.

SETTING UP THE RIGHT TEAM

66 *"Talent wins games, but teamwork and intelligence wins championships."*

—Michael Jordan, one of basketball's greatest players, led the Chicago Bulls to six NBA championships (1991–93, 1996–98)

IN THE NEXT FEW SECTIONS, I will go into the nitty-gritty of how to rethink your team if you are a small company, from a solopreneur startup to a large corporation.

As a small startup, you might think having such an organizational structure is unnecessary. And yet, I bet you already intuitively have a "kitchen cabinet" of friends and family in place supporting your endeavor, and when you need help, they are there to support you.

You probably also have a "brain trust" of people in various roles to help you move forward. While it may seem overwhelming and not applicable to small companies to set up this kind of organizational structure, I recommend small and large companies consider it, because the framework can easily scale up or down and provide the support needed to thrive in the Fame Revolution.

At first, many roles are combined and performed by one person. When you have a startup, you wear many hats. If you are the founder, you start as the CEO, web developer, administrative assistant, and social media manager, and as you grow, you delegate the roles. But as you grow, adopting strategic thinking regarding organization and scalability becomes increasingly important. It's about figuring out the most effective way to structure your operations so that you can grow successfully and sustainably.

Interestingly, former CEO Eric Schmidt of Google implemented the chief of staff position and stated it was a game changer. Harvard University and Oxford University have newly partnered with the Chief of Staff Association. And they are now offering educational programs to train leaders to consider having a chief of staff to manage the new demands of being a CEO.

When setting up new ventures for our clients, be it a non-profit, educational program, or campaign, our first hire is always the chief of staff. We recommend investing in a role that can provide executive decisions and is crucial in reducing your workload as a Public Figure. Interesting to note, many startups begin with two founders, where one takes on a role similar to that of a chief of staff. This pattern is evident in the founding of major companies like Apple and Microsoft. Steve Jobs had Steve Wozniak, while Bill Gates had Paul Allen, with one playing more of the visionary role and the other focusing on operational excellence, technological development, and internal management.

The Fame Revolution requires new thinking, and the Public Figure way is not about fixing what is broken but finding new ways to create an effective operation. I am not saying it is the only way; I am showing one way that has proven effective and has a track record in Washington, D.C. and Hollywood.

Let me reiterate: if you are feeling overwhelmed, I understand. It seems like a lot, especially if you have not taken the time to strategize and assess everything you are doing and everything you need to do to position yourself for success in the Fame Revolution. You don't have to have everything all at once. Build upon each aspect and facet daily and ensure you are writing things down and keeping track of where it takes you. I encourage you to search for people and consultants who can help you create your Public Figure Strategy.

YOUR BRAIN TRUST

"All great leaders choose great advisors, people they really trust for their governance."

—**Tom Payne,** English actor

"In the multitude of counselors there is safety."

—**Proverbs 11:14 (KJV)**

WHEN THERE IS A SHIFT in the political winds, there is a need for a "brain trust" to ensure that all minds are on deck to plan and strategize.

During the presidential election of 1932, when the United States was still struggling with the Great Depression ignited by the 1929 stock market crash, the winds shifted, and there was a chance for change. For eighty years, the Republicans had been in the presidential seat, and with the Great Depression in its high season, there was a sense in the air that it could turn. The Democratic presidential candidate Theodore Roosevelt did not leave it to chance and, I believe, won the election because he had gathered advisors far and wide to provide the socioeconomic solutions needed to move America forward. He collaborated with academics from Columbia University, such as Raymond Moley, Rexford G. Tugwell, and Adolph A. Berle, Jr. The members were primarily responsible for shaping Roosevelt's policies and strategies that were pivotal in addressing the challenges of the Great Depression. The gathering of these men captured the attention of journalist John F. Kieran, who coined the gathering of advisors as the "brain trust."

Roosevelt won the election and ushered in the Democratic Revolution that set the foundation of American policy for the next sixty-two years, until, in 1994, the winds shifted again. At that time, Newt Gingrich, like Roosevelt, created a "brain trust" as he saw the opportunity to change the direction of the country. He gathered many different advisors, including Arianna Huffington, founder of the HuffPost, Frank Luntz, the pollster, House of Representatives Dick Armey, John Boehner, and Jim Nussle, to name a few, and created the legislative agenda known as the Contract with America. With his brain trust, Newt Gingrich led the Republican Revolution and became the first Republican speaker in fifty-two years. **Each of these men, Roosevelt and Gingrich, created a thinking machine into which they could throw any problem and have it pass through the minds of trusted advisors.**

In the book, *Creativity, Inc.*, co-founder of Pixar Animation, Ed Catmull, discusses using a brain trust as a tool to "push toward excellence, and root out mediocrity" in their films like *Toy Story*, *Up*, and *Finding Nemo*. Catmull believes the brain trust is important, because in many cases, the film's director becomes so immersed in their own work that they can lose sight of the bigger picture. They benefit from having the perspective of intelligent colleagues who can look at the film from different angles.[76]

Catmull writes, "If Pixar is a hospital and the movies are the patients, then the brain trust is made up of trusted doctors. In this analogy, it's important to remember that the movie's director and producer are doctors too. It's as if they've gathered a panel of consulting experts to help find an accurate diagnosis for an extremely confounding case. But ultimately, it's the filmmakers, and no one else, who will make the final decisions about the wisest course of treatment."[77]

Consulting a trusted panel for problem-solving and feedback will improve the quality of your work or message. As Catmull puts it, "The brain trust is valuable because it broadens your perspective, allowing you to peer—at least briefly—through others' eyes."[78]

SO, WHAT IS A BRAIN TRUST?

The *Oxford Dictionary* defines it as "a group of experts appointed to advise a government or politician." It brings together diverse knowledge and expertise to inform decision-making and policy development. In most of the positions I have held in my career, I have set up brain trusts for clients and utilized this method—I establish more informal groups and help gather advisors, academics, and experts from non-governmental agencies (NGOs), sports, and entertainment to provide insights into the issues we are facing. Brain trusts have been instrumental in bringing countless great ideas to life.

The power of the brain trust is in its combination of both the formal and informal nature. The concept of a "brain trust" goes far beyond mere brainstorming. It embodies a strategic gathering of trusted advisors and key staff members, including the kitchen cabinet, chief of staff, voicewriter, champions, and those in charge of promotions and strategy. This inner circle of advisors provides a wealth of knowledge, insights, and advice, substantively contributing to the decision-making process.

In uncertainty or upheaval, having many advisors to provide the different vantage points from your peripheral vision is wise. It provides a 360-degree view and helps find the right solution to ensure maximum impact.

HOW CAN THIS WORK FOR YOU?

In the Fame Revolution, collaboration is the currency, and I believe that forgoing a brain trust is missing a real opportunity to test and fine-tune ideas. Members of your brain trust are free to critique your ideas, because, unlike boards of directors, they have no fiscal responsibility for your business. They are particularly valuable in the early stages but can also contribute to long-term, sustainable innovations.[79]

Mentors, colleagues, and even competitors can give you the perspective you need to thrive. Cultivate people to listen to your ideas, help explore possibilities, and take things to the next level.

CHIEF OF STAFF

- **Navigator:** Charts a course through difficult waters and helps steer the organization's strategy and ensures that it avoids potential pitfalls.
- **Conductor:** Harmonizes various elements of the organization by coordinating different departments, initiatives, and personalities, making sure that everyone is aligned and working together effectively toward a common goal.
- **Counselor:** A confidant and advisor to the leader, offering insights, advice, and perspective on a wide range of issues.

CHAMPION

- **Outreach:** Initiates and builds relationships with stakeholders, media, and community groups to share key messages and establish connections.
- **Engagement:** Actively interacts with diverse audiences to foster dialogue, community, and loyalty through platforms like social media and events.
- **Collaboration:** Partners with organizations, influencers, and industry peers to jointly achieve goals and amplify message reach and impact.

YOUR BRAIN TRUST

KITCHEN CABINET

- **Catchphrase:** Crafts concise, memorable phrases to encapsulate and communicate a brand or individual's core message, resonating with the audience.
- **Storytelling:** Creates engaging narratives that emotionally resonate with the audience, reflecting their values and experiences.
- **Framed Messaging:** Strategically shapes information presentation to influence audience perception, utilizing tone, context, and emphasis for impactful communication.

VOICEWRITER

- **Unified around the Vision:** Ensures complete alignment with the vision, gaining 110% commitment from all members.
- **Diverse:** Embraces diversity in occupations, perspectives, genders, races, ages, and creeds, especially valuing insights from different age groups for campaign success.
- **Respectful Disagreement and Agreement:** Fosters a culture of respect and honesty in feedback and insights within a diverse group.
- **Trust:** Creates a comfortable, informal environment where members can be themselves, offering protective support, feedback, and counsel to present the best way forward.

YOUR KITCHEN CABINET

> *"The power of the kitchen cabinet is not just in its collective wisdom, but in its collective belief in your potential."*
>
> **—Unknown**

YOUR **KITCHEN CABINET** is part of your brain trust. While your brain trust is comprised of expert advisors who help you raise your game and hold you accountable to keep your integrity, your kitchen cabinet is a smaller, more intimate group of people you trust and admire who share advice and personal insights with you. The members of the kitchen cabinet have a personal interest in you. They embrace **candor, which targets the issue, not the person.** They are part of an inner circle, and their contact with you is frequent.

The term "kitchen cabinet" comes from the era of President Andrew Jackson. Rather than relying solely on his official cabinet, Jackson leaned on an informal group of confidantes for guidance. Tradition recounts that their discussions often unfolded in the White House kitchen, leading to being coined "kitchen cabinet."

"Candor is a compliment; it implies equality. It's how true friends talk."

—Peggy Noonan, Pulitzer Prize–winning author

WHAT IS IT ABOUT THE KITCHEN?

I don't know about you, but whether I am hosting or attending a party as a guest, the kitchen is the center of it all where the most interesting discussions occur.

Faith Durand, editor-in-chief of Kitchn, a website focused on home cooking, kitchen design, and gatherings, stated to NPR that the messy informality of the kitchen has its own draw, "In the kitchen, you can relax. . . . You can bump up against a counter, not worry about putting that glass of wine down. There might already be some mess."[80]

This idea of having a cabinet of advisors is an intimate circle of advisors, regardless of their formal roles.

During my leadership time, I understood the profound significance of such a trusted advisory group. My kitchen cabinet has been different at certain points in my career. I prefer a more informal format. One cabinet I had while leading a nonprofit met every six weeks over breakfast. These meetings were crucial touchpoints—a space where I'd share updates on my leadership journey, from managing interpersonal dynamics with staff to strategizing on fundraising. They, in turn, offered insights, guidance, and sometimes necessary challenges on a spectrum of issues, ensuring that we stayed true to our vision. Over time, our professional interactions during these breakfasts laid the foundation for deep-rooted friendships.

CRAFTING YOUR OWN CABINET

Envision your kitchen cabinet, not as storage for utensils but as a reservoir of wisdom and guidance. These individuals, hand-selected by you, bring a breadth of perspectives to the table—a potluck of sorts. It can be a group as informal as your spouse, family members, or friends or maybe you can recruit a professional you admire. Personally, I have had most success when meetings were organized and regularly planned with people I admired. Everyone brought something to the table, and everyone was heard. It worked because they believed in the vision of the organization.

You can make this group a "resume builder" and name it a "Board of Advisors." Whatever you decide, a kitchen cabinet should have no more than a handful of people, three to five being optimal. You want just enough people to fit around the kitchen, talking over some chips and salsa, keeping a tight-knit vibe.

To have an effective kitchen cabinet, keep the channels of communication open, encouraging genuine dialogue and constructive critiques. Key qualities to look for are:

Unified around the vision: First and foremost, it is about the vision. Make sure they are 110 percent behind you.

Diversity: Choose people with different occupations, perspectives, gender, race, age, and creed. I have found the more diverse, the better, and stacking the cabinet with people from different age groups is crucial. I have personally been so grateful for the younger generations as they provide unique insight and have saved me multiple times when it came to launching a campaign.

Respectfully agree to disagree: With a diverse group, it is important to be founded on respect for one another and to be honest with the feedback and insight.

Trust: With a cabinet, you can be informal like a late party when you end up in the kitchen. You kick off your shoes, loosen your tie, and show up as yourself with all your foibles. The informality encourages openness and new ideas. Because these are meetings of equals, everyone is heard and valued. You know that the people surrounding you are there to protect you, provide feedback, and provide advice that will ensure that you put your best foot forward.

The cliché that it takes a village to accomplish something is true more now than ever. So, find your kitchen cabinet and your brain trust. This will provide a full breadth of advisors and people to help ensure that you have a 360-degree vantage point of who you are, what you are to be known for, and how to position yourself in the marketplace of ideas.

· ·

CHOOSE WISELY

· ·

YOUR CHIEF OF STAFF

"You can focus on the 'Chief', or you can focus on the 'of Staff'. Those who have focused on the 'of Staff' have done pretty well."

—**James A. Baker III,** former chief of staff to presidents Reagan and G. H. W. Bush. Notably also served as secretary of state (Bush), treasury secretary (Reagan), and commerce secretary (Ford)

EVER WONDERED HOW entrepreneurial powerhouses like Ryan Reynolds and Jennifer Lopez juggle their many roles? For smaller businesses, and especially for serial entrepreneurs, navigating complex personal and professional lives demands expert management. That's where a chief of staff steps in, ensuring seamless information flow and maximizing the principal's time and decision-making. It's a game-changer for effective leadership.

Google took a page from the Washington, D.C. playbook when they brought on Silicon Valley veteran Ann Hiatt to be the first chief of staff at Google for Eric Schmidt, chairman at Google. The experiment was supposed to last one year but lasted nine and a half years.

In an interview with *Business Leader*, Ann remarked, "I invented the chief of staff role at Google." She was inspired by her interactions during meetings with the Obama Administration on behalf of Google, where she saw firsthand the effectiveness of such a role. After their first year working together, Eric told Ann that her contributions had added ten times his impact to the organization.[81]

In the realm of business support functions such as marketing, HR, and communications, the ultimate desire is to secure a place at the executive leadership table and be recognized as a vital core of the business. Personally, it's my passion to identify the most effective ways to contribute and propel the business forward. Often, these functions intersect and sometimes clash due to overlapping areas of responsibility. Branding might overlap with marketing and communications, internal communication might cross into HR territory, and even the CFO can touch upon various domains. A chief of staff sees the interplay more clearly than the leader as they are a confidant to the principal, that is, Public Figure/CEO/business owner, and the people reporting to them. They also see what is missing in the execution. They have the unique role of seeing all the players and being able to go in and play when necessary but also have the bird's eye view. This unique role has the power to ensure that silos are broken and to guarantee an interplay of collaboration and steady flow of information.

I suggest following Ann's example at Google and taking inspiration from Washington's playbook by appointing a chief of staff for your operation. What's interesting is that an increasing number of corporations are adopting this role.

What about a small operation or an influencer? I would say that this model works for the smallest of organizations that want to scale up. One of the requirements of chief of staff is to understand all of the company's roles and be able to step in when necessary.

THE GROWING TREND OF CHIEF OF STAFF

As Dan Ciampa aptly puts it in *Harvard Business Review*, "The purpose of the chief of staff (CoS) is to make time, information, and decision processes more effective."[82] I would also emphasize that they serve as a crucial line of defense against silos forming within an organization.

The chief of staff is a growing phenomenon. Boston Consulting Group conducted a study that indicated companies with a chief of staff or equivalent had at least $2 billion in revenue. The chiefs of staff for large companies also tended to have greater breadth of responsibilities and duties.[83] While researching this, I discovered that there's a chief of staff association that offers a certification in partnership with Oxford University and Harvard University. Members of this association hold influential positions in over forty-five countries.[84]

In D.C., one can witness the significance of the chief of staff role and its power in streamlining an office. When I served under Senator Hatch, the Chief of Staff was a formidable figure who efficiently managed the operations. She was among the few who could match the senator's pace. Senator Hatch had multiple chiefs of staff during his time in office, each contributing significantly to his office's accomplishments. Largely due to their collective efforts, the office achieved a great deal. According to the *National Journal*, by the time of his retirement, Senator Hatch had passed more laws than any other living senator, with well over 750 of Hatch's bills becoming law.

You might be thinking, "I am not a big corporation, celebrity, or politician," yet this framework of having a chief of staff can help you. Implementing a chief of staff function substantially improves operations by showing a 360-degree vantage point, which is a challenge for a single CEO or leader.

The benefit of the chief of staff is being attuned to the leader's needs, and the ability to handle more sophisticated situations that require a deeper level of understanding and discretion than an executive assistant. I personally advocate having both an executive assistant and a chief of staff. This dual setup creates a powerful team to ensure that the Public Figure is always looked after, ensuring everything runs smoothly and efficiently.

YOUR VOICEWRITER

> *"Speech is the representation of the mind, and writing is the representation of speech."*
>
> **—Aristotle,** Greek philosopher, and polymath

"SO, HOW SHOULD I ATTRIBUTE you in my book?" stated a client to me. "You have been my thought partner and have helped nurture my vision."

I replied, "I am your voicewriter," and explained, "I reflect what you aim to express. Together, we found your voice, and I helped articulate it in a way that aligns perfectly with your vision and voice for the book."

He said, "I have never heard of a voicewriter, but I like it. It fits."

The voicewriter is a new concept created by Lisa Duncan who found the terms ghostwriter and speechwriter limiting, and I agreed. Lisa and I have been working on several books where I have been the lead editor and needed someone to come alongside our clients as they themselves saw their limitations in finding their voice and fully expressing their vision.

The benefit of using a ghostwriter is that you do not have to reveal that you have had assistance, and yet, now the climate and expectation are to give some credit to the person who is assisting you with finding your voice. In politics, there is a tradition of giving credit to the speechwriters, and a voicewriter models that but goes beyond the speeches. Some might call them content writers, but again, that role is limited to creating content and not necessarily in the voice of the Public Figure.

When I worked for Senator Hatch, I remember being assigned to write talking points for a live interview with CNBC right after 9/11 on the state of the economy. I researched and wrote what I thought would work. The talking points were then sent to the legislative assistant on finance and taxes (the person in charge of monitoring key legislative issues and responding to policy, drafting policy, and speeches on that issue). Next, the talking points were sent to the communications directors and chief of staff and returned to me with edits. It was not just one round but several rounds to ensure the accuracy of the senator's viewpoint and voice. As a young press assistant, I was annoyed and kept asking myself, "Why is it taking so long to get the message approved?"

On the day of the interview, I was assigned to assist. Having received the talking points the previous night, Senator Hatch used our brisk fifteen-minute walk from the Senate Hart building to the Capitol to familiarize himself with them. During the interview, he skillfully adapted the points we prepared and added his own insights.

While Senator Hatch entrusted us with preparing initial talking points due to his busy schedule, he actively engaged with the material, ensuring it aligned with his perspectives and knowledge. This collaborative approach was a testament to the trust he had in his team to provide well-researched, accurate information that he could then personalize and present."

IS IT ETHICAL?

Some say yes, and some say no. Having a ghostwriter and speechwriter has been a standing tradition for Hollywood and D.C. Speechwriter Ted Sorensen helped President John F. Kennedy with his inaugural address that included the famous statement, "Ask not what your country can do for you, but what you can do for your country." President Reagan and President G. W. Bush leaned on Peggy Noonan. In contrast, President Obama counted on Jon Favreau, the current host of the podcast *Pod Save America*, at the beginning of his presidency, and later relied on Cody

Keenan. Speechwriters often grow close to their speakers, and President Obama would refer to Jon Favreau as his "mind reader."

We see this practice expanded outside of politics with key influencers from Guy Kawasaki to Andrew Sullivan who have admitted to having people write for them. Critics of ghostwriting raise concerns about authenticity and deception. They argue that ghostwriting can mislead the audience, especially when the presence of a ghostwriter is not disclosed. This lack of transparency may lead the audience to attribute the eloquence, wisdom, or humor in a speech directly to the speaker, potentially creating a false impression of their capabilities and character. The criticism hinges on the belief that personal authenticity and direct authorship are critical for trust and credibility, particularly in public discourse. When a speech, assumed to be a personal expression of the speaker, is found to have been written by someone else, it can undermine the speaker's credibility and the audience's trust in them.

It is interesting to note that when it came to preserving President John F. Kennedy's legacy, his wife Jackie Onassis requested all drafts of the inaugural speech with the famous line, "Ask not what your country can do for you—ask what you can do for your country," to be destroyed. She wanted to ensure the speech was credited to President John F. Kennedy. The development of this inaugural speech involved a team of writers and strategists, making it difficult to attribute specific contributions since everything was intertwined. And yet, it was Kennedy who delivered the speech and put his name on the words spoken. It was his speech as he delivered it.

I can understand the disappointment and the feeling of betrayal of knowing that someone was there to "help," and yet, when you become a Public Figure, doing it all by yourself is not practical. The key is to build the brain trust of people who can respond and write on your behalf—hence, the reason it took so long to draft the right talking points for the

CNBC interview with Senator Hatch.

Each person reviewing the talking points asked, "Is this what the senator can stand behind? Is this in his voice?" Because Senator Hatch had been in the office for more than twenty years, there were years of trust built with his team, who stayed by his side for decades. I imagine he glanced at the talking points and had no question about confidently going out and saying them publicly.

On the issue of being ethical, I believe the workaround is to admit that you have the brain trust of people helping you articulate your vision, voice, and ideas. And remember, you are ultimately responsible for the words written or said in your name. Again, the reason why Senator Hatch's brain trust took the time with the talking points was to ensure that it reflected Senator Hatch. With this kind of trust comes great responsibility, yet the responsibility stops with Senator Hatch and you as the Public Figure.

MY BRAIN TRUST

I could not have written this book without my brain trust. Within that group, I have had many advisors and editors, and yet, I found a voicewriter to be the overall best solution for me. The editor typically focuses on refining what you have already written, whereas a ghostwriter often takes over the entire writing process. Lisa, my voicewriter, was the ideal middle ground, as she was able to adapt to my voice and help me find ways to express my vision.

I discovered the power of the voicewriter when I was about one hundred pages into my book and felt my draft was in the weeds. I would fervently explain my thesis and idea, but the editor could not see beyond the confines of what I had written, that is, rearranging the furniture. I did not need a ghostwriter as I had already written the first draft. The problem I had was going too far into certain aspects of the book, and few could decipher what I wanted to communicate. Lisa truly listened, brainstormed, and helped provide feedback on streamlining the book. It was the igniter that got me to rewrite the book, and since then, we have bounced off ideas and this is the result.

WHO GETS CREDIT?

Well, my take is that if you are a voicewriter or speechwriter for a Public Figure, I prefer Obama's way of giving credit to Jon Favreau as the chief speech writer. We do not know what specific lines Jon wrote, rather we know that Jon was part of the first presidential campaign and inaugural address.

It reminds me of Dolly Parton and Whitney Houston regarding which singer gets credit for the song, "I Will Always Love You."

Dolly Parton wrote and originally recorded the song in 1973, so she obviously gets credit and copyright ownership of the lyrics and royalties of the rendition of the song she sang to number one in 1974 and 1982 on *Billboard Hot Country Songs*. However, Whitney Houston recorded a soul-ballad arrangement of the song for the 1992 film, *The Bodyguard*, the world's best-selling single of 1992 with accolades and awards and the version most people think of first.

This example shows that a Public Figure "performing" should get credit. It is not just the words on the paper. The person delivering the message and standing behind it is key. And we interpret the message of a speech or article by the presenter as this person's voice and brand which frames our interpretation and reception of it.

I believe there is a place for all to get credit. When we look at President Kennedy's inaugural speech, we know that Ted Sorensen was one of the speechwriters, and the main credit should go to President Kennedy as he approved the message and performed it sharing his thoughts with the public. To me, this model seems fair.

Giving credit is tricky, and the Public Figure should decide what is best for them. I am, as always, in favor of collaboration, and having another person who can bring ideas to the table is invaluable. However, many ghostwriters prefer anonymity such as the ghostwriter for Britney Spears's memoir, whom she acknowledges simply as, "You know who you are."

WHAT EXACTLY IS A VOICEWRITER?

A voicewriter is a professional skilled in articulating and adapting the unique voice and tone of a Public Figure, ensuring that their messages are conveyed in an authentic and compelling manner.

To get a better understanding, I wanted Lisa to tell her version of why the voicewriter matters.

LISA DUNCAN'S VOICEWRITER
ANALYSIS: THE VOICE, NOT THE GHOST

"Find your voice, and inspire others to find theirs. Don't ignore that longing to make a difference."

—Stephen Covey, author of international bestseller: *The 7 Habits of Highly Effective People*

I LOVED IT—UNTIL I DIDN'T. "Ghostwriter" is a cool title. It invites a lot of questions. The first several books I wrote were exciting. I loved shaping the words to fit the "author." I loved finding the perfect way to make a story stick. I loved the appreciation of the authors who felt heard.

I still love all of these things. What I no longer love is being a ghost.

Did you know that the French word for "ghostwriter" is very close to their word for "slave" when translated into English?

When I learned that, my stomach dropped. I don't know that I would use that word to describe my experience, but as I got more work as a ghostwriter, I began to feel smaller and smaller. I was tucked away like a dirty secret. I was nameless and yet, without me, these "authors" had no books at all.

I knew the deal going in, but the longer I went along with it, the worse I felt.

I thought the cure would be to write something for myself. I had ideas. I had lots of stories to tell.

What were they again?

I came up empty.

I took a writing class for inspiration.

I followed writing prompts.

I meditated.

I sat wordless day after day.

Had I given all my words away?

I finally started a project of my own that I fell in love with, and I also realized that not only do I want to write for myself, but I also want to collaborate with the people for whom I write. I want to write for people who are excited about what they do and who have moral standards I match with and admire. I want to work with people who understand that writing is a creative process and that they will benefit if I want to work with them. I want a mutual agreement and respect.

As a voicewriter, I amplify your voice: I don't take it over. I give depth and color to your story and message. I develop it all with you, helping you research facts, quotes, and theories that lend authority and authenticity to your words.

I am re-setting the table and shifting boundaries. I am no one's slave and I am certainly not a ghost.

THE ROLE OF THE VOICEWRITER IN THE FAME REVOLUTION

Yes, I've gone the route of the ghostwriter, and frankly, it doesn't agree with me. I have to show my own authenticity, and I need to be known for what I do, or I won't get the kind of work and recognition I want.

Lisa Duncan, voicewriter, needs to be a Public Figure too. I don't get a pass on that in the Fame Revolution.

I use my skills and experience in a way that adds clarity and power to messages and thought leadership, as well as capturing passion. When public figures need help getting their message across because they lack the time or writing expertise, I am the person they call.

Put simply, a Public Figure strategist like Torund is a story maker. They assist leaders in finding and shaping their stories to connect with the people.

A voicewriter is a storyteller. We help public figures put their stories into words.

In the world of literature, your voice isn't just about the writing on the page: it is what makes your words connect with the audience. Think of it as the literary equivalent of an actor's stage or screen presence. Whether you are here to persuade, explain, narrate, or simply describe, a voicewriter is your wingman, getting more of your voice out to play in a way that is instantly recognizable. The power of your words and voice is your linguistic signature.

A voicewriter is a chameleon of sorts, like an actor who can take on your manner of communication and expression. You speak through your voicewriter and are understood the way you want to be. Your unmistakable voice shines through and consistently engages your audience.

Learning to write well, like any other creative pursuit, demands dedication and time. While expertise in your subject is essential, it's only the foundation. Transforming knowledge into compelling words involves an understanding of your brand and audience. Effective writing requires finesse—it should exude style, possess depth, maintain accuracy, and simplify intricate concepts without oversimplifying them. This is the synergetic work between the Public Figure strategist and the voicewriter that brings you into the spotlight with confidence.

YOUR CHAMPION

"Advertising is saying you're good. PR is getting someone else to say you're good."

—Jean-Louis Gassée, former executive at Apple Computer

WE ALL NEED CHAMPIONS. Usually, our greatest champion is our mom or dad, and we might be embarrassed when we hear them telling their friends about our grades, sports, or music accomplishments. We say we hate it, but deep inside, I know that I did appreciate the praise, even though at times it was over the top and cheesy. I find myself doing the same thing to my nieces and nephews. They turn red and deflect my bragging about them, but I believe that deep inside they appreciate my admiration for them.

In the family, as elsewhere, it is more powerful when Mom or Dad tells someone about my accomplishments what I have done than when I would come running home excited about getting an A on a test. I know that my aunts and uncles put more credibility on what my parents said, and I know that if my brother came home beating his chest about getting a grade A on his test, I would judge it as bragging. Still, when my parents retell the story of my brother's test results, it influences me and those around us differently.

BRAGS VERSUS FACTS

Ever find yourself in a situation where you have done something fantastic, but you have no idea how to let it be known without seeming conceited? Most of us lack the vocabulary for self-promotion. We have all witnessed people who claim greatness without a shred of talent to prove it. On the flip side, some genuine experts are buried under layers of modesty, their impressive skills hidden behind humility. In this age of the famous commodity level where everyone is clawing to get to the next tier, you may want to tell everyone how you have the best service and best product. You might even resort to humble bragging or straight-out telling people how great you are.[85]

This issue resonates with countless public figures when it comes to self-promotion. Many believe they can handle publicity and public relations on their own, dismissing the idea of hiring a professional.

Enter the champion, your ultimate hype-master! Not only do they have connections with the media, but if they love what you're doing, they can pitch you in ways you might find hard to muster on your own. They're your cheerleaders, armed with the perfect words to let the world know how fantastic you truly are.

Navigating the fine line between self-assurance and arrogance is tricky. That's where your publicist steps in. They transform your accomplishments into a compelling narrative, showcasing your product, company, or talents without a hint of boasting. They bring the spotlight to your achievements while you focus on what you do best.

It's a win-win.

In the journey of the Public Figure, authenticity is your guiding light. Being true to yourself and embracing your unique energy becomes the magnet that attracts kindred spirits. As clichéd as it may sound, **your vibe truly does attract your tribe.**

Culture and Self Promotion:

It's interesting to note the cultural nuances in how people talk about their achievements. As a Norwegian American, I can appreciate both cultures.

Americans are much more inclined to talk about their accomplishments, while my Norwegian counterparts are different. I remember when a Norwegian friend of mine visited me at Wheaton College in Chicago. My classmate, who was on the varsity swimming team, found out that my friend was a swimmer as well. But when asked about his prowess, my Norwegian friend stated, "I'm okay, fairly decent." It later emerged that he was just a hair's breadth away from joining the Norwegian National Swim Team. As a friend, I did not know how great he was!

Each culture has their own rules of how it is acceptable to talk about their accomplishments. In Norway, downplaying with a deflective comment is culturally accepted, while I have found that in the United States, it is better to be straightforward with what you have done.

And when all is said and done, the most effective approach is to have someone else speak about your greatness.

Both the entertainment and political industries have a solution for this where they use intermediaries or "go-betweens" to champion and advance their public figures. Historically, in the realms of movies and music, having an agent was crucial for discovering your talent. While today's digital age allows talent to be noticed online, once signed, a manager and publicist become essential to sustain and elevate that success. There are various reasons for this dynamic, but a standout reason from my experience is that it's often more effective for someone else to champion you.

Many journalists I know have expressed a preference for direct contact with experts. This direct interaction is increasingly becoming the norm. However, in my experience, having someone who maintains consistent relationships with the press and key figures, effectively "singing your praises" is the most effective strategy.

This champion could be an in-house hire or someone on retainer. It could even be a student or recent graduate who wants to sing your praises and pitch your expertise. Yet, what's even more impactful is a steady stream of fans who are constantly cheering you on.

KYGO EXAMPLE

In the entertainment industry, it's often more credible when someone else speaks to your talents. A great example of this is the musical artist Kygo, who would not be as famous today if he had not taken on someone unknown to manage his affairs in 2013.[86] While studying in Edinburgh, American and Floridian Myles Shear stumbled upon a Norwegian Kygo on SoundCloud at the tender age of twenty. Myles reached out to Kygo on Facebook, expressing his admiration and vision for the musician. Their enthusiastic Skype conversation sealed the deal, and just like that, Shear began managing Kygo in 2013. Myles, even without a background in artist management, embraced the mantra, "No experience is the new experience."

Almost immediately after he and Miles started working together in 2013, Kygo quietly rose to prominence, becoming one of the world's most prolific hitmakers. By 2015, he was celebrated as Spotify's "Breakout Artist."

Myles championed Kygo throughout this journey, culminating in a pivotal "worldwide talent development partnership" with Sony Music Entertainment announced in 2018. This partnership showcased both Kygo's musical prowess and Myles's strategic aptitude, solidifying their place in the music industry.[87]

A champion, that is, a publicist, does not necessarily have to be a traditional agent claiming 15 percent of your earnings or be a public relations specialist with a retainer. It could be an in-house staff member dedicated to pitching stories or telling about key accomplishments, as I did during my time in Congress and for clients. Having personally managed such responsibilities, I see the limitations of self-promotion and how powerful it is to have someone else, either paid or unpaid, do the bidding.

As Bill Gates states, "If I was down to my last dollar, I would spend it on PR."

OVERVIEW OF A CHAMPION

UNPAID CHAMPIONS:

Fans: *These are individuals who genuinely like and support a product, brand, or Public Figure. Their advocacy is organic, driven by their personal enthusiasm and loyalty. They might share content on social media, recommend products to friends, or participate in fan communities.*

Surrogates: *In politics and advocacy, surrogates are individuals who support a candidate, cause, or campaign and speak on its behalf. They're not typically paid; their support is based on personal or ideological alignment. They can include influential community members, experts, or celebrities who lend their voice to amplify the message.*

PAID CHAMPIONS:

Public relations professionals: *These are individuals or agencies hired to strategically manage the public image of a brand, organization, or individual. Their work includes crafting messages, handling media relations, crisis management, and overall image shaping. They're paid to create and maintain a positive perception.*

Influencers/endorsers: *These can be celebrities or social media influencers who are paid to promote a product or brand. Unlike fans, their promotion is part of a business agreement, though the most effective endorsements often come from those who also have a genuine love for what they're promoting.*

YOUR PEOPLE AND YOUR WAY

> *"Citizenship is the chance to make a difference to the place where you belong."*
>
> **—Charles Handy,** Irish author/philosopher specializing in organizational behavior and management

THINK BEYOND YOUR CLIENT. You belong to a family, local community, and possibly a business association and are a voter who can decide the next leader and petition issues to your congressman.

Being engaged in the community is a vastly underutilized strategy for businesses and building a leadership profile. A business shouldn't standalone but should be deeply integrated into the community. While many companies support local school sports teams, there's a treasure trove of untapped opportunities. **We're not just businesses, we're people. And it is people who drive business growth.**

This perspective became even clearer when I heard Grant Cardone, renowned financial influencer, and multiple *New York Times* best-selling author, emphasize that business growth isn't just about increasing sales or margins and hiring and leveraging human talent. That's where the real-time leverage lies—people.

As I was building my business during the pandemic, I wore many hats. I coded websites, crafted content, handled marketing, and led sales efforts. But there are only so many hours in a day. My real growth came when I started hiring people, partnering with people, and volunteering to serve people.

And yet, it is so easy to commoditize our relationships. Have you been at a networking event fashioned from the 1980s? You will greet one another and exchange business cards, and immediately, the question is posed: What do you do? And the underlying feeling you get from the person across you is, what can you do for me? The conversation is brief. If neither of you can see a mutually beneficial path, you will quickly move on to the next person.

We get so caught up in the transaction that we forget the person, and, ironically, we lose the transaction because we were transactional.

People are the lifeblood of anything you want to accomplish. The temptation we face is that we see the consumer, not the person. We measure the consumer on what they buy or do not buy, follow or not follow, like or not like, if they comment, or not comment on our social media post. Ironically, we leave a lot of money on the table by not being relational and not seeing things beyond the client, customer, or consumer.

Be the giver, that is, the civic citizen
The better path I have found is to be intentional, to view oneself from a 360-degree point of embracing service, and to be the kind of Public Figure who embraces the role of the civic citizen and is intentional in being service-oriented. As I like to say, "Think beyond your client," and "Embrace the role of a civic citizen."

What does it mean to be a civic citizen?
A civic citizen is someone who actively contributes to their community by giving their time, talent, and resources to support various social and cultural causes in order to enhance the communal well-being.

Happiest are the givers
The happiest individuals consistently possess a deep-seated desire to help the world around them. This profound insight was uncovered by Dr. Emma Bradshaw of the Australian Catholic University, who analyzed multiple studies involving over 11,000 participants worldwide.

Bradshaw shared, "These individuals emphasized the value of selflessly assisting others. They see themselves not as isolated entities, but as integral threads in a global fabric."[88]

What struck me about this was the realization that contentment doesn't require sacrificing material goals. Instead, **finding a balance and ensuring personal growth goes hand in hand with community upliftment and global betterment. True fame is an avenue to make a meaningful difference.**

Givers are more interesting and receive more

There is nothing like spending an evening at a dinner party with a great conversationalist, and when you are on your way home, you ponder what made the conversation so great. At the same time, sitting next to someone who mostly talks about themself, and their business, is a great annoyance.

A giver is like a great conversationalist as you are more interesting because you are not one-dimensional and only talk about your business. Instead, you are multi-dimensional and can vacillate from topics such as your charity, volunteerism, sports, or community activities, and you are automatically more interesting and newsworthy.

I remember facing the challenge of securing a B2B business profile for AGR Group, renowned as the world's largest independent oil services company in the mainstream media. Winning a million-dollar contract might intrigue a trade paper, but it generally doesn't capture mainstream attention. However, we managed to get a mention in Norway's *Financial Times* (*Dagens Næringsliv*) for our contract and company profile, thanks to being able to pitch the ski prowess of our quintessential Public Figure, CEO, and owner of AGR, Sverre Skogen. He was known not just for his business acumen but also for his commitment to health, by being one of Norway's top amateur skiers. His achievement in the Birkebeiner race, completing it in a record time of 3:04:42, caught the media's attention. It got us a profile in the paper and an opportunity to share our company's story.

We went a step further. Sverre and I made a bet that if I could recruit twenty staff members to race the Birkebeiner, we would get to have a couple of training sessions with Bjørn Dæhlie, one of the greatest Winter Olympic athletes of all time with eight Olympic golds and a total of twelve Olympic medals. I am Norwegian, but I had not skied in seventeen years and thought, "If I can complete the marathon, I can ski." That was a complete misconception, and I have never trained as hard in my life. Thankfully, I did complete the race and also ended up completing the following year and improving my time by thirty minutes. Many in the company were betting behind my back that I would not make it across the finish line. In fact, it became a company conversation that brought the team together. We even ended up on the front page of the *Wall Street Journal* of Norway (*Finansavisen*) with a full spread in the paper.

If you aspire to be a CEO in Norway, Birkebeiner is an excellent way to stand out and gain notice. The Birkebeiner race is the leading cross-country skiing event of fifty-four kilometers, commemorating the 1206 journey of the Birkebeiners who skied through harsh conditions to save the infant heir, Håkon Håkonsson, from rival factions, a pivotal moment in Norwegian history. The event has become a gathering of CEOs, politicians, and executives to compete and show their prowess.

You become interesting by having fun at work and focusing on being civic-minded as a person and company. The key is intention. You are not doing it for the recognition; you are civic-minded, because it builds the business and culture. And yet, by doing such activities, sharing, and giving of yourself, recognition comes.

One caveat—whatever you do needs to be genuine and fit the vision and values of you and your company. Most people can sniff inauthenticity from a mile away and will know if the charity or activities you represent are first and foremost about profile and attention.

Ways to serve:

Academic and intellectual engagement:

Engage in academic discussions, join clubs, participate in research, attend conferences

Community service and volunteerism:

Volunteer locally, engage in cleanups, support local advocacy, homeowners' associations, and school boards, and volunteer at school

Civic participation and leadership:

Attend town meetings, serve on local boards, and participate in voter drives

Educational and cultural involvement:

Educate on key issues, mentor peers, promote cultural understanding, and play in band and local sports

Fundraising and philanthropy:

Support and raise funds for various causes

Arts and health advocacy:

Join community art initiatives and engage in health and wellness activities

Digital engagement:

Participate actively and responsibly in online communities and discussions[89]

Ways to contribute: philanthropic equity and sweat equity

"Sweat equity is the best equity."
—Mark Cuban

There is philanthropic equity and then there is *sweat* equity, two ways to contribute to society. The philanthropist focuses on donations (equity), while the civic citizen focuses on the giving of time and talent. Both are integral in furthering society.

> When we talk about equity, it is not about the traditional equity within the area of diversity, equity, and inclusion (DEI) or equity values of company shares. We are defining equity as part of either giving of time, talent, or resources.
>
> - *Philanthropic equity:* The funds a philanthropist provides to drive social change and support community initiatives.
>
> - *Sweat equity:* The personal time and talent an individual invests in community service and the greater good.

Benefits of sweat equity

Yet, I have found sweat equity to be the most underutilized. There is so much value in work performed in lieu of payment. When I was in college, my professor Lyman 'Bud' Kellstedt in American Politics was praising the opportunity to volunteer on political campaigns. I ignored him until my internship overseas fell through and I ended up volunteering for the first female gubernatorial candidate, Christine Todd Whiteman, of New Jersey. It was the most amazing experience of my life. I got to see up close the power of volunteers giving their time, as well as experience the personal craziness, excitement, and anticipation of being in the eye of the storm of a political campaign. I saw how the electoral system really works—giving life to what I read in textbooks, which can be so dry. It was a master's class in American government, and I found out that no class can ever prepare you for a campaign. And it is so amazing to see that our governmental system would not be possible without the countless volunteers—those people giving their energy, ready to use their hours to hand out leaflets, make calls, and engage the voters. The democratic system is founded on the civic citizen.

Intriguingly, this internship paved the way for a position in Steve Forbes's presidential campaign that in turn led me to Washington, D.C. Thanks to the networks and connections I established, job offers came through word of mouth and personal references. In fact, I didn't actively seek employment until I relocated to New York eight years later. I believe this was due to cultivating the people around me and also being civic-minded. I led with service and in turn I was entrusted to great opportunities.

The benefits of sweat equity do not just apply to politics. I have volunteered for religious organizations, nonprofits, and associations, and the relationships I have cultivated have been rich with many opportunities that have resulted in an exciting career. For instance, in volunteering with Girl Geek Dinner Oslo, helping more woman to enter the technical industry, I learned about program robotics, AI, and podcasts before they were mainstream. The women I met have become friends for life as we use our time to invest into the future together.

For example, a biproduct of service is to get noticed. Friends whom I volunteered with at Girl Geek Dinner Oslo have gotten noticed for their services by national leaders and have been recruited into lucrative and influential positions.

Philanthropic benefits

But we cannot forget the philanthropist, the person who seeks to promote the welfare of others by the generous donation of money to good causes. Philanthropy is a powerful tool to help the community, and businesses can position themselves well if they are strategic in their investment. It is fine to invest in the local sports team, but I would recommend looking beyond and view donations through the lens of equity, to know which organizations can be good strategic partners and to help move the company and the issue you are aligned with forward. The key is to invest in what aligns with the mission and vision of your company. To invest in something that sounds nice but does not align with the goals, I say, is a waste of time.

Giving is good for business

During my tenure as an event director at World Vision, I had a unique vantage point to watch the (RED) campaign unfold from the sidelines. This initiative, a major campaign to raise money for AIDS research, was a brainchild of U2's Bono and Bob Shriver under the *ONE Campaign*, which captured global attention. Major corporations like Apple, Starbucks, and The Gap championed the cause, creating products with the product (RED) logo.[90] A portion of these sales was designated for the Global Fund. It was an impressive blend of commerce and cause marketing.

While my musical taste has always leaned toward Depeche Mode rather than U2, Bono's transformation from rock icon to global advocate caught my attention. One unforgettable moment during my time with Senator Hatch was Bono's visit. His objective was clear: to solicit support for African Debt Relief. Following his visit, Congress moved to pardon nearly $6 billion in debt, with the UK quickly echoing this decision. Bono's advocacy further shaped the President's Emergency Plan for AIDS Relief under President Bush, a significant initiative credited with saving around

17 million lives. Bono got the taste of the power of philanthropy and co-founded that (RED) campaign to make an even greater impact.

> ### New kind of giving: Pledge 1%
>
> *One of my favorite philanthropic and civic citizen initiatives that our company is part of is the Pledge 1%, which encourages and empowers companies of all sizes and stages to donate 1 percent of their staff time, product, profit, and/or equity to any charity they choose. Marc Benioff, the founder of Salesforce, initiated Pledge 1% when he started in 1999. He committed to donating 1% of the company's annual revenues, dedicating 1% of its employees' time, and contributing 1% of its product value to nonprofit organizations yearly. Since the founding of Salesforce, they have given over $240 million in grants and 3.5 million hours of community service and provided product donations for more than 39,000 nonprofits and educational institutions. And Pledge 1%, which has over 18,000 members in 100 countries, has used Pledge 1%'s flexible framework to ignite half a billion dollars in new philanthropy.*

THE DOWNSIDE OF GIVING

The downside of giving is when a charity has gone bad or has been canceled as their downturn in reputation affects yours.

Like all grand ventures, (RED) was also scrutinized; *Advertising Age* magazine highlighted a potential gap between the campaign's advertising expenses and its fundraising results. They stated that most went to advertising and not the cause they promised.[91] This assertion was promptly challenged and disregarded from outlets like the United Kingdom's *The Independent*.

The lesson is to conduct thorough due diligence on any charity you want to align with. A few good places to look are Charity Navigator and Trust Pilot to review the ratings of the charities. If you are making claims to give, have a process of transparency and be able to document on a moment's notice where you are giving and how much.

Nevertheless, (RED)'s approach of intertwining philanthropy and marketing advanced cause marketing, influencing corporate fundraising, and is still going strong today, making an impact.[92] And when you look up ONE Campaign, part of the (RED) campaign, in Charity Navigator, they have the highest rating of four stars.

RADICAL TRANSPARENCY: CHARITY: WATER

One charity that understands transparency, branding, and donor relationship is Charity: Water. In 2006, their founding year, I was privileged to be at one of the early gatherings to hear Scott Harrison; the former promoter passionately shares his bold mission to bring clean water to every person living without it.

Scott's approach to charity is simple yet revolutionary. Every single cent donated by the public for clean water projects would go directly to the cause. As for the administrative costs, Scott devised a smart plan. They would raise money for operations through separate private fundraising events.

I was shocked, amazed, and impressed when I heard, for the first time, about his model to divide the charity into two categories where the money raised for the water would go 100 percent to providing water, and they would separately raise the administrative and overhead expenses.

Drawing from his past as a nightlife promoter, Scott brought an array of unique skills to the table. Many would've thought that they were an odd fit for the world of charity. But, as he once shared, "In the beginning, we spent most of our money on photo/video gear and trips to Africa, creating video and writing stories." Not your average charity beginnings, and yet, Scott knew the significance of stories. He wanted to show the real, human side of those dealing with unsafe water.

"Conventional wisdom says that you don't start a charity by prioritizing content, but I believed we needed compelling stories about real people who were drinking bad water. Without them there would be nothing to talk about."

—Scott Harrison

Scott dreamed big, aiming to become the "Richard Branson of philanthropy." His inaugural event mirrored his background—a nightclub bash attended by celebrities like Mark Ruffalo, Joaquin Phoenix, and Lauren Bush.

By 2011, Charity: Water was likened to a disruptive startup, with accolades pouring in from outlets like *USA Today*, *Inc. Magazine*, and CNN. While other nonprofits experienced a decline in donations, Charity: Water's contributions surged by a staggering 395 percent. Their administrative costs were covered by a program called "The Well," further underlining their commitment to transparency.

The core of Charity: Water's success?

Undoubtedly, it was Scott's unwavering commitment to transparency and ensuring that every donor knew their entire donation went directly to water projects, and more importantly, his skill as a promoter in understanding intuitively the Public Figure Strategy. He interwove the personal, entertaining stories with straight up hard sell to donate to save lives.

Zoom out sixteen years, and what do you see? A monumental $740 million was raised, powering 137,000 water projects across twenty-nine countries and impacting over 17.4 million lives. Beyond the impressive statistics lies the heart, innovation, and tenacity of individuals of Scott Harris, a true Public Figure who has channeled his passion for ushering in waves of change.

BENEFIT OF THE CAUSE

Consumers today are discerning and conscientious. An overwhelming 85 percent have a more favorable view of companies that actively contribute to charitable causes. And this isn't a passive observation: 90 percent are keen to understand exactly how businesses support these causes. Today's consumers seek out businesses that resonate with values, and they're willing to put their money where their heart is.

And charity is good for employee retention. A massive 93 percent of the employees who participate in company-sponsored charitable initiatives express happiness with their employer.

Both Millennials and Gen-Zers grew up in a world that encouraged recycling and social good. Instead of donating money directly to causes they care about, shoppers under the age of forty prefer to give back through where they shop. When partnering with a charity, you should see this not just as a financial expense but as a holistic investment that aligns and furthers with your purpose.[93]

THE BENEFIT OF INVESTING IN ACADEMIC INSTITUTIONS

If charitable giving does not fully align with your company or purpose, working with academia might. It is another way of charitable giving, sharing knowledge that can benefit society and uplevel the thought leadership contribution of both you and your company.

Being at the forefront of your industry and positioning yourself within the top 4 percent is crucial. One approach I've consistently employed, with the agreement of my employers, is to forge partnerships with universities or research institutions. These academic hubs possess a wealth of knowledge, offering fresh perspectives that can be pivotal for a company's success. Interestingly, academic institutions often fall short in marketing their expertise and opportunities for collaboration. By reaching out and expressing a willingness to invest in research that resonates with both their objectives and the company's vision, you can harness immense potential.

The academic option possesses the capacity to cultivate and broaden the innovation essential for your company, extending beyond just technical or engineering aspects.

For me, the focus has always been on communication—deciphering how we catalyze action through words. While working for the Gassnova, part of Norwegian government with its mission to help realize a carbon capture and storage (CCS) infrastructure, under the leadership of the CEO, we created an informal alliance of leading experts from academia, NGOs, authors, political leaders, football (soccer) manager, and policy experts to find solutions on how to communicate about CCS. The challenge was that solar and wind were the favored climate solutions, and CCS was seen as a less sexy alternative, even though it has been cited as one of the important climate solutions to combat greenhouse gas emissions.

We partnered with the Center for Communication at BI Norwegian Business School to research CCS and language. The question we wanted answered was: How do we ignite action and support for CCS among the public and policymakers? Engaging a communications agency for such work could have cost three times as much. This alliance allowed us to convene a workshop, gathering leading figures in CCS. We established a language framework that resulted in international media coverage, igniting CCS into the spotlight as a pivotal measure against greenhouse gas emissions. This research also led to the opportunity of co-authoring a paper with Professor Peggy Brønn and presenting our findings at the IEA GHGT-14 in Melbourne, a premier global conference on CCS.

After I left Gassnova, the alliance continued and expanded its reach and created a strong momentum. And if we look at the numbers, I believe this initiative was one of the contributing factors to its current success. In 2016, there were twenty-two CCS facilities,[94] and now, there are twenty-seven fully operational CCS facilities and 135 commercial CCS facilities in the project pipeline (from a diverse range of sectors, including cement, steel, hydrogen, power generation, and direct air capture).[95]

I strongly advocate that you consider having your business explore partnerships with universities and research bodies or leading professors interested in the same topic. The expertise can bring fresh perspectives to your business. Engaging with academic institutions isn't exclusive to major corporations. Businesses of all sizes can discover substantial value through such partnerships. It's an avenue worth considering.

MAPPING YOUR 360

> *"When we are fully and totally networked, we ARE."*
>
> **— John Maxwell,** an internationally recognized thought leader on leadership, is a #1 *New York Times* best-selling author who has sold over 30 million books in fifty languages

THE COVID-19 PANDEMIC upended business as usual and helped make sustainable investment mainstream. Companies are not only serving the shareholder, but the stakeholder. As CEO and Chairman of Black Rock Larry Fink stated in his letter to CEO in 2021 "The more your company can show its purpose in delivering value to its customers, its employees, and its communities, the better able you will be to compete and deliver long-term, durable profits for shareholders."[96]

> *A stakeholder is someone who has a vested interest in a company or Public Figure and can either affect or be affected by the operations and performance. Typical stakeholders include investors, employees, customers, suppliers, communities, governments, or trade associations.*

Dennis Larsen, founding partner of leading international reputation management consultancy Reputation Inc., states, "People expect businesses to fix major societal challenges, not make them worse. New generations of employees will increasingly only lend their time to companies that share their values. Investors scrutinize corporate cultures and ESG ratings as thoroughly as financial statements. Suppliers refuse to work with companies that can't live up to their own ever-stringent codes of ethics and compliance. Regulators are struggling to regulate increasingly complex and democratized industries. Meanwhile, geopolitically, the dominant force is shifting towards Asia, and the stabilizing power of multilateral institutions is waning."

What to do?

Map your people. The key is knowing who your people are, investing in them, and engaging with them.

Dennis states, "The new world demands new approaches to stakeholder management and engagement. Novel, inquisitive ways to uncover trends and learn from those who are shaping new paradigms. And to carve out the rightful position of each company in addressing matters people really care about."

To be one step ahead is to take the time to do stakeholder mapping and stakeholder management. To explain it another way, it is basically mapping all the people in your ecosystem who touch and impact your company. By understanding the movements of your ecosystem, you will be able to monitor your network better, anticipate the coming trends in your industry, anticipate your client's needs and wants, and help assess the best way to engage and invest in your community. Stakeholder management is a long-term investment in your reputation and is an insurance policy for your success. When a crisis hits, by having already invested in your people inside and outside of the company, when you need help, people will be there. I tell my clients that it is too late to expect much help from someone in your network if you have not engaged with them regularly.

I highly recommend you map out your people. It is an invaluable asset for your business and managing campaigns, and it helps you better understand how to manage their expectations effectively.

Even small businesses and solopreneurs should do this. What makes the world go around is people, and you never know where the next opportunity lies.

Being actively engaged with your stakeholders can provide the most amazing professional opportunities. And in the end, working and partnering with people saves time and resources. I have hacked many obstacles by having the right people in my circle.

Many opportunities you encounter in human engagement would never come your way otherwise. What you do not know, you do not know. Knowing arises from encounters with friends, colleagues, or even a chance meeting with a stranger at a cocktail party or charity event. These interactions can bridge the gaps in your understanding and ultimately save time and money.

The image below shows a list of places where you can connect with possible like-minded people. Some groups might apply, and some might not. I might even be missing a few groups. But knowing who is in your circle will help assess who your support is and how to build your business or become famous for what you do.

SOCIAL

RELIGIOUS GROUPS
"YOUR KITCHEN CABINET"
SPORTS CLUBS
NGO'S & THINK TANKS
SOCIAL ORG.
ACADEMIA

PERSONAL

FAMILY
FRIENDS
SOCIAL MEDIA GROUPS
MENTOR
TEACHERS
CLASSMATES

YOUR 360°

COMMUNITY

MEDIA
FEDERAL GOVT.
ASSOCIATIONS
MEDICAL ESTABLISHMENT
STATE & LOCAL GOVT.
LAW ENFORCEMENT
AGENCIES

WORK

EMPLOYEES
INVESTORS
CONTRACTORS
SUPPLIERS
THOUGHT LEADERS
COLLEAGUES
JOINT VENTURES
SHAREHOLDERS
INDUSTRY LEADERS
CLIENTS/ CUSTOMERS
BUSINESS PARTNERS

THE POWER OF COLLABORATION

"Collaboration is the new currency."

—Amy Blankson, author of *The Future of Happiness*

NOW THAT YOU KNOW that you should think beyond your client and have a full bouquet of people and organizations you can tap into, what is next? Tap into the power of collaboration.

We are now in an era where strategic collaboration is key, and businesses that succeed often do so by forming partnerships across different sectors. This approach has always been around, but its effectiveness became particularly evident in a somewhat unexpected context: the music industry.

Puff Daddy led the effort to complete an album to honor the life of The Notorious B.I.G., whose life was cut short by a drive-by shooting in 1997. Puff Daddy didn't want his debut album, in collaboration with the late The Notorious B.I.G., to be buried with Notorious, especially knowing he didn't have the gravitas to carry an album alone. Therefore, he assembled a group of renowned artists from that era, including Busta Rhymes, Mase, Lil' Kim, Carl Thomas, Jay-Z, Black Rob, The Lox, Ginuwine, Twista, Foxy Brown, Faith Evans, and 112, to pay tribute to The Notorious B.I.G. Using a new practice, each artist was given credit in the title of the song instead of just being in the footnotes.

The first release, "I'll Be Missing You," featured by (ft.) Faith Evans and 112, topped music charts worldwide for twenty-four non-consecutive weeks, debuting at number one on the Billboard 200. **And "Featured" was born and also captivated the imagination of the power of collaboration.**

> ⌕ *"Feat." or "ft." in music indicates a guest appearance by another artist on a song.*

HOW COLLABORATING BENEFITS YOU
Boosts your brand

Rihanna was the good girl next door and needed a song to redefine her brand from being a good girl to becoming more edgy. The song was "Umbrella"; however, producer and songwriter Christopher Tricky Stewart was not convinced until Def Jam CEO-rapper Jay-Z added his rap to the song. Jay-Z lending himself as a featured artist took Rihanna out of the good girl image and set her brand as edgy and sexy. The song "Umbrella" was a global success, topping the charts in seventeen countries and thrusting Rihanna to global status.

Benefits you: One powerful approach is to align with key leaders in your industry, not necessarily clients but changemakers who resonate with your vision and values. Their endorsement can serve as a massive boost to your product or service, acting as a megaphone to your brand's values and purpose. Statistics reveal that 82 percent of the customers are drawn to brands that mirror their values, and 83 percent are more inclined to buy from brands they trust. So, identify a company or leader that can elevate your brand's standing.

Opens new opportunities

While Usher and his team grappled with the *Confessions* album, feeling the absence of a compelling lead single, they knew they needed a fresh direction. Seeking a breakthrough, Usher collaborated with the dynamic producer Lil Jon. To elevate it even further, Ludacris was brought into the fold, creating the iconic "Yeah!" Marrying crunk and R&B in a style Lil

Jon dubbed "Crunk&B," this track marked a pivotal moment in Usher's career. As the lead single from *Confessions*, "Yeah!" didn't just top charts—it dominated them, reigning over the *Billboard Hot 100* for a remarkable twelve weeks and selling over 4 million copies. Even today, "Yeah!" remains Usher's most iconic track, solidifying his place in music history.[97]

Benefits you: If you ever find yourself stuck or plateauing in your business, considering partnerships or joint ventures might just be the game-changer you need.

Access to new markets

Collaboration has evolved and become the new currency in the realm of digital entrepreneurship. This trend is evident among celebrity entrepreneurs who have carved a niche for themselves on the Internet.

For instance, Grant Cardone, renowned financial influencer, and multiple *New York Times* best-selling author, started hosting events and summits sharing the stage with other industry celebrities. Instead of monopolizing the spotlight, he collaborates with experts like Jenna Kutcher, known for her adept digital marketing strategies, and Russell Brunson, the brain behind the successful sales funnel software, ClickFunnels.

Another prime example is Tony Robbins' shift towards collaboration. Before the pandemic, Tony's events and programs primarily centered around him as the central figure. However, in recent times, he has expanded his approach by partnering with individuals such as Russell Brunson and Dean Graziosi, both online celebrity entrepreneurs, real estate investors, and best-selling authors. Tony has also broadened his platform to host the first Women's Summit and personal development course, featuring Karissa Kouchis (KK) and other leading women. The list continues. . . . Brendon Burchard, a leading figure in personal development and high-performance training, often collaborates with best-selling author and motivational speaker, Jay Shetty, among others. These strategic cross-promotions amplify their reach exponentially, offering value to a much broader audience.

Bringing people together and collaborating can be a powerful tool. It is recommended that you go back and look at people in your ecosystem and assess who you can work with.

Can you cross-pollinate with a person, company, or non-profit and create a stronger service?

When Madonna collaborates, you take notice.

I remember when I was at SONY, and Madonna was reaching 50 years old. She got on the collaboration train with her 2008 album "Hard Candy." To stay relevant, Madonna collaborated with contemporary mega talents Timbaland, Justin Timberlake, Pharrell Williams, and Kanye West. She featured other artists in her songs for the first time in her 25-year career. Three singles were released from the album. With "Hard Candy," the collaboration resulted in Madonna weaving new genres and cementing her relevance with millennials. Her song "4 Minutes" was a worldwide success, topping the charts in 21 countries and becoming Madonna's 37th Billboard Hot 100 top-ten hit.

Your story should embody
who you are and why you
started this quest. The
creation story helps your
superfans understand
and empathize with your
journey. It is the first step to
wooing superfans to believe
in you and want to belong
to your cause, product, or
service.

CHAPTER FOUR

HOW TO BECOME FAMOUS: PURPOSE

It all starts with what you want. In this brief chapter, we talk about your purpose and how important it is for you to have one to be a successful Public Figure.

Note: Many of you already know what gift you want to showcase to the world . . . so skip and go to the next chapter.

For the rest, who kind of, sort of, know where they want to go or have an inkling but are too embarrassed to claim it, this part is for you.

We will help you take it one step further and help you solidify your purpose.

We will pause to find what you are looking for, longing for, and wanting to be known for.

All public figures have a dream. Everyone has a gift to share with the world.

And we will help you go higher and be daring to 10x your purpose and find your Big Bold & Boundless Dream.

The purpose of this section is to find it, claim it, and be ready to live it confidently.

PURPOSE OF YOUR GIFT

*"Where there is no vision, the
people perish."*

—Proverbs, 29:18 (KJV)

THE FOUNDATION OF BEING a Public Figure is to know what you want. Having a purpose and a vision will be the fuel that drives you to your goal, and your purpose will get you through the valleys of life.

At my consulting company, Diotima Strategies, one of our central services is to help align the purpose for our clients as we develop their Public Figure Strategy. We tailor their purpose to what they want to become known for. I believe your purpose is your gift, and where your focus should be.

Each individual possesses not just a single gift but many. In the early stages of your journey, it's recommended to concentrate on one main gift. This gift can evolve into the cornerstone of your purpose. By developing a vision and mission centered around the gift, and grounding it in the pillars of your values, you can be propelled toward your goal. This approach enables you to utilize your talents effectively, laying the foundation for a fulfilling path that resonates with your core strengths and beliefs.

At this point, you might feel stressed and challenged and say to yourself, "I do not know my purpose." Many feel the pressure and put too much into finding their purpose, but let's simplify the process.

I define purpose as the gift you focus on, wanting to invest time and resources to hone.

Eventually, your purpose grows and becomes your vision, formulates your values, and becomes the mission in your life.

So, the first question to ask is: What are your gifts?
A good start is to select your top three gifts. To qualify which gift, ask yourself in which gift you regularly invest time and resources.

- You might have the gift of singing in a local band with friends and playing small gigs on the weekends. It is fun as a hobby, but it might not be the gift you want to be known for.

- On the other hand, you have a gift for teaching and a passion for helping teenagers build their self-esteem, so you might want to become known as the leading teacher or go a step further and establish a nonprofit.

- Or you might be a psychologist passionate about helping leaders with their stage fright and becoming known for having a transformative course.

If you are still stalling, here is a good exercise inspired by Robert Murray, a leading international brand strategist from the UK. He often discusses the importance of having both a "Selfish Why" and a "Selfless Why," which resonated with me.

To put this into the framework of purpose ask what is your public purpose versus your private purpose? You will find your true purpose in the intersection of these two questions.

Purpose framework	
Personal purpose (impacts you):	**Public purpose (impacts others):**
Ensures your well-being	Enhances others' lives
Attracts financial stability	Draws in people
Elevates your quality of life	Improves life for others
Boosts your happiness	Spreads joy to others
Personal growth	Inspires growth in others

For example, I have a client who is a psychologist specializing in youth mental health. His public purpose is to raise awareness, stop the silence about mental health issues, and normalize solutions.

His private purpose is to become a thought leader among other distinguished and progressive research doctors in the global pediatric mental health community.

The power of balancing between the selfish and selfless:

"The most successful brand owners are selfish.

They know when to focus on themselves.

They set goals that keep them optimistic, passionate, and driven.

They have a star to shoot for, and they don't let others knock them off course.

The most successful brand owners are also selfless.

They give for a greater cause.

It's causes bigger than you that attract others. It ensures your customers feel seen, heard, and valued.

By balancing being both selfish and selfless is what builds great brands.[98]

—Robert Murray

You can build out your mission, vision, and values from purpose, which will be the cornerstone of your Public Figure Strategy. Knowing your gift and why this is your gift, you can determine where you want to go and have a purpose-driven strategy to start on the journey to become famous for what you do.

THE FRAMEWORK OF A PURPOSE-DRIVEN STRATEGY

In shaping a strategic plan that truly captures the spirit of your organization or you as a person, focus on these essential components.

Your Purpose: "Why do you exist?" Look deeper than just the profit motive. Why do you do what you want to do? What greater impact are you aiming to achieve with your gifts? Why does your business exist? What is the deeper impact you or your organization are aiming for?

Your Vision: "Where are you going?" Clearly define your future goals. As a Public Figure, what legacy do you want to leave? Imagine the ultimate goal for your organization.

Your Mission: "What actions will you take to reach your vision?" List the practical steps and strategies you will use to reach your vision. Your mission could involve personal growth initiatives, business expansion strategies, or community engagement plans. "One Purpose: Many Missions" is a phrase that brings it to life for me.

Your Core Values: "How will you behave?" Identify and describe the principles and behaviors that guide you and your organization. What is important to you? What traits do you value in your team? It could be innovation, fairness, integrity, or teamwork, just to name a few examples.

Your Origin Story: "Your humble beginnings" Tell the story of your organization's beginning or how your gifts were first found and nurtured. The origin story is a window into what truly motivated you or led to the birth of your business.

Finding Your Unique Edge in Your Roots

If you are struggling to pinpoint your gift or the uniqueness of your organization, go back to where it all started. The early days often shed light on what ignited the why. It's not always about grand ideas; sometimes, it's as simple as seizing a good business opportunity. As seen in the case of AGR's founders, Arve, Geir, and Reidar, their individual styles and leadership shaped the company's culture.

As you might recall, earlier in the book, Jim Stengel, former CMO of Procter & Gamble, uncovered the essence and purpose of brands like Max Factor by digging into their historical roots. This exploration of Max Factor's origin revealed a unique connection to Hollywood glamor, which became a key differentiator in its market strategy and success.

Reflect on the beginnings of your journey
- Who was with you?
- Why did you choose them?
- What were your motivations?
- What problem did you want to solve?
- What gifts did you want to share and why?

Digging deep into these aspects can be incredibly revealing. It's about identifying the unique parts that separate you and your organization. This exploration into your history is not just about reminiscing; it's a strategic examination to uncover and embrace your distinctive place in the market.

FRAMEWORK HIGHLIGHTS

- Your Purpose: Why do you exist?
- Your Vision: Where are you going?
- Your Mission: What actions will you take to reach your vision?
- Your Core Values: How will you behave?
- You Origin Story: What ignited your start?

BUT MY COMPETITION HAS TAKEN MY IDEA!

I remember attending Business Mastery with Tony Robbins to learn how to start a business in executive branding. However, I was unsure if I could start, because companies already offered the service I wanted to set up.

A conference partner smiled, reminded me that competition is good, and stated, "Look to Coca-Cola and Pepsi. Yes, they have the same product but tell a different story and appeal to different kinds of person. So, if someone has taken your idea, that is a good sign. There is still room for you."

He was right. When I look back, I am not sure what my hang-up was.

A product can be almost identical and yet so different; the difference is the core. When we look deeper at Coca-Cola versus Pepsi, we see they are both colas but very different.

Why?

They have created experiences that are completely different because their core is different. Finding your core is finding your gift; by finding your gift, you find your purpose and values, which will automatically exude a different experience.

GO HIGHER

> *"Up high I feel like I'm alive for the very first time.*
>
> *Set up high I'm strong enough to take these dreams and make them mine."*

—**Creed,** an American rock band; song: *"Higher"*

ONE OF MY FAVORITE BOOKS is *Built to Last* by Jim Collins and Jerry Porras, and I loved their concept of the "Big Hairy Audacious Goal." The idea is to have a clear, compelling goal that seems unreasonable and slightly out of reach, but you believe you can achieve it. It was a great start, and I liked the concept, but I personally felt that the "goal" part was restrictive and switched it up and used the "Big Bold & Boundless Dream." To me, "dream" taps more into the limitless imagination.

When you dream bigger, you fast-track your goals because dreaming big ignites a powerful force within you. Also, the other difference from "Big Hairy Audacious Goal" is that you keep the Big Bold & Boundless Dream a secret and instead share the milestones until you get closer to reaching your dream.

What I have discovered through my work with leaders becoming public figures is that when we set the Big Bold & Boundless Dream and establish concrete milestones for the next three to five years, we often achieve them in half the time. This process is a game changer and the secret sauce of our agency. By engineering ourselves to pursue the Big Bold & Boundless Dream, we unlock untapped potential and accelerate the path to success.

The power of this approach lies in its ability to ignite passion, focus our efforts, and push us beyond our perceived limits. When we put our dreams on paper and break them down into milestones and actionable steps, we create a roadmap that propels us forward with purpose and determination. So, embrace the Big Bold & Boundless Dream, set ambitious goals, and witness the transformative impact it can have on your journey to becoming a remarkable Public Figure.

By dreaming bigger, you tap into your true potential and unlock the power to achieve your goals faster than you can ever imagine.

TO FIND YOUR BIG BOLD & BOUNDLESS DREAM, FOLLOW THESE STEPS:

- Imagine there are no limits or rules. What is your wildest and most exciting dream?
- What activities or experiences make you feel incredibly happy, fulfilled, and alive? What gets you leaping out of bed with excitement?
- If you had all the support, resources, and opportunities in the world, how would you make a positive impact and leave your mark?

Once you've identified your dream, please take a moment to write it down and keep it in a special place. This serves as a reminder of your Big Bold & Boundless Dream and keeps it close to your heart. While keeping your dream sacred and personal is important, we encourage you to share it selectively with those who will support and uplift you on your journey.

Consider confiding in your closest friend, your trusted "kitchen cabinet" of advisors, and key individuals who can help propel your dream forward.

In my experience working with clients, I have encountered a diverse range of aspirations and ambitions. While some clients may aspire to be like Oprah or Tony Robbins, others have their own grand visions, such as being invited to speak at prestigious global events like the United Nations. These aspirations are often deeply personal and may not be openly shared with others.

THE DREAM

When working with entrepreneurs and authors in the U.S., the most common Big Bold & Boundless Dream I encounter involve sitting on Oprah's couch or speaking at Tony Robbins's Business Mastery event, proudly holding a *New York Times* bestseller and discussing their achievements.

Many hesitate to express their dream, but when they claim it and write it down, we create a strategy document. Things move fast. I love working with leaders who are bold and willing to pull up their sleeves and go for their dream and together set the plan in motion. I also love working with people who are hesitant, and we go on a treasure hunt to find their gift within, dust off, and spotlight it for the world to see. In the span between the two, it is a beautiful process to see the leader or company we work with become its fullest self. I have yet to get someone to sit on Oprah's couch on *Super Soul Sunday* but have witnessed individuals achieve remarkable milestones, including speaking engagements at various influential national and international platforms. The power lies in understanding and embracing your dreams, regardless of their scale or perceived audacity. By tapping into your passions, talents, and purpose, you can unlock extraordinary opportunities and make a significant impact in your chosen field.

The true essence of success lies not in simply achieving *The New York Times* bestseller status or having a one-time experience on Oprah's stage. Instead, the essence lies in the transformation of oneself into becoming a person who is genuinely deserving of an invitation into the conversation, capable of forging meaningful connections, and committed to making a lasting contribution through their ideas. The Big Bold & Boundless Dream assumes the role of a guiding star, propelling them relentlessly on a boundless journey of continuous growth and profound impact.

A BIG BOLD & BOUNDLESS DREAM: SIT ON OPRAH'S COUCH

"The guests who come on my show have a unique ability to touch hearts, ignite change, and remind us of the remarkable potential within each of us."

—Oprah Winfrey, American talk show host

A dear friend worked on Oprah's talk show during the late 1990s when her television show was at its peak. Hearing the behind-the-scenes stories are thrilling and inspiring. Sitting on Oprah's couch is a metaphor and guide to any Big Bold & Boundless Dream. The key lesson I gathered from my friends is that there are two kinds of guests—the one-hit wonders and the guests who come back. To achieve the latter, you must become the person to be worthy of sitting on the couch. Remember, it's not about meeting Oprah, it's about becoming the person worthy of sitting in her chair. Embrace the audacity of your dream and watch as it guides you toward remarkable achievements.

The first lesson on the journey is this: I must first become it to achieve what I desire. It all starts with cultivating the right mindset that embraces growth, resilience, and endless possibilities. For years, the transformation may go unnoticed by others, but it is in becoming the change that real progress takes shape.

But here's the second lesson: dreams can be even grander. I've realized that my aspirations have often fallen short of their true potential. They were not big enough to ignite a fire within me. So, I dared to dream beyond the limits of comfort and security. In fact, I've penned down a dream so audacious, it's too embarrassing to share. And that is what I tell my clients: the Big Bold & Boundless Dream should be secret and embarrassing. It's a dream that pushes me to the edge of my capabilities and stretches my imagination to new horizons.

Yet, I've learned that this dream is best kept secret until it's on the cusp of realization. Until then, I'll continue to work diligently, fueling my determination and embracing the journey of growth and self-discovery.

Remember, the key lies in becoming the person you aspire to be. Develop the mindset, take inspired action, and allow your dreams to expand and flourish. Through this transformative process, you'll witness your own evolution and inspire others to do the same.

What must you become?

To be newsworthy and sit on Oprah's couch or share the stage with Tony Robbins, I've identified five criteria that can help you reach the highest level. You do not need all of them, but the more the better.

STEP 1: BE EXCELLENT. Showcase mastery, innovation, or exceptional impact in your accomplishments. Push the boundaries and be different.

STEP 2: INSPIRE TRANSFORMATION. Your craft should have the power to inspire, touch lives, spark inspiration, and uplift individuals and communities. The best avenue is to do this through mentorship, education, or advocacy to make a positive difference in the world.

STEP 3: BE AUTHENTIC IN ACTION. Be genuine, transparent, and true to yourself. Demonstrate authenticity in your words and actions.

STEP 4: HAVE NATIONAL OR GLOBAL IMPACT. Highlight the far-reaching effects of your work. Demonstrate how your contributions have made a significant impact on a broader scale, spanning nations and continents.

STEP 5: HAVE A COMPELLING PERSONAL STORY. Weave your accomplishments into a captivating personal narrative. Engage the hearts and minds by sharing the story behind your journey—the obstacles you've overcome, the pivotal moments that shaped you, and the milestones you've achieved. Craft a narrative that resonates with universal human experiences, allowing the audience to relate to your story.

Lastly, it's important to note that if you decide to pitch Oprah's producer or a similar person, you have a higher chance of being recognized if you get someone else to vouch for you. Simply reaching out to Oprah's producers and saying, "Hey, I think I should be on your show," in my experience, is not effective. The finesse lies in being endorsed or recognized in such a way that Oprah cannot help but want to invite you. This is the key differentiator when it comes to embracing the role of a Public Figure—you need others to promote you and tell your story. It's crucial that others mention your achievements in a manner that piques Oprah's interest. This can be achieved through media coverage, testimonials from influential individuals or by being acknowledged for your remarkable accomplishments. The recognition you receive from others adds credibility and effectively catches Oprah's attention.

Remember, receiving an invitation to join Oprah's conversation should be more than just being a one-hit wonder and only experiencing as single appearance. It should be about becoming the person who will stay and be a frequent guest who makes an enduring impact.

ANYTHING CAN HAPPEN IN FIVE YEARS.

Graham C. Weaver, a distinguished Stanford business lecturer, owner of a private equity firm, and TikTok sensation, wisely says, "Anything can happen in five years." And he's absolutely right. A lot can happen when you commit to your Big Bold & Boundless Dream and consistently take action toward it. He recommends writing down your five-year dream daily, along with three tasks you are doing today that will help you reach it tomorrow.

> ### Quick Tip for Your Big Bold & Boundless Dream:
>
> Every day, write down your five-year Big Bold & Boundless Dream and jot three tasks you're doing today to move you closer to it tomorrow. Simple, focused, and effective!

As a Public Figure, setting a position toward our goal in the dynamic fame landscape is both an art and a science. Just as the captain of the sailboat sets the course toward a destination, businesses and leaders set their position aimed at a specific goal.

CHAPTER FIVE

HOW TO BECOME FAMOUS: POSITIONING

Before setting our sails toward our Big Bold & Boundless Dream, we must chart the course and position ourselves in the direction of our destination. As the famed Roman philosopher Seneca stated, "If one does not know to which port one is sailing, no wind is favorable."

Like a captain on a sailboat, you must constantly readjust the sails and course in response to changing weather conditions to reach your Big Bold & Boundless Dream. Similarly, in business, market conditions and technological advancements are our "weather" and the "sea" is our people, including our customers/clients, constantly in flux and often unpredictable. Long gone are the days when a five-year strategic plan was sufficient. The Fame Revolution requires a new strategy to adjust the sails of our constant changes.

This section is to ready the sailor for the journey. The art of positioning is to become agile and responsive to immediate changes in the "weather" while maintaining a steady course toward the larger, enduring dream.

"It is not the ship so much as the skillful sailing that assures the prosperous voyage."

—George William Curtis, American writer and public speaker

POSITIONING FOR SUCCESS

👀 *"The wind and the waves are always on the side of the ablest navigator."*

—Edmund Gibbon, English historian, best known for his six-volume history of the Roman Empire

AS A PUBLIC FIGURE, setting a position toward our goal in the dynamic fame landscape is both an art and a science. Just as the captain of the sailboat sets the course toward a destination, businesses and leaders set their position aimed at a specific goal. However, in today's rapidly changing conditions, it is important to have a plan that is flexible and yet provides the right direction.

While writing this section, I asked myself how I could use a metaphor to explain brand positioning. Being Norwegian American, it felt natural to look to the sea for inspiration as I was brought up by the sea and frequently went fishing with my dad and sailing with my friends.

BEFORE YOU SET SAIL

Before any adventure, you need to know that you have a ready team and a sturdy boat. For this adventure, you also need the gift you want to become known for, which can be a trait, a product, or a service.

We already have the compass ready, which we dealt with within the "Purpose" chapter—vision, mission, values, and your Big Bold & Boundless Dream. The compass serves as an indispensable tool and symbolizes your strategic direction and vision, ensuring that every decision and action taken aligns with the overarching objectives providing clear guidance and direction toward the Public Figure and the organization's long-term goal.

Also, the compass presents the values that steer the organization through both smooth and turbulent waters, ensuring integrity and responsibility in all its endeavors.

Know your surroundings and stakeholders

When you know the destination, it is then a matter of designing the position to get there. If you are aiming, as we recommend, to achieve the Big Bold & Boundless Dream that will take five-plus years to reach, you will need to break down the dream and create milestones.

A client who wants to be recognized by winning their industry's equivalent of the Oscar award will choose milestones that can lead them there. One such milestone might be writing and publishing a book to become a top industry leader in their sector. Another milestone could be joining their peers' panels, speaking publicly, or volunteering at their industry association.

When we set milestones for our clients, we set them for one to two years with regular touchpoints where we meet to go through the strategy and plan. A few years back, we would revisit the strategy once a year with our client, but because of today's ever-shifting climate, we see that it is necessary to revisit at least every quarter. We also go through a thorough analysis annually, while remaining flexible when a gust of wind causes us to shift tactics. If necessary, we go back to reassess if we are on the right track.

The weather (surroundings and market)

The first task in preparing for the sail is assessing the weather conditions. In business, you will want to take a temperature check on your industry sector and public sentiments, review the market, technological trends, and forecasts to help anticipate, assess, and prepare for what lies ahead, much the way sailors rely on weather reports to foresee upcoming conditions. By understanding potential shifts in market dynamics, customer behaviors, and industry trends, you can strategically position yourself to either brace for challenging times or maximize opportunities.

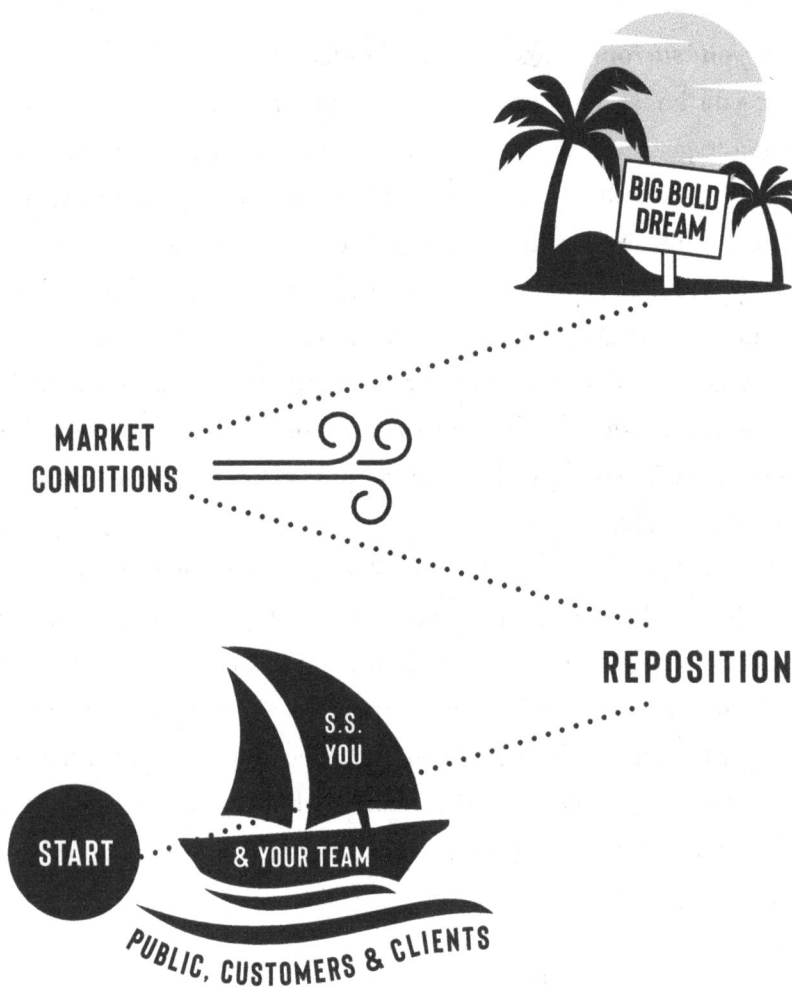

The ocean (people: clients, customers, and public)

The vast and diverse ocean perfectly symbolizes the wide and varied people base you face as a Public Figure. Like the waves, people will either pull you backward or thrust you forward toward your destination.

(Note that there is one exception to this sailing metaphor: your team of people is part of the sailboat. They are part of the operations to make you a Public Figure, while all other people are the ocean that will move you toward your destination with ease and grace or be the choppy waves creating delays.)

As the ocean is filled with different currents and waves, the people's landscape is characterized by varied preferences, needs, and behaviors. In the business world, understanding and navigating this diversity is crucial.

We tend to forget that we need to think beyond our client. The sea of people does not just hold the customers or clients that directly buy from you but also the potential clients. People who are indirectly part of your universe can open the door by building up your reputation or endorsing you because they just like you. For example, let's say Mary, who you are connected to on LinkedIn, sees one of your posts. She doesn't need your service, but she likes the article you wrote and shares within her network. By sharing your post, she is endorsing you. Or there's John who is on the board of directors with you at a nonprofit to save the children. When someone asks John about whether he knows anyone in your area of expertise, you are on top of mind, and John tells this potential client about you.

To thrive in the Fame Revolution, we must be adept at adapting to all the people, that is, stakeholders, and their approaches to meet evolving needs and expectations. Your potential client/customer is your first priority, and yet to thrive, it is important to have an eye on the rest of the ocean of people. Customers are not confined in just one part of the waters; they intermingle with your other stakeholders. They can greatly influence your reputation and the willingness of other potential customers to buy from you.

What I like the most about the sailing analogy is that no matter what wind and weather you face, you can still reach your destination if you have the right plan to deal with the people who impact your business.

"We cannot direct the wind, but we can adjust the sails."

—Bertha Calloway, activist and historian

Plotting the position

We like to imagine that we are the only ones at sea, but if we are close to the harbor, we can see that we have many competitors. Sometimes you are by yourself, and that is when you are sailing in the "Blue Ocean Strategy," as coined and developed by W. Chan Kim and Renée Mauborgne, professors at INSEAD and the authors of the international bestseller *Blue Ocean Strategy*.

The idea of Blue Ocean Strategy is simple: find a place with little or no competition. Open a new market space and create new demand. That is the Blue Ocean. On the contrary, the red ocean is a commodity where you fight for margins like Coke and Pepsi do. To be first in a new ocean and take the risk, even if it fails, is better than not doing so because you were first.

Finding the Blue Ocean and claiming the stake will put you ahead of everyone else. And remember, the key is to be within the top 4 percent, but being number one is better. I like what the founder of Click Funnels, Russell Brunson, says: "You can find a Blue Ocean within a red ocean." It involves identifying a common product or service and carving out a unique niche within that market. For instance, the Dollar Shaving Club found a niche where men shave but do not like to shop and do not like to spend exorbitant amounts of money on shaving. So, what does the Dollar Shaving Club do? They sold blades for a dollar via mail. The business took off in 2016 and was sold to Unilever for $1 billion.[99]

I am a big fan of the concept of the Blue Ocean Strategy and have expanded to think of the Blue Ocean message, the Blue Ocean gifts, things that set you apart. I have found that building upon the Blue Ocean

Strategy is not just about finding the product and service that will put you in uncontested waters. I believe that you *are* the Blue Ocean. Tapping into your differentiator and finding ways to utilize it creates new opportunity and growth.

Positioning can mean two things. As we have covered above, it can be about setting the position toward your destination. Still, there is a second definition that Al Ries and Jack Trout wrote in their authoritative book, *Positioning: The Battle for Your Mind.* They state, "The easiest way to get into someone's mind is to be first," meaning capture space in their mind for your service, product, or idea. However, sometimes, we cannot be first, and as seasoned navigators of the seas, we want to utilize the tools to help find ways to chart the course with competitors. We can be the first to claim a unique position and be a desirable alternative. The priority is to create a memorable space in people's minds.

"You would not sail to Hawaii in a dinghy," stated Neil Beam, a seasoned sailor and friend. He reminded me that when setting sail, make an honest assessment of your capabilities and team. The boat can grow bigger as you get closer to your Big Bold & Boundless Dream. You might start with a dinghy and end with a cruise ship.

The question is, how can we ensure that we are on top of mind in the ever-shifting marketplace?

As with sailing, we need to map out our course, and in business, setting up a Public Figure Strategy means developing a comprehensive plan and market analysis that underpins a successful enterprise.

It is similar to a captain's chart, outlining a business's intricate course to realize its ambitions. This map clarifies the contours of the market landscape and provides insights into environmental conditions and potential challenges. The map is our Public Figure Strategy; by going through each phase, you have a plan and will be ready to set sail.

THE PUBLIC FIGURE STRATEGY

I believe in simplicity and have taken what I learned in strategic communication at Columbia University and added a few components. Strategic communication is about the right message, time, channel, and audience. Along with that, we also need to incorporate strategic marketing and ensure that we also focus on achieving branding business goals (market expansion, audience growth, sales channel activation, etc.).

And when we want to forge a Public Figure path, having the right team and outcome and staying on the offense are important. Staying on your toes and being prepared to respond to criticism or crisis with a team behind you are paramount.

The components of the Public Figure Strategy include:

- **Outcome:** Driving the desired action to create lasting positive impressions, elevate status, and achieve tangible results.
- **Message:** Weaving together verbal, visual, video, branding, and personal facets into a compelling narrative.
- **Channel:** Utilizing a range of platforms from events and nonprofits to books and broadcasts, from social media shorts to sponsorships to tell your story.
- **People:** Engaging everyone from fans to associations, from ambassadors to endorsers, all the while nurturing these relationships.
- **Time:** Capitalizing on current events, trends, and the pulse of the audience to strike when the moment is right.
- **Team:** Cultivating a harmonious and collaborative internal environment, focusing on clear communication, alignment with vision, and shared objectives.
- **Be on the Offense:** Proactively countering "cancel culture," building and safeguarding the reputation of the brand, and ensuring that the narrative remains positive and undamaged.

We are now ready to set sail with the compass leading us to our destination. You will undoubtedly face unchartered waters, but you are as prepared as possible.

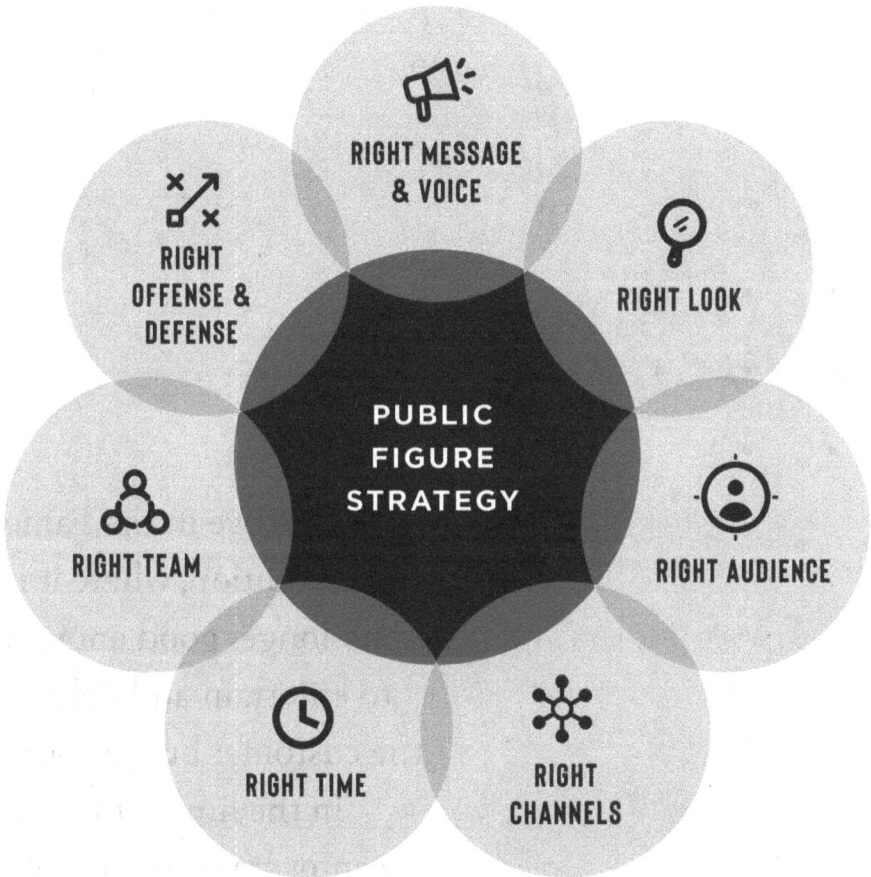

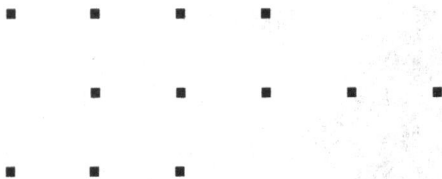

We live in the Fame
Revolution, where it is
no longer good enough
to entertain and delight
the customer but to stand
in the limelight, take
center stage to promote
your product, and inform
on an important issue.
To be different. To be
authentically you.

CHAPTER SIX

SAFEGUARDING YOUR FAME

When we leave the fortress of safety to share our purpose, our gift, and our authentic selves, we are vulnerable to attack.

How do you safeguard yourself from being hurt, bullied, or canceled? You can't, but you can mitigate the impact.

It is like a mother removing the training wheels from her child's bike for the first time. You are never fully ready, and you know falls will happen.

As a child, you think you are invincible as your whole biking experience has been on a steady bike ride, and you believe nothing could go wrong.

As the training wheels come off, the child will experience the bike for the first time as unsteady and not as sturdy as before; the bike wobbles, and when the child tries to pedal, the bike will shake, wobble, and after a few treads, it will suddenly tip and fall.

This section is to help you prepare for and manage the fall.

Because it is not a matter of IF you fall, but WHEN.

STEPPING INTO THE ARENA

"Toil and risk are the price of glory, but it is a lovely thing to live with courage and die leaving an everlasting fame."

—Alexander the Great, one of the greatest military strategists and leaders in world history spreading Hellenistic culture through his conquests of the Mediterranean, Persian Empire, and parts of India

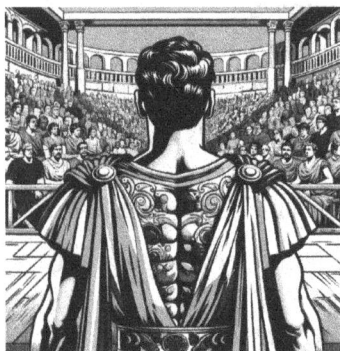

DISCUSSING THE CHALLENGES of embracing the spotlight or distinguishing oneself from the crowd, many turn to the words of President Theodore Roosevelt. Delivered in Paris before French leaders and an audience of 2,000 at Sorbonne University, the speech titled "Citizenship in a Republic" would be famously dubbed "The Man in the Arena." It celebrates those audacious enough to champion their beliefs. Roosevelt's words resonated deeply, with the speech selling thousands of copies in mere days and later inspiring global leaders like Nelson Mandela. Here's part of *The Man in the Arena* speech:

"It is not the critic who counts;
not the man who points out how the strong man stumbles,
or where the doer of deeds could have done them better.
The credit belongs to the man who is actually in the arena,
whose face is marred by dust and sweat and blood;

who strives valiantly; who errs,

who comes short again and again,

because there is no effort without error and shortcoming;

but who does actually strive to do the deeds;

who knows great enthusiasms, the great devotions;

who spends himself in a worthy cause;

who at the best knows in the end the triumph of high achievement, and

who at the worst, if he fails, at least fails while daring greatly,

so that his place shall never be with those cold and timid souls

who neither know victory nor defeat."

Many refer to this speech, and rightfully so. It underscores the dangers of fame. When we share our achievements, critics, without fail, will linger nearby, ready to pull us down. These backseat drivers of life discourage many from even attempting to step into the spotlight. Yet, while there is always a risk, the old saying goes: nothing ventured, nothing gained. The jeers and critiques from the sidelines should be ignored as they do not dare to present their own ideas openly.

One of the courses at the Institute of Media and Entertainment (IME) was on how to manage talent. We interacted with top executives from media giants like MTV, VIACOM, and CNN, plus filmmakers, songwriters, directors, and the talents themselves. I recall when a famous opera singer visited our class to share her struggles with stage fright and the immense pressure of being in the spotlight. And yet, she had a calling and an ardent passion to share her gift. The professor wanted to remind us that even those who seem confident on stage often battle their internal demons. It's crucial to find healthy ways to manage your emotions and handle the pressures that come with being in the public eye. What became clear from that course is that while managing or representing talent, one must always remember the risks taken. Being in the spotlight makes you feel naked, alone, and freezing in the glaring light, revealing your innermost self. Managers or publicists can provide a shield against criticism, but they cannot always fully protect from its impact. Some talents resort to coping mechanisms, like drugs or alcohol, to manage the sheer vulnerability they feel. This reflection of being in the arena resonated with me: when you support someone's cherished project, idea, or vision, you are a support to the Public Figure, but **you as the Public Figure standing in the arena bear the most risk of the critiques, while you as the Public Figure standing in the arena bear the most risk of the critique, while also receiving the most applause.**

SAFEGUARDING YOUR GIFTS

> *"Above all else, guard your heart,
> for it is the wellspring of life."*
>
> **—Proverbs 4:23** (NIV)

WHEN YOU FULLY DARE to be authentic in sharing your gifts, a sign of success is, ironically, the critic. The critics come out from the woods and attempt to downgrade your gifts with a shrug, a snide comment, ridicule, or worse. They may even bully you or go so far as to become vigilantes with an obsession to gather momentum and banish you from the public square.

Some ~~trolls~~ people just have nothing better to do.

As the saying goes, **safeguard your heart, because it is the wellspring of life.**

Does that mean being confined to the ivory tower, shriveling up, and having your gift die, never to see the light of day? That sounds a bit dramatic, but it is how we feel when we first experience the onslaught of criticism. We want to hide from the world.

And yet, that is not living.

Most of us can still recall the first time we were embarrassed by our classmates, laughed at, ridiculed, or bullied. We felt shameful and might have been tempted to hide behind our mothers' skirts, never to resurface. That first moment of being burned in the spotlight is, most likely, a scar etched in our memories—some carry it their whole lives, unable to shake it off.

Sharing our message with the world can be a daunting task, as it means exposing our strengths, frailties, and weaknesses to the public eye. The closer we get to the limelight, the more visible our imperfections become, making us want to hide or even resent the exposure. Risks are involved in becoming known, and the criticism that often follows can be harsh and overwhelming.

In this era of the Fame Revolution, many people are eager to bombard social media with their messages without fully understanding the potential consequences. However, it's important to be prepared for emerging critics, as handling them is key to surviving and thriving in the limelight. And know that it is possible for the critic to become a fan. I have seen it happen many times.

A REGULAR GUY DISCOVERS INTERNET TROLLS

I came across a regular guy in my YouTube feed who became a social media personality with several videos with over 2 million views and over 150K subscribers on YouTube; like his fans, I was impressed with his research citations and the way he explained complex issues in a folksy, down-to-earth manner. I noticed that the post I had watched was posted seven years ago and went to his channel to discover that he had abruptly stopped posting his regular videos. What was the reason?

I went down a rabbit hole and visited Reddit and Quora and discovered that the critics and trolls became too much for him to handle, and it was mentioned in various threads that he had ended up in the hospital due to panic attacks. He had abruptly stopped the whole operation of providing enlightening and informative content. I thought this was so unfortunate, because he seemed to love sharing his insights. He even had T-shirts that he sold on his website with a regular blog. His website, blog, and shopping cart were taken down except for the YouTube channel. I imagine, even though the critics got him to stop posting, he did not want to let go of all the insightful work. And even today, you will see new comments wishing he was back. So many fans, but a few trolls stopped him.

How do we safeguard our hearts and share our gifts, knowing full well that we will fall and be ridiculed or possibly canceled?

Contrary to the conventional wisdom, retreating from the scene is not the answer. The solution is to be even more brave, stand your ground, and share even more.

The worst kind of incident is the one we are not prepared for. Most of the people I see sharing on social media are not mentally prepared for the trolls. And the first critic we encounter on social media can feel like a sniper attack. A fellow author who just released his book was completely devastated when he received only two stars with no explanation. "The person could not have read the book. I just released it. And why did they give no explanation?" He went on to lament how hard he had worked.

The solution is to be prepared for the critic, the troll, and the canceller to come knocking on your door. Most importantly, be mentally ready.

"If you have no critics, you'll likely have no success."

—**Malcolm X**

THE CRITIC IS YOUR GREATEST ASSET.

If there is any consolation prize, I have found that the stronger the critic, the more valuable and unique your gift is. A gift shining in the light will bring out the detractors at first; they will ignore you, then they will fight you, and if you persist, you will win.

The hardest part to watch is when your good intentions trigger someone else to be your detractor. I say "detractors" because they try to detract the radiance of your gift, but you will only shine brighter if you persist.

I like what one blogger wrote: **"If everyone likes you, you aren't being real enough..."**[100]

Authenticity requires you to have critics.

I have found my greatest critics, detractors, and bullies to be my best friends, but not in the sense that I would want to sit and hang out with them. No, they make me stronger and better, and I excel because I listen to them. When they highlight a shortcoming, I ensure the gap they highlight is filled as much as possible. And if that is not possible, I make sure to be prepared with an apt response.

In this age of the Fame Revolution where the prerequisite to thrive is to become famous for what you do, the downside is the sting of the limelight. We have a great saying in Norwegian, "Medaljens Bakside," meaning "the shadow of the gold medal." With glory, there is a shadow we need to come to terms with. Knowing this and being prepared mentally is half the battle.

"First, they ignore you. Then they ridicule you. And then they attack you and want to burn you. And then they build monuments to you."

—Nicholas Klein, American labor union advocate, best known for his speech to the Amalgamated Clothing Workers of America in 1918

THE EMOTIONAL RESPONSE CYCLE

> *"When you REACT, you are giving away your power. When you RESPOND you are staying in control of yourself."*
>
> —**Bob Proctor,** Canadian self-help author of *The New York Times* best-selling book *You Were Born Rich* and a contributor to the film *The Secret*

WHEN THE CRITIC COMES, the first line of response is not to react but feel the emotions. Allow time to breathe, reflect, and assess the situation before responding.

In our agency, we make room for clients to react in a safe space.

Do not fall into the temptation to immediately react with a post or comment. Give yourself some time. As the age-old advice goes, count to ten. We might feel that we do not have time to count to ten, but instead of reacting, use that time to call a friend or your support group or reach out to your folks in the "kitchen cabinet."

BE EMOTIONALLY PREPARED

Before the critic comes, I recommend being prepared and having a list of people you can call to make room for you to vent your emotions and brainstorm with you to find a constructive response.

As it says in the Old Testament (Proverbs 15:22 ESV), "Plans fail for lack of counsel, but with many advisers they succeed." Seek counsel. Do not react on your own. The reaction can make it worse.

To help manage a response to being criticized on social media, small to large critiques, a great tool that has helped us in our agency is to map out our client's state of mind through the Emotional Cycle Overview. Assisting clients in recognizing the typical stages of emotional reactions to criticism, like shame, defensiveness, and anger, is key. Understanding these stages can prevent extreme reactions and make it easier to calm them down, allowing us to collaboratively develop an effective response strategy.

The Emotional Cycle Overview shows the five stages we face when a critique comes. **First, there is the immediate reaction to the attack.** We might be appalled and shocked as the incident sinks in.

Then, **in the second phase, we enter the protective mode,** become defensive, and say to ourselves, "That is not me," "That is not what I meant to say," and "How can they say this?" As we continue to contemplate, we might enter **the third stage, where emotions intensify,** and we are tempted to immediately come back with a reaction of anger, or we cry or pull the victim card. This stage is the most dangerous, and it is crucial to know that when you are in this stage, you delegate the strategy of response to someone else. The recommendation is to have a professional with crisis communication experience on standby to help.

Stage four involves resisting immediate reactions and self-regulating to craft a considered response, while **stage five is about integrating the incident,** learning from it, improving for the future, and moving on.

The Emotional Cycle Overview is a guide to become aware of the natural cycle of the stages we go through when we face a critic or troll. It reminds us that it is human to react, to be angry, to want to be aggressive, and then, eventually to breathe, seek support, regulate ourselves, cool down, and proceed forward. Our emotions are not as predictable or clinical as the Overview, but the five stages are meant to provide awareness, and half the battle is in knowing where you are so you can give yourself grace and find a solution that is not destructive but constructive.

EMOTIONAL RESPONSE CYCLE - FROM SHOCK TO GROWTH

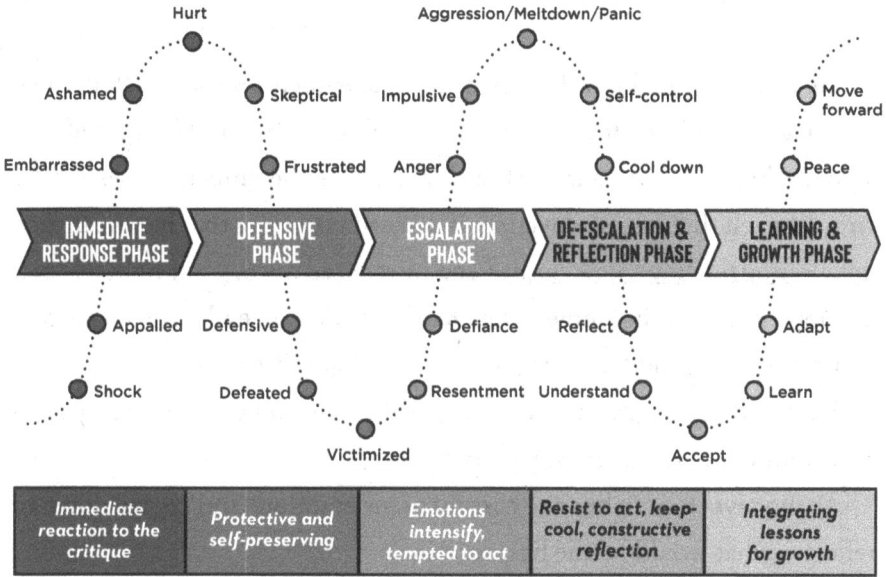

Immediate reaction to the critique	Protective and self-preserving	Emotions intensify, tempted to act	Resist to act, keep cool, constructive reflection	Integrating lessons for growth

THE EMOTIONAL RESPONSE: THE EMPEROR'S NEW CLOTHES[101]

We are taking you back to the end of the famous tale of H. C. Anderson when the emperor has been fooled by two con artists. They convinced the emperor and his trusted advisors that they were weaving the finest clothes, so fine that they were invisible to the commoner's eye. In reality, it was a hoax; there were no clothes.

Embarking on the procession, the king showed off his new clothes; a boy in the midst blurted out what no one else dared to say: *"But he hasn't got anything on."*[102]

At first, the emperor was **shocked** that the boy would say such a thing, and he and the crowd were **appalled**.

The boy's father immediately stated, "Did you ever hear such innocent prattle?" as he did not want to get in trouble. But the spell of believing the illusion that the emperor was wearing new clothes broke. *"And one person whispered to another what the child had said, 'He hasn't anything on. A child says he hasn't anything on.' And then the whole town cried out loud, 'But he hasn't got anything on!'"*[103]

We can imagine the rush of emotions the emperor must have felt. First, **embarrassed** and **ashamed**. He was **skeptical** of the boy and **frustrated** that a young kid could exclaim such a thing, but as the emperor assessed the crowd, he felt that he was shivering. It dawned upon him that he was, in fact, not wearing the finest new clothes, and he realized the boy was right. He had no clothes on, and he immediately felt **hurt**, **victimized** by the con artists and his advisors, and felt all alone in the spotlight. What to do?

He could get **angry** or utilize his royal power to punish someone, but that would only reflect poorly on him.

As the royal leader, he took **control** of his emotions and **cooled down** to reflect—what would be the best solution?

Unfortunately, his trusted advisors were not there to tell him what to do, because like the emperor, they had been fooled and did not want to admit that the invisible clothing was not real.

As the crowd looked upon the emperor and he felt their stares of disbelief, the best solution after a moment of **reflection** was to **accept** the situation and proceed like he was wearing new clothes. He thought, *"This procession has got to go on."*[104] So, he walked more proudly than ever as his noblemen held high the train that wasn't there at all.

We can imagine that when the emperor returned to the castle, some of the emotions he had to hold back were unleashed. He probably was **angry** and **frustrated** and might have even thrown a wine glass or vase on the ground. I know that I might do something like that when feeling betrayed. But after a moment, he would **cool down** and realize that the con artist had appealed to his vanity, a weakness that had gotten him into this crisis. To keep this from happening again, he would work on his vanity issues, reassign the poor advisor to less powerful positions, and immediately hire new advisors to assess the best course of action to rehabilitate the emperor's image, brand, and reputation.

Like the emperor, emotions e.g., someone embarrassed by critics or con artists will experience emotions that will go up and down like a roller coaster and will not go in a chronological order as above. Anger might resurface, hurt and feeling victimized may come up again and again, but that is okay. Let the emotions flow, feel, and let them go and think to yourself, "This too shall pass."

HOW TO PREPARE?

"Your response—and not the crisis itself—can become the story."

—Dr. Steve Goldman, course director, Crisis Management and Business Resiliency, Advanced Business Resiliency, at Massachusetts Institute of Technology (MIT)

Lesson one: embrace your shadows

Assessing the skeletons in your closet and creating a plan to address them can save a lot of heartache and headaches. A simple statement can get twisted, depending on the listener, and if it's tied to something in your past, it may cripple you—if you let it. Once you've mapped out your potential skeletons or messages that could get skewed, draft your talking points. Sure, these topics might never pop up, but you want to form muscle memory and learn to respond, not react.

Reacting to something is a quick and natural tendency. But when you take a moment to respond, you give yourself space to understand, plan, and move ahead calmly. There is a huge advantage in using a more evolved approach over an immediate, emotional one.

Lesson two: authenticity is your armor

We like to believe that we're transparent, open books and honest souls just doing our thing. How could anyone get the wrong idea about us? But without preparation, in the heat of the moment, nerves can make us stumble over our words, and boom—we've been misinterpreted.

Lesson three: secure your backup

Think of this as having a PR safety net. Just as you'd call your lawyer for legal troubles, have a PR professional who is already familiar with your plan and can jump right in to manage the situation when you hit one of those sticky communication snags.

Here's the thing:

- There's no blueprint for this. Let common sense be your compass.
- Always tailor any advice to suit your unique needs or organization.
- Sometimes, all you need is a sounding board. That's where the "kitchen cabinet" (your most trusted people) comes in handy.

FIND YOUR FOXHOLE FRIENDS

> *"Most wars are won or lost in our own heads, and when we're in a foxhole we usually aren't alone, and we need to be confident in the quality of the heart, mind, and dialogue of the person hunkered down with us. Because at some point we will need some empowering words to keep us focused and deadly."*

—David Goggins, retired U.S. Navy SEAL and *The New York Times* best-selling author of *Can't Hurt Me: Master Your Mind*

WHO WILL BE IN THE FOXHOLE WITH YOU?

DURING WORLD WAR I, as the conflict between France and Germany stagnated, a "no man's land" emerged—a neutral zone lined with foxholes where soldiers stood guard against the opposing side. The question became, with whom will you want to share the foxhole with? That is, to whom can you entrust your life? Who do you want by your side in a crisis?

Take the time to work with your brain trust to identify your foxhole friends; and while you are at it, identify your foes and fans. Friends come in different shades, as do foes and fans. The key is knowing those few you would want in the foxhole.

This exercise underscores the importance of cultivating meaningful relationships with your team members. Be aware that some friends may only be fair-weather or casual and could potentially become foes.

A foe can become a friend. They can be a simple critic and grow from there. I have been surprised in my career. My greatest adversary becomes someone I respect and later is in the foxhole with me.

MAPPING YOUR FRIENDS, FOES, AND FANS

People mapping is a collaborative endeavor involving research, debate, and discussion. Tap into diverse viewpoints to compile a crucial list of individuals and groups spanning the broad spectrum of associations and relationships. I like to keep it simple and bucket my network into friends, foes, and fans.

- **Friends (supportive stakeholders):** These are allies and partners, including "foxhole friends" who stand with you in tough times and "trusted advisors" who offer guidance and support. They range from investors and collaborators to supportive community members and play a key role in providing resources and backing during challenging times, being integral to your success.

- **Foes (critics or competitors):** This group encompasses competitors and critics who may not necessarily wish for your success. Understanding their perspectives is crucial for anticipating challenges and mitigating potential negative impacts on your business.

- **Fans (loyal customers or supporters):** Fans are your loyal customer base and enthusiastic supporters. They are crucial for positive word-of-mouth and can be powerful advocates for your brand, especially during crisis situations where their loyalty and support can significantly influence public perception.

To map people into these categories, assemble pivotal individuals to contribute to a brainstorming session. This mapping should be specific to each campaign, project, and product or service, emphasizing the individuals' relevance and roles. In this case, we are mapping who will be our foxhole friends in a crisis.

People mapping is good for business

Before launching a product, wouldn't you want to gauge its potential champions? Sometimes, your closest allies and friends can be your strongest advocates. Through people mapping, you can rediscover valuable connections, perhaps overlooked in the hustle of everyday life. Imagine you're hosting a book launch on culinary delights. There might be a vendor you've unintentionally sidestepped who'd be ecstatic to sponsor your event.

Ever organized an event and then realized, all too late, that a cherished friend was inadvertently left out? People mapping can be your safeguard against such oversights.

I advise you to undertake a comprehensive mapping of your entire network. Identify your top 100 most crucial contacts and then categorize the remainder into relevant groups and find the handful of foxhole friends.

Great ideas come when we do not censor ourselves. The brainstorming process can be broken down into the following:

- **Identifying:** listing relevant groups, organizations, and individuals.
- **Analyzing:** understanding the perspectives and interests of these people.
- **Mapping:** visualizing relationships to objectives and other connections.
- **Prioritizing:** ranking the relevance of these connections and identifying issues.

Your foxhole friends come down to the people you can always count on to support you. Your foxhole friends are fierce and faithful. As the old saying goes: "In prosperity our friends know us; in adversity we know our friends."

CRISIS MANAGEMENT OVERVIEW

66 *"Plans are useless, but planning is indispensable."*

—President Dwight Eisenhower, 34th U.S. president (1953–61) and supreme commander of the Allied forces in western Europe during World War

TODAY, TIME IS OF THE ESSENCE. Communicating effectively with both the public and the media is not just a skill that's nice to have; it's a strategic must. In this section, I'll provide an overview of the various types of disruptions that can occur and provide a standard timeline that can help navigate your possible crisis or viral moment. Is viral a crisis? No, but going viral is an unexpected disruption, even if it can be a positive windfall. Viral moments will require extra manpower, strategy, and planning to manage well. A viral disruption can become a crisis if you are not ready for it.

RANGE OF DISRUPTIONS

To simplify, I categorize three main types of disruptions: crises, cancellations, and viral disruptions.

Crisis: A crisis is an unexpected and significant event that poses a serious threat to an organization or individual, requiring immediate attention and action.

Cancellation: Cancellation refers to the public and often collective decision to stop supporting or engaging with an individual or organization due to perceived misconduct or disagreement.

Viral disruptions: Viral disruptions are sudden, widespread events or phenomena, typically accelerated by social media, that capture massive public attention and significantly impact normal operations or public perception.

Each of these areas require different ways of managing the disruption, but here is a sketch of a timeline showing on how this disruption can unfold. This is a bird's eye view of the key milestones in a crisis from the first hour.

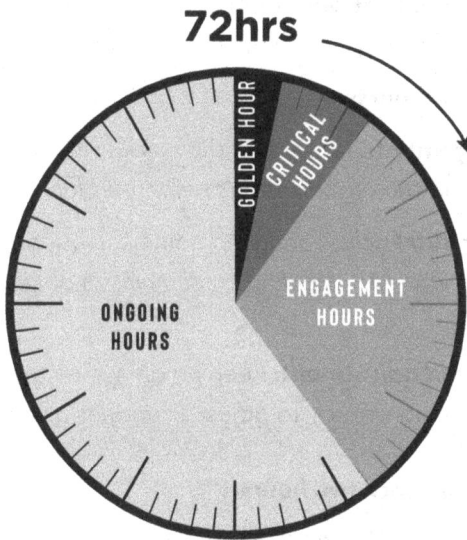

Critical Response Timeline: Managing the First 72 Hours of a Crisis

The golden hour (first hour after disruption):

- **Immediate assessment:** *Quick evaluation of the situation to understand its severity and potential impact.*

- **Holding statement release:** *Issuing a brief, initial communication to acknowledge the crisis and inform stakeholders.*

- **Crisis team activation:** *Mobilizing a dedicated crisis management team to handle the situation.*

- **Initial communication to employees:** *Ensuring internal stakeholders are informed and aligned.*

Next few hours (one to six hours after disruption):

- **Gathering information:** Collecting detailed information about the crisis.

- **Strategy development:** Formulating a response strategy based on the gathered information.

- **Ongoing communication:** Continually monitoring the situation and updating stakeholders with new information.

First twenty-four hours:

- **Media engagement:** Addressing the media with more detailed information and the organization's response plan.

- **Stakeholder outreach:** Continued communication with all relevant stakeholders, including customers, employees, and partners.

- **Monitoring and adjustment:** Keeping an eye on the situation and public reaction, ready to adjust strategies as needed.

Forty-eight to seventy-two hours:

- **Detailed analysis:** Conducting a thorough analysis of the crisis causes and effects.

- **Ongoing communication strategy:** Implementing a longer-term communication strategy to manage the ongoing narrative.

- **Stakeholder engagement:** Deepening engagement with key stakeholders to rebuild trust.

One week and beyond:

- **Review and adaptation:** Reviewing the crisis response effectiveness and adapting future crisis management plans.

- **Reputation management:** Focusing on long-term strategies to repair and enhance the organization's reputation.

- **Lessons learned:** Identifying key learnings to improve preparedness for future crises. [105]

THE GOLDEN 15

> *"Death and life are in the power of the tongue, And those who love it and indulge it will eat its fruit and bear the consequences of their words."*
>
> **—Proverbs 18:21** (AMP)

IN TODAY'S FAME ECONOMY, experts say you have fifteen minutes or less to a crisis. **That means not reacting but responding.** Find a way to self-regulate and not let emotions get the better of you. Then respond factually and with decorum, steering clear of anything hasty or angry.

The Emperor's New Clothes showed how a mature leader who could respond instantly with grace despite being exposed, laughed at, and ridiculed. I imagine his response will give his subordinates, the public, and the commoners a newfound respect for him, even though he caused this disaster.

In crisis communication, the first hour of any crisis is called the Golden Hour, when a Public Figure or organization has the best opportunity to establish the facts, shape the narrative, and persuade the public impression in its favor. In reality, the growth of digital and social media has dramatically reduced the golden hour to a few minutes to create a response. I like to call it the Golden 15.

I believe the first hour is still important, but it is within those first fifteen minutes that you will be able to best shape the story, establish your position, and set the pace for the information flow throughout the crisis.

In today's world, it's absolutely critical for any Public Figure or organization to issue that initial holding statement within the first fifteen minutes of a crisis. **It is make or break**. And within that crucial first hour, it's essential to gather as much information and as many facts as possible, to activate the crisis management plan, and begin building the narrative with drips of information and action.

> A holding statement is a brief, pre-prepared, fill-in-the-blank template communication released immediately in response to a crisis. The intention is to inform, reassure, and manage the stakeholders' expectations for a response. It also buys time for the team to assess the situation, collect the facts, and ultimately issue a more detailed response.

However, responding within fifteen minutes does not mean you must provide any information that will expose you and force you to react. **Sending out a holding statement informs all parties that you are aware and in control of the situation. It also buys you time to assemble your team,** to better understand the situation, collect the facts, create a strategy, and ultimately issue something more detailed. If you do not put out a holding statement, the media, the public, and your team, internally and externally, will start creating their own stories of what happened. This is when rumors will start to fly, and you will have lost the chance of shaping the narrative. Then you can be put into a defensive mode throughout the crisis.

Leading crisis strategist Davia Temin states in *Forbes Magazine*, "When a crisis hits, how you respond in the first fifteen minutes may make or break your organization—and your reputation. I have found that in those first fifteen minutes of a crisis, your response must be exactly the right message. As well as being delivered in exactly the right words, to the right audiences, and in just the right way. Or you will have to deal with your mistakes for days, weeks, or even months."[106]

With one video or one statement going viral, your reputation and your company's future could be hanging in the balance. With the prevalence of "cancel culture," a moment of poor judgment or a misguided comment can lead to swift and severe consequences. The potential for irreparable damage to your personal and professional brand, as well as the bottom line of your company, is very real. That's why reputation management has become more important than ever, and why businesses are investing heavily in strategies to monitor and manage their online presence and response.

The Golden 15 is just the beginning. But in that moment, you must hit the ground running to manage the crisis. You are working against time, but taking action within the first fifteen minutes will give you grace and breathing room and help you stay as far ahead of the story as possible.

I strongly recommend having a sort of "insurance policy" in place. This means setting up a proactive plan and assembling a dedicated team to manage potential crises or legal challenges that could arise from increased public exposure. Being prepared in this way can provide a vital safety net as you navigate this evolving landscape and help protect your rights and reputation in the digital age.

Are you feeling a bit daunted by the timeline I have laid out?
I totally get it—it can look a bit overwhelming at first. But don't stress over it. Think of this as your friendly guide, not a set-in-stone timeline. The intention is to help you out if you ever find yourself in a tricky crisis. Just remember, having this timeline means you won't be caught off guard. It's like having a heads-up from a good friend, so you can handle whatever comes your way with a little more ease and a lot less surprise. Waiting for disaster to strike is the biggest mistake you can make. The significance of swift, frequent, and articulate communication in the wake of an impactful event cannot be overstated.

You'll sleep better at night with these plans in place. Trust me.

WHY AM I A STICKLER FOR PLANNING FOR A CRISIS?

Crisis came to me while working as a press assistant and webmaster for Senator Hatch in Washington, D.C. And it was September 11, 2001 (9/11), when nearly 3,000 people were killed in a series of attacks in the United States. The planes did not hit the U.S. Capitol building, which we thought would happen after a plane hit the Pentagon. The shock, the fear, and the frantic moments of thinking that my then-boyfriend had possibly died in the Pentagon attack are something I will never forget. Amid the frantic moments, I felt one person stood steadfast and calm: Senator Hatch. While most of the staff were unsure and afraid, he was calm in his office with a select few of his advisors. We, the staff members, were eventually dismissed to go home to our loved ones.

At the same time, Senator Hatch stayed and became one of the de facto spokespersons when President Bush was not available to issue a comment. I have never been as proud to work for the senator as during those moments, and I got to relive them when I was assigned to contribute to the post-report by reviewing all the media statements and footage that the senator made in the first seventy-two hours to various reporters and TV channels. My recollection from reviewing the footage was how calm Senator Hatch was amid a crisis. What struck me is how effective he was as a communicator even though he pretty much repeated the same information over and over again to different interviewers. But, we who were transfixed to the television for the first seventy-two hours could hear the same information and be comforted by it. I like to call this the "non-information information strategy."

Non-information information strategy: *A communication method for filling the void and controlling message flow, often used to reassure the public. It involves making announcements or statements that repeat information or explain issues without adding new crucial details. The intention is to maintain a presence, control the narrative, and offer comfort in sensitive situations.*

It is a handy tool to use when having to respond to a crisis. Sometimes, the best thing to do in a crisis is to fill the void with non-information information to provide comfort and trust that it will all work out. A month after 9/11, we navigated an anthrax attack where letters containing anthrax spores were mailed to several news media outlets, including Senator Daschle's office, on the floor above us. The attack killed five people and infected seventeen others. I remember the day when it happened. Again, I was in shock, fearful, and this time paralyzed about what to do. I was afraid of being so close to an anthrax attack, fearing that it would impact my health. Luckily, it didn't.

This attack, however, was a far worse crisis to manage than 9/11, as we were displaced from our office for months because the Hart Senate Office building needed to be cleaned and repaired from the spores of anthrax. I felt like I was in a post-war zone, sharing offices with about twenty-five web developers crammed in a computer room close to Union Station, a fifteen-minute walk away from the U.S. Capitol building, and a similar distance to the other staff members displaced in other locations, all the while trying to continue business as usual. Looking back, the post-anthrax attack reminds me of the pandemic, as we discovered new ways to continue business operations, though at that time, we did not have the luxury of working remotely.

Since then, I have worked on various crises, from cancel culture incidents to terrorism, and I even worked at IntraPoint, a crisis and risk management software company. During my time at IntraPoint, we saw firsthand that the software we provided was instrumental in managing a terrorist attack, fires, and weather disasters. Seeing up front how effective it is to have a software tool and process to manage a crisis is a *night and day* experience.

First and foremost, you are mentally prepared for the disruption, because you have trained for that moment. And when the crisis hits, your training is in your muscles, and the muscle memory kicks in. You are on autopilot, able to regulate your emotions, act and respond with intention, remain calm, and ensure minimum damage. In responding to the terrorism crisis, our clients utilized the IntraPoint Crisis Manager Software. Tragically, there were casualties and significant facility damage. The company's approach, marked by calm composure, respect, and deference to the families of victims and employees, as well as its responses to the media and government, was exemplary. In the post-crisis period, the company not only saw a swift rebound in profits but also built unprecedented trust with its clients, the media, and government agencies.

You probably don't have a looming terrorism crisis coming. Still, sitting down for a half day and assessing your potential crisis scenarios, such as the death of an employee, cancellation, viral moment, embezzlement, or energy disruptions, will help you be as ready. Doing this right could save your business; doing it wrong could result in loss and even bankruptcy.

You will sleep better at night when you take what you say and present on social media seriously with a crisis plan in place.

THE POWER OF TRAINING

How many times have you lost your keys? It's usually at the most inopportune times, right? I know I've lost mine many times and it's such a helpless feeling, especially if you have to be somewhere important and you're running late. So, I have conditioned myself to place a key in a bowl by the door. It takes some initial awareness but after a while, the habit is formed. This is a small-scale crisis plan. Whenever I move to a new house, I need to consciously remember where my "key bowl" is. At first, it demands effort, but over time, it embeds itself into my muscle memory, becoming second nature. When ingrained deeply, best practices naturally kick in, even when the mind is overwhelmed by "fight or flight" instincts. When you scale up the crisis, the actions will have to scale accordingly, but I wanted to show that it's not just the big situations that you should plan for. Smaller things like where you put your keys so that you remember are important, especially in an emergency situation. Here are some training modules you can consider:

- **Tabletop exercises:** Interactive simulations where team members discuss their roles and responses to hypothetical crisis cancellation, or viral scenarios.
- **Media training:** Sessions focusing on how to effectively communicate with the media, including handling interviews and press conferences.
- **Facebook live training:** Practice sessions in a private Facebook group, where team members can train on delivering live video updates and responses.
- **Social media simulations:** Creating mock social media crises or viral disruptions and practicing how to respond quickly and appropriately on various platforms.
- **Feedback and review sessions:** Analyzing past crisis responses, viral disruptions or theoretical scenarios, followed by constructive feedback to improve future communication.

PREPARE WITH A CRISIS PLAN

Crisis and emergency management is a whole field of study. I was privileged with my job at IntraPoint, to attain a certificate for Crisis Management and Business Continuity at MIT. I highly recommend this course to any company with over a million or more in revenue. It is a two-day program that helps set the foundation for the range of crises and how they can disrupt business as usual, and more importantly, how to thrive and mitigate the damage. If you cannot take the course, I recommend having a professional conduct an audit and prepare a crisis and business continuity plan for the long term.

A crisis management plan is a structured strategy or set of procedures designed to prepare an organization for an unexpected and potentially damaging event, guiding the organization's response to manage and mitigate the impact effectively.

Why? Because it is smart business, and it does not have to cost much time or money but still provides peace of mind and gives you the tools, strategies, and plan to get out of the crisis as safely as humanly possible.

CRISIS COMMUNICATION PLAN

Check for risks: Look at what could go wrong in your business.

Plan for problems: Create a plan for each thing that could go wrong, including a to-do list.

Know what to say: Pick the main points you need to share, making sure they're clear and truthful.

Know your audience: Figure out who you need to talk to supporters, critics, or loyal customers.

Pick your tools: Choose the best way to talk to each group, like email or social media.

Who does what: Decide who in your team will do the talking when trouble comes.

Get ready: Make draft messages you can change quickly when needed.

Practice: Run practice drills to see how well your plans work.

Keep updating: Keep giving new information to everyone as things change.

Listen and respond: Make sure you have a way to hear back from people and answer their questions.

THE BULLETPROOF RESPONSE

I am a fan of simplicity, and that's exactly why I greatly admire Molly McPherson's approach to crisis management, particularly as outlined in her book, *Indestructible*. Her three-step process, detailed in this work, is refreshingly straightforward and incredibly effective.

I highly suggest you give it a try. Below, I've outlined these steps along with explanations to help you understand and navigate each one with confidence:

Step one: Own it. You must acknowledge, accept, or apologize.

- *Explanation:* Your crucial first act in the drama of crisis management or cancellation is to acknowledge the ripple effects of your actions, understanding their impact on others. Just saying, "I'm sorry," and calling it a day is not good enough. You start by acknowledging your actions, accepting the consequences and delivering a heartfelt apology that resonates with sincerity.

Step two. Clarify it. Put the issue into context.

- *Explanation:* Now that you've laid the groundwork with a solid apology, it's time to switch gears into the "explainer" mode. You should paint the full picture for your audience, giving them the context they need to understand what went down. Here, you are the narrator of your own story, filling in the gaps and helping everyone see the bigger picture. It is your chance to answer the whys and hows, shedding light on the situation and guiding your audience through the maze of events that led to the crisis.

Step three. Promise it. Announce your commitment to the plan, prioritize the plan and adjust it if needed so that you can ensure you stick to your promise.

- *Explanation:* After acknowledging the past and clarifying the present, you're now looking to the future. This final step is like making a pact for a better tomorrow. You're not just saying you'll do better; you're laying out a roadmap of how you'll prevent a repeat performance. This is where you make commitments, set new standards, and promise to implement changes that ensure that history doesn't repeat itself.

There is so much more I could say on the topic of being on the offense. My advice is to stay ahead by taking all the signals around you seriously and mitigate a crisis or potential cancellation by implementing best practices. Yet, the plans and training all needs to fit you and your business. What I leave you with is an invitation to be vigilant and find the practice that fits you. Be ahead of the curve and be ready for any disruption. Be prepared for the crisis and the success.

If a crisis should occur, here are some good rules from the Federal Emergency Management Agency (FEMA):

- **BE FIRST.** The first source of communication often becomes the source against which all others are measured.
- **BE RIGHT.** Accuracy is critical to credibility.
- **BE CREDIBLE.** Honesty is fundamental to maintaining trust.
- **EXPRESS EMPATHY.** Emotion cannot be countered with facts. People must first know that their leaders care.
- **PROMOTE ACTION.** Giving people something specific to do restores a sense of control over out-of-control circumstances.
- **SHOW RESPECT.** A lack of respect for the public in crisis undermines trust.[107]

Source: https://emergency.cdc.gov/cerc/ppt/CERC_Introduction.pdf

BE ON THE OFFENSE

> "*Your response—and not the crisis itself—can become the story.*"
>
> —**Dr. Steve Goldman,** internationally recognized expert in crisis management and business continuity and course director, Advance Business Resiliency, MIT (Massachusetts Institute of Technology)

EACH DISRUPTION TAKES US out of the relative normal life and forces us to act. You have a choice when it comes to this action. For some, the temptation is to bury their head in the sand and ignore the problem, hoping it will disappear (it won't). Some will get defensive and act rashly (a strictly regrettable move). But the strategic Public Figure will have a process in place to respond and to be on the offensive.

I firmly believe that the wise Public Figure will continually be on the offensive and be ready to respond. They will not be frantic and reactionary. They will be prepared to give a response that is measured and delivered in the right tone of voice, with the right message, and at the right time.

When a crisis hits, there is not much time to devise a plan. The person and/or company that has planned for months or years in advance will be the one that comes out unscathed. They may even be able to create a new opportunity out of the crisis that never would have existed otherwise.

My first recommendation is to recognize that you cannot do this by yourself, and it is unlikely that you will be able to behave as calmly as the "naked emperor," unless you practice and plan. He took control of the situation and responded with deliberate action, because he had practice. He had been in the public eye all his life and knew intuitively what to do.

Another temptation when a crisis hits is to wait without a response. This can worsen the situation, so training on authenticity and learning an appropriate level of response are key.

THINGS THAT MAKE YOU GO "HMMMM"

Have you had that moment where you noticed something and stopped and said, "That is strange," and later found out that whatever it was became a crisis, trend, and/or went viral?

Well, it all starts with the "hmmmm . . ."

Things That Make You Go Hmmmm . . . was a running gag popularized by talk show host Arsenio Hall. Apparently, it all started while Arsenio was on a long drive, pondering certain thoughts and referring to them as "things that make you go hmmmm . . ."

This catchphrase was immortalized in the song, "Things That Make You Go Hmmmm . . ." by C+C Factory in 1991. The song topped the charts and soared to the number-one position on both the Billboard Hot Dance/ Club Play chart in the United States and elsewhere in the world. The lyrics are about our suspicions and following that gut feeling that something is not quite right.

To me, things that make you go hmmmm, are an indication that where there is smoke, there is fire. Do not ignore the hmmmms in your life. We want to capture our hmmmms and stay on the alert as much as possible, because a crisis usually starts with a hmmmm. Staying alert in the business world and as a Public Figure is like having a secret superpower. It's not just about keeping your eyes open; it is also a vital part of your readiness toolkit to outsmart challenges and continue to shine in the spotlight.

Being on the alert will help safeguard your professional reputation and personal safety. It will fuel top-tier decision-making as you will know where your competition is going and what topics are trending in your field. This will equip you for newsjacking, handling media interactions, and public appearances.

The hmmmm test

First rule: Do not ignore your suspicion. Mention it to your team, assess it, and imagine if this hmmmm were ten times larger, what would it lead to? What kind of crisis or viral moment would it be?

The hmmmm is the start of it all; it is a sign you can recognize. If you find that something is not quite right, you will want to discuss, investigate, research, and decide if it is an identified issue you want to monitor, take action on, or let go. Here are a few steps to consider:

1. Identify
2. Analyze
3. Decide to discard, store, or monitor

When monitoring and assessing, ask yourself: will it grow in significance, remain the same, or decrease?

In monitoring, you look for trends, anomalies, positive feedback, performance fluctuations, market changes, sentiment shifts, cultural or behavioral changes, risk indicators, comparative data, and consistent patterns to identify potential issues or opportunities. Outsourcing a team to manage this will help you find ways to increase business and prepare for a potential crisis.

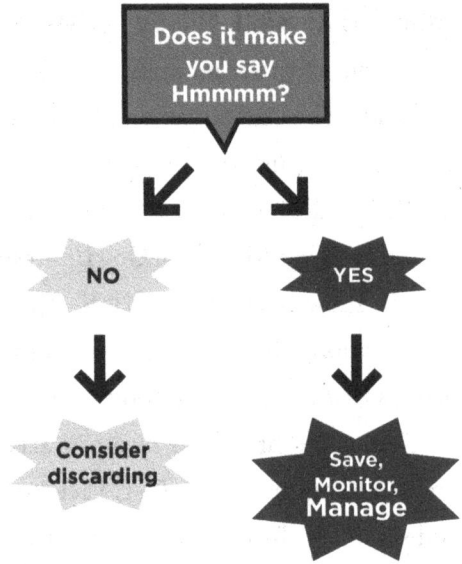

Legal Implications of Public Figure Status on Social Media

When assessing the future of being out on social media and embodying the Public Figure status, I believe it is only a matter of time before we will all be legally designated as a "Public Figure." The reason: we are actively pursuing the visibility once held for traditional celebrities and public officials that can now be obtained by anyone.

The Fame Revolution has greatly expanded the number of people in the public eye. As you post content online, it is critical to understand that you are stepping into a public forum. If your content "goes viral," it will likely propel you to another level of recognition, and it could be believed that you thrust yourself into the public eye, inviting people to chime in with their opinions and comments, good or bad.

> _Legal definition of a Public Figure,_ according to the U.S. Supreme Court in Gertz v. Robert Welch, is an individual who has assumed roles of special prominence in the affairs of a society or has thrust into the forefront of particular public controversies to influence the resolution of the issues involved. Public figures also include individuals who have achieved pervasive fame or notoriety. Whether a party is a Public Figure is a question of law for the court.[108]

This can have serious ramifications, particularly in terms of privacy and defamation. For instance, suppose you have a cute video of you and your hamster that unexpectedly goes viral. Suddenly, millions of people are talking about your video, recognizing your face, and you might even be dubbed 'The Hamster Whisperer.' Whether intentionally or not, you may have become a limited-purpose Public Figure in the context of viral hamster videos. This means that the standard for proving defamation is higher if someone were to make a defamatory statement about you related to this context. You would need to demonstrate that the statement was made with "actual malice" – that is, knowing it was false or with reckless disregard for the truth – for a successful defamation claim.

The term, "limited-purpose public figure," was coined by the United States Supreme Court (*Gertz v. Robert Welch, Inc.*) in 1974. These figures are individuals who have gained prominence in a particular field or connection with a particular controversy. It implies that private individuals can morph into the legal definition of Public Figure in relation to a specific public controversy or issue, hence being exposed to a lower degree of protection and privacy.[109]

With social media bringing us instant visibility, the private becomes public so easily. Once something is shared online, it must be assumed that it will live there in perpetuity and cannot be taken back.

As social media continues to integrate deeply into our daily lives, I believe we're heading toward a significant shift in how legal systems perceive public figures and private citizens. Currently, there's a level of protection for private citizens that public figures aren't necessarily allowed to enjoy, especially in terms of privacy and exposure to public scrutiny. However, with the pervasive nature of social media, there's a growing possibility that these boundaries could blur. If laws evolve to consider regular social media users as public figures, it could lead to a substantial loss of privacy rights for many.

YOUR REPUTATION

"It takes 20 years to build a reputation and five minutes to ruin it. If you think about that you'll do things differently."

—Warren Buffet, chairperson of Berkshire Hathaway and one of the best-known investors in the world

WHILE IT IS DIFFICULT to quantify the value of a reputation, the Reputation Institute's Global RepTrak® 100 study has found that companies with strong reputations had a 2.5 times higher likelihood of outperforming their competitors in the stock market. Similarly, a person with a good reputation may have more opportunities and greater success in their personal and professional life than someone with a poor reputation.[110]

Oxford Analytica states in their 2019 Risk and Reputation Report, "Firms with strong reputation equity can outperform the market by over 100%."[111]

WHAT IS THE PRICE OF A REPUTATION?

On March 19, 2023, there was a shotgun wedding between two Swiss banks, UBS and Credit Suisse, to avoid a reputation meltdown. We have this idea that Swiss banks have the highest integrity. What would happen if one of the largest banks collapsed? Could Swiss banks survive such a demise?[112]

Key Swiss leaders, government, and bankers believed that they could not. As a result, with the urging of the Swiss government, both banks got "married." UBS acquired Credit Suisse to prevent its impending collapse as it was hemorrhaging deposits, with shareholders dumping its stock and creditors rushing to seek repayment. The travesty is that Credit Suisse, formed in 1856, was considered one of the most prestigious investment banks in the world, with a reputation for strict bank–client confidentiality and banking secrecy.

There was a "dowry's cost," i.e., UBS agreed to buy Credit Suisse for 3-billion Swiss francs ($3.2 billion) in a government-supported, discounted deal. Although this merger may have saved the banks from collapse, it has forever changed Switzerland's reputation.

As Octavio Marenzi, CEO of Opimas, stated in a research note, "Switzerland's standing as a financial center is shattered. The country will now be viewed as a financial banana republic."[113]

Reputation counts.

SOCIAL MEDIA AND ITS POTENTIAL DAMAGE TO YOUR REPUTATION

Social media has made reputation management crucial. According to AON's 2019 Global Risk Management Survey, reputation damage ranks as the second-highest risk among the fifteen identified. The survey, based on responses from 2,672 decision-makers in sixty countries, highlights that in the age of social media, a single inappropriate tweet from a CEO, employee, or client can swiftly go viral, causing instant harm to a company's reputation.[114]

Dr. Deborah J. Pretty of Oxford Metrica stated in Reputation & Value (Oxford Metrica, 2019), "Technological developments have heightened reputation risk by making it easier, cheaper, and faster for people to spread news.[115]

BENEFITS OF A GOOD REPUTATION AND BEING KNOWN FOR WHAT YOU DO

There are major upshots to having good a reputation and being famous for what you do.

Increased visibility and exposure: A musician with a solid reputation may be invited to perform at larger venues and festivals, which can increase their visibility and exposure to new audiences. This, in turn, may lead to more opportunities for collaborations, sponsorships, and other partnerships.

Improved credibility: A scientist who becomes a well-known expert in their field may have more credibility when applying for research grants or presenting their findings at conferences. This can help them attract new collaborators and expand their research.

Greater influence: An environmental activist who has a solid resume and is known may have a significant influence on others and may be able to leverage their name to promote positive change and raise awareness for important environmental causes.

Higher earning potential: A social media influencer who has a solid reputation and good name may be able to earn significant income through sponsorships, partnerships, and advertising. This can provide financial stability and the ability to pursue creative or entrepreneurial endeavors.

Opportunities for personal growth and development: A CEO who is a leader in his field may have access to high-quality coaches and training, which can help them improve their skills and grow as a leader and CEO.

Access to exclusive events and experiences: A business executive may be invited to exclusive events, such as award shows or celebrity parties, which can provide unique experiences and networking opportunities.

Increased social capital: A business owner who becomes famous may have access to influential networks and stakeholders, such as venture capitalists or high-level executives. This can help them attract funding and support for their business ventures.

Reputation builds trust, and trust is the fastest route to solidifying your base—be it customers, employees, or partners. The trust you build directly impacts your business's bottom line, ensuring that your audience stays with you, supports you, and contributes to your sustained success, especially in challenging times.

"A good
reputation is
more valuable
than money."

—PUBLILIUS SYRUS,
(FLOURISHED FIRST CENTURY
BC) LATIN MIME WRITER

PART 03

The Exploration of Fame

As we navigate life, we often find ourselves drawn to communities that reflect our values and interests. This might lead us to join a church, become active in associations, or, if we have children, connect with other parents—perhaps even coach a little league.

CHAPTER SEVEN

DIOTIMA'S LADDER OF FAME

In the next few chapters, we will go through the progression of fame and show that we were all born to be famous and that fame is part of our DNA. In fact, to become famous is integral to our society and culture. It has been a fixation since the times of Ancient Greek philosophers.

We will explore Diotima's Ladder of Fame to provide a better understanding of the levels of fame and what it takes mentally, emotionally, and even spiritually to reach the highest levels.

We are living in the best of times and worst of times. It's the worst of times for those who want anonymity and to stay only within their social circles. It is the best of times because you can be anything you want.

Today, there are few gatekeepers to hold us back. Now, you are in control of your visibility and relatability.

It is a process; this section will help you understand how to reach each level, where you are on the ladder, and where you want to go.

Enjoy.

FAME FROM THE ANCIENTS

❝ *"Fame is the perfume of heroic deeds."*

—Socrates, Greek philosopher from Athens, credited as
the founder of Western philosophy

"WHY DO WE STOP ON red and not green, Daddy?"

"Why is a stop sign red?"

"And why is a stop sign not square like the other signs?"

As an annoying five-year-old, I sat in the car's front seat with my dad, asking these questions, and my dad was patient, feeling like a broken record as he kept telling me, "That's just how it is."

Eventually, I learned to ask better questions, and in later years, I found a friend in the master of questions, Socrates. "Examen Philosophicum" (Exphil) is a required Norwegian university course designed to provide students with foundational insights into philosophy, the history of science and ideas, critical thinking, and scientific methods.

I liked Socrates because he was the bomb thrower of ideas and shaped society from the street corners of Athens. He was fat, and some would say quite ugly and poor, and yet his ideas became the conversations of all levels of society. He was even condemned to death for his power to question.

My favorite thing about Socrates is that he gave honor where honor was due and in Plato's *Symposium*, this curmudgeon of a man honored his coach, priestess, and mentor—a woman—for teaching him about the nature of love. Her name was Diotima.

Not only did Socrates give her credit, Plato, the student of Socrates, also ensured that Diotima's name was etched in the *Symposium* for future generations to come. He retold how she made a speech among leading men of Athens, teaching them about the *Ladder of Love*, which was the central insight of the symposium. Diotima taught Socrates and the men at the symposium that the pursuit of love is in the form of a ladder and the highest form of love is a way to get closer to God. She taught them that the goal of love is immortality, which can be achieved by having children or making beautiful things.[116]

SIDENOTE **A Woman Almost Erased from History**

Have you ever heard of Diotima of Mantinea?

If not, you're not alone. Despite being a mentor to Socrates and giving the famous speech on the Ladder of Love, this brilliant woman was almost erased from history by skeptical men in academia.

But don't worry, Diotima can't be erased that easily. In fact, our agency is named in her honor—Diotima Strategies. And with good reason.

You see, when Plato wrote about Diotima in his Symposium, he invited her—the only woman—to speak among the notable men of ancient Greece on the subject of Eros. She gave the speech that formed the foundational thought on love in Western philosophy, but men in academia couldn't believe that a woman could come up with such a grand idea.

In 1485, Marsilio Ficino, a priest and historian, was the most important advocate of Platonism in the Renaissance. He questioned Diotima's

existence, and for over five hundred years, her historical reality was doubted. However, feminist scholar Professor Margaret Urban Walker confirms that Diotima was indeed a real person who had the conversations with Socrates recorded by Plato.

I appreciate that this topic has been taken up in recent years. Dr. Mark Setton, the co-founder and CEO of The Pursuit of Happiness, a multi-educational platform centered on human happiness, stated, "So you might say that Plato is once again making things up, inventing the person of Diotima, and along with Diotima, a very sophisticated and thought-provoking form of dialogue, to introduce his own ideas. But if you did, you would have to concede that he invented Socrates too."[117]

Diotima couldn't be erased from what was written in the original text, but Ficino's written critique on her continues to cast doubt on her existence. So let's continue to honor and celebrate women like Diotima, who paved the way for generations of women to come. And let's make sure that their stories are not only told, but also believed and valued.

Note: Right or wrong, truth or a lie, words on paper have lasting impact. Take responsibility for what you write, as your words have the potential to outlive you and influence the world for years to come.

I imagine Diotima, draped all in white, serving as a soothing force for Socrates's hot-headed mind filled with ideas, helping him formulate his philosophical ideas, brainstorming with him, imparting her wisdom, and helping him navigate the intricacies of the influential circles of Athens.

When writing this book, I went back to the source and read the *Symposium* and discovered that not only did Diotima come up with the *Ladder of Love*, but a few pages before the *Ladder of Love*, there is the second ladder, which I call *Diotima's Ladder of Fame*. What she calls in the text immortality, I call Timeless Fame. The desire to be known beyond ourselves, to have our name etched in perpetuity, is part of our nature. We have an innate and deeply human desire to be recognized for our gifts and contributions to society.

In the ancient texts, Diotima describes a journey to immortality and alludes that only philosophers can reach the highest level of Fame. It is at this part of the journey where Diotima and I depart. I build upon her ideas of Fame and love and take the artistic license that fame is not just for philosophers but for everyone—and that we go subconsciously up the ladder, not just for love, but toward building timeless Fame.

Many would prefer I use the word "legacy" rather than "timeless Fame," but our research for a client on a separate issue revealed that "legacy" often carries negative connotations, being associated with outdated or obsolete systems, such as legacy software. Therefore, I use timeless Fame.

Fame courses through our DNA, compelling us to etch our names in various forms so as not to be forgotten. The fear of being erased from memory drives us, sometimes subconsciously, to work toward being remembered. While some people are more deliberate in this quest, others may simply harbor dreams of leaving something by which to be remembered.

Before Diotima's eloquent discourse in Plato's *Symposium*, we see her outline different stages of Fame, exploring the innate human desire for immortality by becoming known through creative innovations. Just as there are levels of love, from eros to agape, so too is there a ladder to achieving Fame and becoming a Public Figure.

The yearning to leave a mark on this world is a uniquely human trait. I would even argue that it is a basic human need. We erect monuments, write books, produce films, champion causes greater than ourselves, or have children—all to ensure future generations remember our significance. We aim to prove that we once existed, and fame provides humans with a kind of afterlife.

According to author Joseph Epstein, 81 percent of Americans believe they have a story to tell, a book inside of them just waiting to be written.[118]

In Plato's *Symposium,* Diotima speaks of the various stages of reaching immortality through our gifts. I see these as five stages where each builds upon the other in a personal quest to build a name and become a Public Figure.

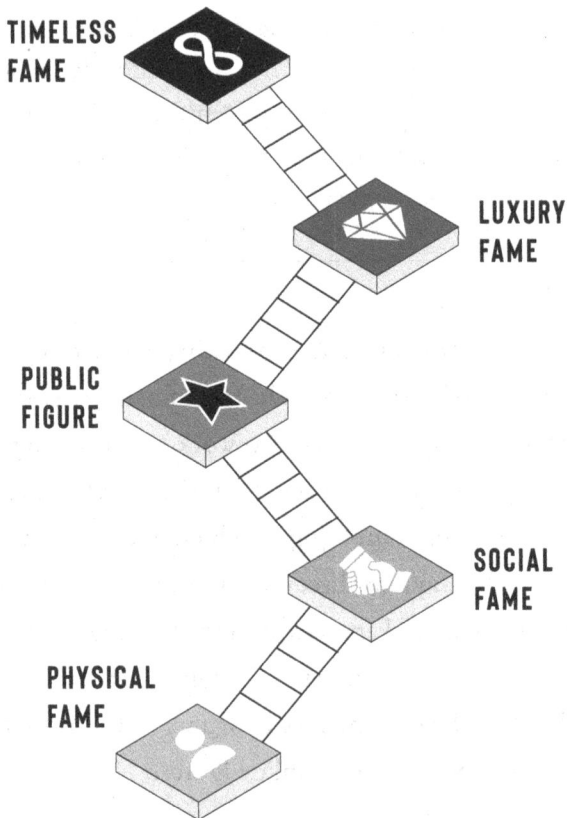

TIMELESS FAME

LUXURY FAME

PUBLIC FIGURE

SOCIAL FAME

PHYSICAL FAME

Similar to the *Ladder of Love*, we begin with the physical stage and gradually ascend into the spotlight. Each stage presents its challenges, with each step building upon the previous one.

1. **Physical Fame:** We are born. We procreate. In this step, we manifest Fame through biological means, such as birthing the next generation, ensuring the family lineage is preserved and perpetuated.

2. **Social Fame:** We identify ourselves with a specific social circle, group, or community, immersing in the group's culture and ethos such as identifying ourselves as Catholic, Democrat, or New Yorker. You may be a member of a specific sorority, an activist for Greenpeace, or an employee at Google, Tesla, or Starbucks, or maybe you are a Navy SEAL. Our personal brand is defined as part of the group and as such, we are willing to advocate for the group's cause or even go to war and die for the cause.

3. **Public Figure Fame:** We step away from the group to forge a unique path to be recognized for individual actions and contributions such as writing a book, leading a podcast, or founding a business or nonprofit organization. At this level, the individual step to become a Public Figure gains recognition or prominence in society, due to an individual's work, achievements, or public activities.

4. **Luxury Fame:** Building on the concept of a Public Figure, Luxury Fame entails being highly recognized as a leading figure (within the top 4%) in one or several niche markets, while also retaining the ability to remain anonymous, when desired, in the public at large.

5. **Timeless Fame:** The pinnacle of recognition, this signifies the classical notion of Fame, the enduring impact and widespread reputation that remains celebrated and remembered across different eras This kind of Fame doesn't fade with time but endures.

THE LADDER OF FAME IN THE FAME REVOLUTION

The passage from Physical Fame to Social Fame to Public Figure Fame requires steps of transformation. One can achieve Physical Fame by having children, building the family name, and the next generation. You can stake your claim in Social Fame, by exerting your identity as part of the group, community, or business. Most would be content to remain in Social Fame. The challenge now is that you are in the Fame Revolution, and it requires more of you.

In the next few chapters, I will cover each step on the pathway to the levels of fame.

"True good fortune is what you make for yourself. Good fortune: good character, good intentions, good actions."

—Marcus Aurelius, Roman emperor from 161 AD to 180 AD and a Stoic philosopher

STEP ONE: PHYSICAL FAME

> *"The fruits of your labors may be reaped two generations from now."*
>
> —**Henri Nouwen,** author of *The Prodigal Son* and a Dutch theologian

DIOTIMA REASONED THAT the first level of fame was birthing children, which can satisfy our desire for immortality. Reproduction brings us the closest to permanence of all forms of fame, as a part of us will bodily live on through our children. This desire is deeply embedded in our biology, manifesting as a physical urge to have children, commonly known as the "biological clock."

"It's the family name that lives on. That's all that lives on. Not your personal glory, not your honor, but family."

—**Tywin Lannister,** Game of Thrones

The greatest achievement of fame throughout history was to have children. Children continue through their DNA to perpetuate your name. You are part of the lineage of the past, present, and future. To have children was of great status at all economic levels.

As Zen master Thich Nhat Hanh used to say to people he met, "When I meet somebody, I never meet that person as an individual, I meet their entire lineage."[119]

> Grandchildren are the blossoms of our lineage,
> rooted in the past, but reaching toward the future,
> ensuring our name continues to thrive.

Even today, we follow with anticipation the succession of royal families. The world tuned into the elaborate coronation of King Charles III and his wife, Camilla. In fact, it was shown in over 125 countries around the world.[120]

Not only do we tune into the coronation, but we also follow who the royals marry. Soon after that, we anxiously anticipate when their first child will arrive. And since it is important to know the offspring, the selection of a mate is under much scrutiny, such as when Prince Harry married the American actress Meghan Markle.

In Norway, it was a scandal in the early 1970s when the current reigning King Harald wanted to marry a commoner. It took nine years before his father, King Olav, finally approved the marriage to his soul mate, Sonia. Traditions in the selection of a mate and the line of succession have changed. It is no longer just the first-born male who can inherit the kingdom; it is now whoever is the oldest, and this new rule of succession has trickled down to smaller estates and land in countries such as Scandinavia, the United Kingdom, Scotland, Japan, and Spain.

And we do not just obsess over the royals: we scrutinize who our siblings or family members date, marry to have children, and perpetuate the family name. Our whole lives and culture revolve around marriage, birth, and succession.

Throughout history, women have been condemned if they could not bear children. If a couple was childless, the blame and stigma was most often placed on the woman. I recall earlier this year when I read a post from a friend, Anne, on Facebook lamenting the stigmatization of being a childless woman. She often encounters questions from well-intentioned friends and occasionally from strangers about why she doesn't have children. Anne's thoughtful response is that individuals are defined by more than just their offspring. She leads a fulfilling life, is happily married, and is blessed with two "bonus" sons. (In Norway, stepchildren are affectionately referred to as "bonus kids," because all children are seen as a gift and bonus in life.)

Anne's post resonated with me, as I have felt pressure to continue the family lineage. "When will you have children?" was the oft-asked question. Like Anne, I did not complete the first level of Physical Fame and skipped right to level two as I chose not to have children. I am grateful my brothers carried on that tradition and provided our family with nine nieces and nephews. The social pressure outside my family added to the demand for children. It led me to appreciate Diotima's idea that there is a desire to perpetuate the family name beyond having kids—a ladder to climb.

STEP TWO: SOCIAL FAME

> *"So many of us feel like we're misfits until we finally find our tribe - the other people who are strange in the same way - and suddenly everything clicks."*
>
> **—Jenny Lawson,** *New York Times* best-selling author, journalist, and blogger

AFTER HAVING CHILDREN (or deciding not to), we often yearn for something greater, seeking recognition beyond our family circle. We look for causes to strengthen our family name and carefully consider where to attach our reputation. By associating with influential leaders, causes, or companies, we use our names as currency to convey our values and beliefs to future generations.

As we navigate life, we often find ourselves drawn to communities that reflect our values and interests. This might lead us to join a church, become active in associations, or, if we have children, connect with other parents—perhaps even coach a little league. These groups and activities become integral to our identity, mirroring the values and passions we resonate with. It's during these moments that we truly begin laying the foundation for our fame, defining who we are and envisioning who we aspire to be.

In this journey of self-discovery and community engagement, we might naturally gravitate toward leadership roles, such as taking the helm of an apartment association, continuing to shape and refine our impact in these communities.

When it comes to our professional life, for many of us this is a period of cementing our career trajectory, laying it down brick by brick. Whether climbing the ladder and celebrating promotions or facing challenges and unexpected job shifts, we often find paths that align even more closely with our unique strengths. At this stage, we've come to recognize ourselves— our business cards proudly display our titles—and we're acknowledged as experts in our fields. Some might pursue higher education, such as a master's degree, to further hone their expertise.

After perhaps a decade in a particular industry or sector, we've carved out a niche or theme in our professional journey. Our accumulated expertise not only adds weight to our title but also shapes our identity. This identity melds with the organizations we're part of. Take, for instance, an employee at Google I'm acquainted with—their deep connection to the company culture has seamlessly intertwined their brand with the organization's.

When it comes to Fame, we share the glory with our tribe. We are not alone, and during this step, the group is our source of strength. We might become community leaders. We volunteer our time. We protest for a cause that is aligned with our values. We feel comfort in belonging. But what happens when we no longer belong?

Brené Brown is a multiple *The New York Times* bestseller writing about her two decades of research on courage, vulnerability, shame, and empathy and states that there is a distinction between fitting in and belonging. "Fitting in is about assessing a situation and becoming who you need to be to be accepted. Belonging, on the other hand, doesn't require us to change who we are; it requires us to be who we are." [121]

Many corporate leaders dream of something more but find themselves trapped in the comfort of the tribe. They stay because they are not able to envision an alternative path or have a fear of the unknown. However, leaving behind the old, familiar coat of corporate identity, embracing a new level, and becoming a Public Figure is a journey of self-discovery, self-expression, and personal growth.

Leaving behind the familiarity and security of the old coat can be difficult, but your personal and professional evolution must reach the Public Figure stage.

Multi-platinum singer Adele once noted in an interview on *Skavlan*, the most-seen talk show in Scandinavia, that her circle became smaller after becoming a celebrity. When you step out to become what you're meant to be, not everyone will support you. We could speculate that this is because they do not care for our dreams and aspirations. I once read an insightful statement on an Instagram story: the reason your loved ones are not supporting you and might even try to stop your pursuit is because they want time to stand still and yearn for time to remain static, wanting both the past to persist unchanged and for you to remain as you always were. However, as you continue to grow to find your voice, new opportunities will emerge that align with your new identity.[122]

MY STORY

I'm the proud aunt of nine wonderful nieces and nephews and I am surrounded by a rich tapestry of friends from diverse corners of the world: the Scotland, Germany, the United States, Kuwait, Mexico, England, Norway, New Zealand, and Australia. Many are professional women, and our bonds have been shaped by shared experiences and interests. With some, I've delved deep into enlightening conversations at my favorite café in Oslo, Kaffebrenneriet, savoring its exquisite coffee, while with others, I've navigated spirited book club debates in Norway and the United States.

Adventure threads its way through many of these relationships. With some, I have tackled multiple running and ski marathons and embarked on annual 10K runs in different European cities. My biking expeditions, with fellow enthusiasts from Scotland and Australia, have taken me through breathtaking landscapes, introducing us to new cultures in the most sustainable way.

My commitment to empowering women in IT, with my involvement with Girl Geek Dinner Oslo, resonates with many. At my core, I identify deeply as a devoted aunt, a passionate adventurer, and a steadfast friend— these are the anchors of my identity.

On a professional level, after seven solid years in Washington, D.C., I felt a calling for something new. New York seemed like the next logical step. Though I initially wanted to dip my toes in the entertainment sector via IME (Institute of Media Entertainment, now part of IESE Business School), I soon realized its close resemblance to politics and left. But life has its way of presenting opportunities. A lecture at Columbia University introduced me to strategic communication, and I fell in love with it. This passion led me to my VP role at AGR Petroleum Services, a master's in 2014, and various leadership stints, including my proud association with the EACD (European Association for Communications Directors).

One of my proudest moments was my work with the Norwegian government, promoting the importance of climate technology carbon capture and storage (CCS). Alongside my mentor and professor, Peggy Brønn, BI Norwegian Management University, I co-wrote and researched on how to best communicate CCS to the public. This work took me from Melbourne's prestigious IEA GHGT-14 international conference to presentations in cities like Oslo, Paris, and London.

In short, I became the go-to person for strategic communications related to climate tech, especially CCS. This journey, filled with learnings, challenges, and triumphs, had me speaking in front of diverse audiences across the globe. And yet, I still wanted more.

THE FORK IN THE ROAD:
DO YOU STAY OR MOVE ON?

> *"Two roads diverged in a wood and I - I took the one less traveled by, and that has made all the difference."*
>
> —**Robert Frost,** one of the most recognized American poets of the twentieth century

WHICH ROAD WILL YOU CHOSE?

Will you remain on the platform of Social Fame, or will you dare to venture out toward the next step and become the Public Figure you were meant to be?

The greatest challenge in achieving and creating a lasting name occurs when transitioning from stage two, Social Fame, to stage three, Public Figure Fame.

There is a chasm that is vast and wide between stage two and three.

The traits that got you to level two, Social Fame, will not work the same on your way to Public Figure Fame.

The clear distinction between stages is that you are the person up front taking all the risk. You may be standing out on your own, making yourself and your opinions known. But at the same time, you will be the one reaping the most rewards. Opportunities will gravitate toward you.

It's easy to be a critic, but stepping up requires more bravery.

To become a Public Figure, you will need to get some clarity about who you really are, what your talents and skills are, how to move forward, and how to move from Social Fame to Public Figure Fame.

Some questions you might be asking:

- What will I do with my life?
- What impact do I want to have?
- How do I know what I really want?
- What is holding me back?
- Who is holding me back?
- What do I stand for?
- Am I ready for this? If not, what is missing? Or do I just need some time?
- If I do move forward, what are the consequences and rewards?
- If I don't move forward, what are the consequences?

So, which path do you choose? Will you stay in the Social Fame stage? Or will you venture upward?

While I know I just gave you a choice, reality begs the question: do you have the choice, really? The answer for most—is no. Those who act sooner to capitalize on the Fame Revolution and step into their roles as public figures will find the greater success.

WHAT CAN YOU EXPECT?

> *"I am the master of my fate, and I am the captain of my boat. While ups and downs are a part of everyone's journey, how you face it makes you the person or artiste you are."*
>
> —**Jubin Nautiyal**, award-winning playback singer and live performer

TO REACH THE THIRD STEP of Public Figure Fame, the first and main requirement is to be willing to stand out by yourself.

To be a Public Figure takes courage. You embark on that adventure alone, and therein lies its intrinsic reward.

Becoming a Public Figure might take time, and it might not. Some people step into the Public Figure Fame level with ease, while for others, it takes time, like timidly dipping their toes into the water before plunging in fully.

As the era of the Fame Revolution unfolds, more is expected from each of us. Stepping forward becomes imperative for all. Here are some things you can expect on the way toward Public Figure Fame.

First, be ready to let go of your current status to discover yourself

Many seasoned staffers in Congress believe they are more intelligent and capable than the congressmen they serve. Occasionally these staffers attempt to overshadow their leader, only to realize that standing in the limelight demands a unique kind of personality, courage, and talent.

I recall one Chief of Staff who believed he could run for Congress, but after making a few attempts, he discovered that he did not have the stamina, will, and desire to lose his status with his peers to be a congressman. He went back to being a chief of staff for another member.

The challenge of working at the highest levels, whether as a chief of staff in government, a senior executive in the corporate world, or a publicist in the entertainment world, is that to excel in those roles, you often forgo aspects of your unique identity. You assume a serving role and often represent the image of your leader or organization.

An Internet social media strategist and life coach, Mandy Perry, states that it takes time for corporate executives to shed their layers of corporate identity, find themselves again, and embrace their differentiators. Sometimes, the qualities you had to bury or stifle in the corporate world take time to emerge.

When leaving the confines of Social Fame, the first thing you need to let go of is the status quo in the corporate hierarchy, in the organization, or community to rediscover your uniqueness. Russell Brunson, founder of ClickFunnels and author of *Expert Secrets*, states, "Status is the magic word in this business. When someone is presented with an opportunity, their subconscious mind is working on the answer to this question: Is this thing I'm considering going to increase my status or decrease it?" He continues, "Status as I am defining it has nothing to do with how others perceive you, but rather how you perceive yourself."[123]

"What stops people from taking that new opportunity [becoming a Public Figure]?

Fear of decreased status.

What if I try this, and it decreases my status? I feel stupid." [124]

We do not want to look foolish in front of our peers, subordinates, mentors, family, and community.

We do not want to lose the status we have that has been defining and comfortable.

For me, letting go of my role as the behind-the-scenes strategist was very difficult. I cherished my identity as either the marketing and communications department leader or as an advisor to clients from the comforts of the shadow they cast.

But then, something shifted. I started to catch glimpses of my true self, like my own faint shadow on a cave wall. These glimpses ignited a newfound awareness. I reached a crossroads—should I remain in the cave of conformity or summon the courage to venture toward the entrance and step into my true self?

Second, understand and shed the layers that are holding you back

In our experience of self-discovery, we often don't see the need or impact of shedding the layers of external expectations placed upon us by family, friends, peers, employers, and leaders in our circle. It takes strength to let go of those expectations and allow our true essence to shine. But when we do, something remarkable happens—we become a gravitational force, attracting clients, opportunities, and success.

I've witnessed this firsthand while helping leaders become public figures. The more they embrace their authentic selves, the more magnetic they become. Authenticity is a powerful magnet that draws people in. People want to connect with genuine individuals, and they are more likely to buy from or invest in those who are true originals.

Shedding the layers and stepping into your authentic self is not only liberating for you but also serves as an invitation for others to do the same. Embrace your unique essence, radiate your light, and let the world gravitate toward the extraordinary being that you are.

Third, find clarity about who you are and what you want to become known for

Self-discovery and the Public Figure Strategy bring you to a point where you will be asked, "Who are you?" and "What is your vision?" You might be tempted to skim over this, convinced that you already know or perhaps you are too uncomfortable and unsure of the answers. You're not alone; even for me, the path to clarity has been a winding, life-long exploration. To become a Public Figure, you will need to get some clarity about how to move forward and how to move from Social Fame to Public Figure Fame.

Fourth, understand that finding clarity is a journey in itself

It's easy to get lost in a sea of self-help books and online resources promising the formula to find clarity. But let's be real; for many authors, like me, it took writing my own book to attain my clarity. Yet, these resources might lead you to believe that you need to have everything figured out before you start. Remember Marie Forleo's wisdom, "Not starting is the greatest danger."

Consider Marie Forleo herself. I recall her initial branding was somewhat mediocre uncertain and, to me, seemed frivolous. I was wrong to determine that her beginning would be her end. She pushed forward, honed her message and look, and stood true to herself. One decade later, she has a multi-million-dollar platform. Progress always begins with the courage to take the first step. And it's okay if you don't have all the answers. The more you explore, the more you'll discover. Keep revisiting this process, because for most of us, clarity is indeed a life-long pursuit.

In my personal experience, the pathway to clarity often takes unexpected turns, evolving and refining over time. I began three years ago with writing a book titled *Moving Beyond Your Tribe to Reach the Summit of Fame*, which then transitioned to *The Fragrance of Fame*, then to *Fame-ology*, *The New Famous*, and finally culminated in *Fame Revolution*. Similarly, my podcast underwent several name changes, starting as *Moving Beyond Acronyms*, and then transforming into *Moving Beyond Your Tribe*. Each step along the way, I received constructive feedback from my mentors and advisors, allowing the titles and my vision to become sharper. Today, my podcast is simply titled *Become Famous*, and my book is known as *Fame Revolution*. While the *Become Famous* brand may continue to evolve in the future, what matters most is that the journey toward gaining clarity began with the courage to step forward with the clarity I had at each stage. It's through this process of exploration and adaptation that we refine our vision and find our true path.

"Clarity is not the place from which we begin but rather the place at which we ultimately arrive."

—Victoria LaBalme, The Wall Street Journal best-selling author and Hall of Fame speaker

Fifth, know that action breeds clarity

As best-selling author Victoria LaBalme states in her book, *Risk Forward*, "Some of the most celebrated companies and creative endeavors didn't start with complete clarity. . . . They started with an idea, a wisp . . . which the person then followed and explored, often through significant periods of self-doubt."

If you're anything like me, a perfectionist, you might think you need absolute clarity before you can move forward. You may find yourself waiting on the sidelines, paralyzed by the need for precision. My mentor, Michelle Sorro, a former host on TV *Extra: The Entertainment Magazine* and an acclaimed global podcaster of *Fire and Soul*, once challenged me with a simple yet profound piece of wisdom: "Action breeds clarity."

In our agency, we typically dedicate three months to deeply engaging with our clients, who are unsure of what gift they want to be known for. Together, we explore their aspirations, define their unique identities, shape their grand vision—their "Big Bold & Boundless Dream"—and create a package that exemplifies them and a roadmap for their three- to five-year plan. This journey can sometimes resemble a rollercoaster, fraught with peaks and valleys, and it ebbs and flows with clarity and confusion. Yet, through this intense process, our clients gain significant clarity—often through recognizing what they *don't want*. This discernment provides a sharper sense of direction for their next steps, propelling them toward their personal and professional goals.

In my personal journey and my work with clients, I've learned that the path to clarity is often shrouded in uncertainty, like trying to navigate through a dark cave. But each step forward, every action, brings us closer to understanding ourselves and our vision more clearly.

Sixth, manage the dilemma of "I" and "we"

In my quest for self-discovery, I found myself shedding the layers that had confined me, like a corporate coat that no longer fit. It was during my journey from "we" to "I" that I realized the profound impact it had on my life and the lessons I learned along the way.

I remember the pivotal moment when my mentor, David Meerman Scott, challenged me to shift from using "we" to embracing "I" in my LinkedIn profile. It was a daunting task for someone who had been taught that teamwork was paramount. But deep down, I knew it was time to claim my individual voice and take ownership of my achievements.

The transition from "we" to "I" wasn't just about self-promotion, it was also about recognizing my unique contributions and stepping into a leadership role. It required courage to break free from the comfort of the collective mindset and stand proudly as an individual.

I discovered that there is power in both "we" and "I." Collaboration and teamwork have their place, but so do personal accountability and authentic self-expression. Balancing these aspects is essential to becoming a well-rounded leader and achieving true success.

Stepping into the light of authenticity meant shedding the fear of being judged or misunderstood. It meant embracing my own worth and recognizing that my unique perspective has value. It wasn't always easy, and there were moments of resistance and self-doubt along the way. But with each step, I grew more confident in my ability to lead and make a difference.

This journey of self-discovery taught me that the layers we accumulate throughout life can be shed, revealing our true selves. It's a process of peeling back the expectations and societal norms that have shaped us and allowing our authentic light to shine.

So, if you find yourself yearning for something more, I encourage you to reflect on whether you are a "we" or an "I" person. Most of us have a dominant preference and I encourage you to consider making the weaker one stronger. The goal is having both the powers of "we" and "I." Seek the balance between collaboration and individuality. Trust in your unique abilities and let your authentic self guide your path.

Seventh, don't expect everyone to be on board

You are excited about your clarity, developments, and motivating thoughts, but your family, friends, colleagues, employers, and community may not share the same enthusiasm. They mean well, but they want to protect the familiar and keep things as they are. They have their own comfort zones, and as a result, they may not respond the way you hope. Let them think what they want to think, but keep on going in the direction you have been moving.

The bottom line is to expect some resistance, but understand that it is normal and don't let it take too much of your time and energy. Remember your vision and values.

Eighth, expect to come face-to face with your own fears

As you venture into uncharted territory, fears and self-doubt will rear their ugly heads. I remember attending the Insitute of Media and Entertainment (IME), where we learned about managing talent and the importance of providing room and support for individuals who have the courage to step out into the limelight. We were taught to have respect for their bravery and to create an environment that fosters their growth.

MY JOURNEY TOWARD THE PUBLIC FIGURE

I attribute my success to my team of supporters. One of the most influential is Tony Robbins, the guru of all gurus. Being in his ecosystem introduced me to leading coaches, counselors, and advisors who helped me in my pursuit to be the best version of me.

In December 2015, I decided that I needed a change and embarked on a quest and was introduced to various podcasts featuring insights from Lewis Howes, Tim Ferris, Pat Flynn, Michael Hyatt, and Donald Miller. As I delved deeper into books, a pattern began to emerge—many of the authors I deeply respected and found enlightening had once been attendees at Tony Robbins's events. This revelation, paired with high praise from best-selling authors such as Michael Hyatt and Lewis Howes, further ignited my passion and desire to explore the world Tony Robbins had crafted. In the spring of 2016, I found myself at the *Unleash the Power Within* event in London, eager for transformation. From there, I met an ecosystem of mentors, advisors, counselors, and collaborators who have changed the course of my life.

Through this network, I met Michelle Sorro, a former host on *ExtraTV*, podcaster of top-ranked podcast *Fire and Soul,* who urged me to be a better speaker, challenged me to a thirty-day Facebook Live (I ended up doing sixty), and recommended I start my own podcast, which I did.

I met Scott A. Martin, author of *Groundswell* and world-leading marketeer, who was integral in partnering on a project for a client. His cutting-edge idea on marketing and growth hacking was the foundation for our success.

And finally, I met my mentor David Meerman Scott through Tony Robbins's Business Mastery. David challenged me to impart my experience in a more intentional way by writing a book. The idea of writing a book seemed daunting. I wasn't sure I knew how to do it. But I was definitely among the 81 percent of people who believe that they have a story to share. Mine was the same story I tell my clients daily, along with my passion for being prepared for fame. And now you're holding my book.

So, I ask you, what is your story?

Where are you on the Ladder of Fame?

A SIGN YOU ARE BECOMING
A PUBLIC FIGURE

> *"If you have the power to go alone in a restaurant or a cinema hall, then you can do everything in your life."*
>
> **—Leonardo DiCaprio,** American actor and film producer

HAVE YOU EVER DINED ALONE?

IF YOU HAVEN'T, I highly recommend you do. I recall a client sharing how uncomfortable she felt eating alone, to the point of ordering food to her hotel room while traveling.

How many times do we close ourselves off from experiences simply because we're unable to be or uncomfortable in being alone?

To be a Public Figure or a leader in general, the more you can find power within yourself, the better you are. And one of the best exercises to cultivate that power is to come to a point of truly enjoying your own company.

I have always loved to travel, but I often found myself disappointed when friends didn't share the same enthusiasm. Determined not to miss out on the experiences I craved, I decided to reward myself with a cycling trip as a graduation gift for attaining my master's degree. I joined a group to cycle through the picturesque plains of Thailand, explore the ancient wonders of Angkor Wat in Cambodia, and ride on a river boat in Ho Chi Minh, Vietnam.

At the time, I was overwhelmed with fear and uncertainty about traveling alone to such an exotic destination. The fear even manifested as migraines and anxiety. Despite my hesitations, I summoned the courage to take the risk and joined the Exodus Travels cycling group, even though I didn't know anyone in the group.

Little did I know that this decision would turn out to be the best decision I ever made. The trip itself was an extraordinary adventure, but it went beyond that. It opened my eyes to the beauty of travel, the power of friendship, and the profound impact of seizing the moment.

Inspired by my experiences, I challenged myself to overcome what I believed to be the most difficult feat—enjoying a meal alone at a restaurant. Even when I traveled solo, I often confined myself to cafes during the day. But during my first vacation alone in Greece for three weeks, I encountered a sophisticated and confident woman who was enjoying her own company while dining solo. Intrigued, I mustered the courage to strike up a conversation. She shared how her husband didn't share her love for travel, and she had embraced the freedom of exploring the world on her own terms.

I took the plunge and learned to savor a meal alone, finding solace in my own thoughts or immersing myself in a book I love. In today's digital age, technology has made it even easier to find solace in solitude while dining. We can delve into the captivating depths of our phones, whether it's reading an e-book, staying updated on the latest news, or simply indulging in some well-deserved social media scrolling.

I found that taking the risk to dine alone not only strengthened me as a person and gave me a profound sense of freedom, but it also served as a reminder that I have the power to do whatever I want, go wherever I please, and enjoy my own company without relying on others. It was an empowering experience that encouraged me to step out of my comfort zone and embrace the beauty of independence.

STEP THREE. PUBLIC FIGURE: FORGING A NEW PATH

> *"Remember to celebrate milestones as you prepare for the road ahead."*
>
> **—Nelson Mandela,** icon of modern South Africa, a Nobel Peace Prize winner, and one of the most respected world leaders of the twentieth century

YOU HAVE MADE IT to the Public Figure level. You might not have gotten your name in lights yet, but you are here!

Being willing to stand on your own and share who you are is a big accomplishment and a show of fortitude.

Obviously, being a Public Figure isn't a one-size-fits-all situation. Don't be shy about your unique style just because it doesn't fit the traditional mold. The traditional mold doesn't matter anymore. As Sage Toomey, our Gen-Zer, stated earlier, "There are no rules." Rules or no rules, you are building your reputation in your circle of influence.

"Reputation is what other people know about you. Honor is what you know about yourself."

—Lois McMaster Bujold, American fiction writer

I often tell people, for me, as a consultant, the greatest joy is to get *fired* by my clients! I want to see my clients grow into the public figures they were meant to be. By then, they should be fully self-sufficient with the inner knowing of how to move forward and lead with certainty that they no longer need me.

Five signs you know you've made it to the Public Figure Status

1. You know what you want and where you're going.
2. You know which of your gifts to promote and you are able to resist the shiny objects.
3. You know what to share and what not to share.
4. You know what your contributions to society are.
5. You know whom to listen to and who's on your team.

Most people do not know what they want. They listen to what other people say they should want. It's harder to realize what you want because that requires being honest with yourself, and that can be difficult and unsettling. You have to dare to ask uncomfortable questions and learn who you are. You must be bold.

And that's just what you are doing.

So, what's next?

It's time to expand.

At this level, it is about expanding your reach and creating. You'll create meaningful and lasting messages and work that reflects your values, talents, and passions. Artists, writers, musicians, and scientists all create work that becomes a testament to their lives and can influence generations. You can do this as well.

When you have reached the Public Figure Fame stage, there are opportunities to expand and connect with a broader audience. For instance, this is when you can become "discovered" for your work. It may go viral, and your name may reach many different circles.

For example, if you are a professor of math, your recognition may initially be confined to your college, but it can quickly spread to multiple colleges through national conferences. As your theories gain traction and are found applicable to specific fields, such as engineering, you might find yourself speaking at diverse conferences, disseminating and cross-pollinating your ideas to other disciplines. This momentum propels you toward Luxury Fame. After Public Figure Fame you may enter Luxury Fame, and some people even experience Timeless Fame as it expands on what you are known for as a Public Figure.

An example of this is Brené Brown, who was originally known for her research within the academic circles on the study of "shame." When she spoke at TEDx, her ideas went viral, and she was like a meteor star quickly entering the Timeless Fame of being known everywhere. She wrote six number-one *NY Times* bestsellers, hosts a podcast, and continues to share her ideas.

At the Public Figure stage, your ideas have matured, and the chances of reaching wider circles have greatly increased.

Once you have mastered the nuances of achieving the **Public Figure status in one domain, the same principles apply across others**. You have it in your muscle memory and can easily replicate it in a completely different area.

Sir Richard Branson, the founder of the Virgin brands, started with Virgin Records and then ventured into the most unlikely domains, such as airlines, phones, and trains, consistently applying the same strategies.

Starring in roles in hit movies such as *The Proposal* and *Deadpool*, Canadian actor Ryan Reynolds charmed audiences and harnessed his fame to venture into diverse entrepreneurial territories. This phenomenon, aptly called the "Ryan Reynolds Effect" by some, signifies his involvement's transformative impact across industries.

The golden touch of Ryan Reynolds extends beyond the silver screen. While his mere inclusion in a film automatically increases ticket sales, his "effect" goes further. Reynolds acquired a significant stake in Aviation Gin in 2018. His enthusiastic endorsements catapulted the brand into a thriving enterprise. Teaming up with his friend Rob McElhenney, Reynolds purchased the struggling Wrexham football club in Wales. Reynolds began heavy promotions for the club and participated in a documentary about the sport, which prompted higher levels of popularity and participation for Wrexham, and football clubs in general. In 2023, T-Mobile began the process of buying the actor's budget cell service Mint Mobile for $1.35 billion.

Selena Gomez began her journey as an actress before smoothly transitioning into music and later embracing social media. By 2021, her Instagram following surpassed 200 million. The key to her success has been authenticity. Selena openly discusses her personal challenges, championing mental health and other causes she feels aligned with.

My best advice at this or any other stage, is to stay true to your vision and beliefs, keep focused, set yourself free from the opinions of others, and don't take yourself too seriously!

"You are not going to be effective in your actions in the world if it doesn't come within. If there isn't some inner spirit guiding it."

—Robert Greene, international best-selling author on strategy, power, and seduction

NOW, YOU ARE THE SUN

❝❞ *"In the center of all rests the sun."*

—**Nicolaus Copernicus,** Astronomer who
formulated a model of the universe that placed the
Sun rather than Earth at its center

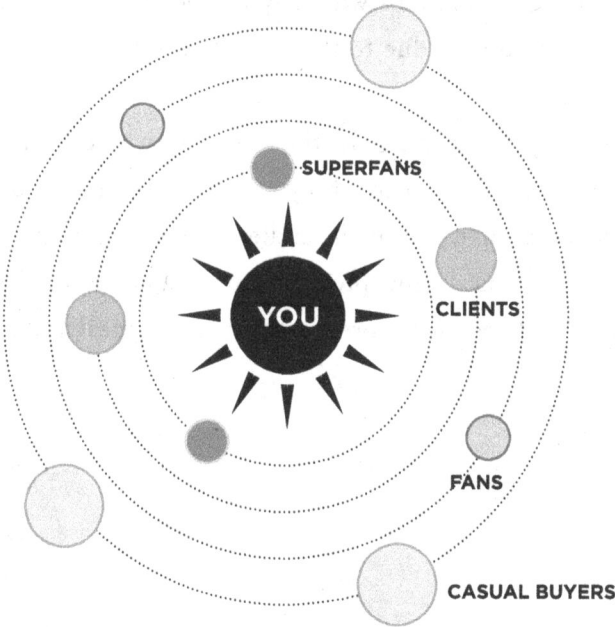

You might raise an eyebrow in skepticism, thinking, "Me, the sun in my own solar system?" But it's true. When you embrace and showcase your authentic self with unwavering confidence, people are naturally drawn to you.

What I've discovered is that when you shine at your full 100 percent, when you express your unique qualities and gifts without reservation, the right clients and opportunities gravitate toward you. **When you deeply**

understand this truth, you open yourself to the gravitational pull of success, making it easier to attract clients, projects, and sales.

When you remain true to yourself, differentiate your product, and strive for excellence, something extraordinary happens. Your fans and superfans will naturally gravitate toward you, just as planets orbit around the sun.

Consider Apple's superfans, the dedicated enthusiasts who eagerly await each new iPhone release. They are deeply connected to Apple's brand identity and values, forming the closest orbit around the company. Beyond the superfans, there are fans who may not be as fervent but still choose Apple over competitors due to the consistent quality and innovation of their products.

What's truly captivating is that as you wholeheartedly dedicate yourself to being excellent in who you are, the services you provide, and the products you offer, your niche audience, your superfans, will naturally gravitate toward you. In this process, your unique offering transcends its niche appeal and becomes more universal in its appeal and impact.

STEPS FOUR AND FIVE.
LUXURY FAME AND TIMELESS FAME
(REACHING *IMMORTALITY*)

> *"What a glorious immortality*
> *I have in the lasting Fame of*
> *other men's tongues."*
>
> **—Gaius Plinius Secundus,** Roman author
> and philosopher

WHAT COMES AFTER you've reached the Public Figure Fame stage? At this point, you know who you are, what you want, and what you do well, and you are making a name for yourself. But how do you move to the Luxury Fame stage? At this stage, you exponentially expand and grow your influence, wealth, and impact, because you're touching more lives and doing everything you need to stay the course. The longer you stay at it, the more people will be drawn to you. Becoming a Public Figure is preparation for moving into the Luxury Fame stage.

The peak of the Ladder of Fame is Timeless Fame, where an individual's achievements, contributions, or influence become so significant that their name is immortalized in history. At this level, people are remembered not only for their work but also for who they were as people.

Examples of people who have reached this peak of Timeless Fame include Albert Einstein, Mahatma Gandhi, William Shakespeare, and Leonardo da Vinci. They have left indelible marks on human history, and their legacies continue to impact the world long after their deaths.

However, even at the peak of the Ladder of Fame, one must remember that the concept of immortality is relative. As time passes, the significance of achievements may fade and the names of famous individuals may be forgotten. As the famous saying goes, "The only constant is change."

On top of the Ladder of Fame is Luxury Fame and Timeless Fame, and that's of course where we want to go. But the purpose of this book is to prepare you for that kind of fame and ensuring your role as a Public Figure. You must know your voice; you must understand who you are. You must be aware of your gifts and be so solidified in them that you can speak with extraordinary confidence. I've found that most opportunities come simply because your certainty draws people to you.

This is one of the reasons why I don't focus so much on who your client is supposed to be. If you focus on who you are and what your gifts are, your clients will come to you. That's why you should be out there becoming known in various sectors.

You have achieved Luxury Fame when you are celebrated within your niche, but you are not being hounded for autographs in the grocery store.

An example of someone who has achieved Luxury Fame is Canadian voice actor, Peter Cullen. Chances are, you wouldn't be able to pick him out of a lineup, but he is a legend in his field, having voiced many well-known characters since 1962. He is perhaps best known for voicing Optimus Prime in the original 1980s *Transformers* animated series and franchise as well as the more recent Michael Bay film series. In late 2023, Cullen received an Emmy Lifetime Achievement Award.

Luxury and Timeless Fame have different strategies, because by the time you arrive there, you've already reached where you want to go. After that it's just about magnifying who you are to bigger audiences and bigger places.

The Ladder of Fame represents our innate human desire to leave a mark on this world. Each level of fame reflects how we attempt to immortalize ourselves, from having children to creating influential works. It is through these efforts that we hope to leave a lasting impact and achieve a sense of immortality.

People do all sorts of things to build a legacy and to ensure that they are remembered long after they are gone. Writing a biography, leaving family heirlooms to children, creating a charity in their name are all ways to achieve this. According to *Psychology Today,* "The reasons behind this desire to leave a lasting legacy are currently under-researched in psychology."[125]

To be celebrated and remembered for one's talents, achievements, or unique qualities entices the human spirit. But there is a dark side of being drawn to fame; immaturity or the need for external approval, stemming from deep-rooted insecurities, can make people reliant on the adoration and validation of the masses.

There is the myth that life is a lot easier for a famous person. People believe that being famous solves all problems: poverty, neglect, rejection, lack, and so on. But being noticed by people does not necessarily mean you'll be loved or respected by them.

"Once you figure out what respect tastes like, you will find it tastes better than attention."

—P!nk, American singer and song writer

There is much to say about this, I could write an entire book on the subject but for now, I will share just this:

Don't trade in your authenticity for approval. Don't let your self-worth to be based on what others think.

In our real lives, we seek out people who are funny, smart, brave, have integrity and emotional intelligence, and are kind, confident, and generous. That's what others are looking for in us too.

CONCLUSION: SALLY FORTH

> *"There is still time to veer, to sally forth, knapsack on back, for unknown hills over which . . . only the wind knows what lies. Shall she, shall she veer?*[126]
>
> **—Sylvia Plath,** American poet and novelist

WE HAVE COME TO THE END—a *tour de force* of the Fame Revolution and how the revolution has democratized fame and provided all of us this unique opportunity to become famous for what we do. We also took a sidestep to Ancient Greece, Socrates, and Plato's *Symposium* in the hopes to convince you that fame is an inalienable desire, as Diotima states, "Mortal nature does all it can to live forever and to be immortal." We are born to proliferate to ensure that our name is etched in history through our namesake or accomplishments.

More importantly, I hope that I have shown you that; you are the Public Figure in your life; you have to think beyond your client, because you are more than your job, and playing full out with all of you and your gifts on the court of life will provide with you the greatest life of influence, wealth, and impact.

There are three things I hope you take with you as I conclude:

First, you are more powerful than you think. Your words and gifts, if shared, will create a ripple effect on your life, community, and society. Your greatest asset is your differentiator. When all of your uniqueness comes together and is showcased to the world, no one can compete with you. The world is your oyster.

Second, you cannot do it alone. A team of advisors from the brain trust to the kitchen cabinet will thrust you to the next level. The Fame Revolution shows that the things we used to do by ourselves are not as easy or even possible today. When you embrace that you are the Public Figure, you will realize you need a team.

Third, have fun, go out there and shine. Yes, our words and actions matter, and we can't be everyone's cup of tea, but doing what you do best and being yourself is your very finest option! Enjoy your time and space in the spotlight.

So, to use my favorite sign-off, *sally forth!*

According to the *Cambridge Dictionary*, "sally forth" means "to leave a safe place and venture out bravely or confidently in order to do something difficult." I like to bend this definition just slightly and say that it means to venture out bravely and confidently in order to do something *extraordinary*.

EPILOGUE: THE FUTURE OF FAME

66 *"The love of fame is a love that even the wisest of men are reluctant to forgo."*

— **Tacitus,** regarded as one of the greatest Roman historians by modern scholars

WILL FAME LAST FOR EVERYONE?

ONLY TIME WILL DETERMINE whether the Fame Revolution spans a few years or decades. It reminds me of Kodak's Brownie camera era. The Brownie was the original social sharing tool long before digital screens and apps.

The Brownie was invented in 1888 and was the smartphone before smartphones and social media before social media. It revolutionized personal photography and set the framework for social sharing. Before the Brownie, photography was confined to professionals and wealthy enthusiasts with specialized skills. The camera was offered for $1 in 1900. There was no need for a license to be a good photographer. The Brownie, with its simplicity and affordability, democratized photography.

A sign of its significant influence was that "Kodak" entered the American Lexicon ("kodaking," "kodakers," and "kodakery"). Kodak created new communities and new forms of expression. With the expansion of these groups, the scope of photography grew beyond the possibility of being restricted by governmental regulations.

Fast forward to groundbreaking inventions such as radio, movies, and TV; instead of making them accessible to the public, the Government confined access to the few with licenses. This move created an economic barrier too high for the average citizen and ushered in the mass communications era, where citizens were transformed to be mere consumers in a one-way communication landscape.

Times shifted once again with the introduction of the personal computer spearheaded by Steve Jobs and Steve Wozniak with the Macintosh. This innovation was the first step to empower the public, and a decade later, Steve Case, the CEO of one of the first web browsers, America Online, was instrumental in bringing internet access to a wider audience. From there came social media, smartphones, video conferencing, and now the Fame Revolution.

WHERE DOES THIS LEAVE US?

We are at a unique point in history when the world is moving faster than ever, and technology is transforming every aspect of life. Right now, fame is for everyone, but will it last? Or will the pendulum swing back to having designated gatekeepers controlling the information flow?

We do not know.

The U.S. government debated banning TikTok in 2023, but pressure from the public delayed the ban. But will they try again? Will AI remain open to the public, or will it be restricted and confined to a few? Only time will tell.

What we do know is that the window of opportunity is wide open for you to share your gifts. So, I advise you to take this unique historical moment and share your gifts liberally with the world.

ENCORE

Credits

As I write, I feel that I have just received the Oscar Award for completing a book in the nonfiction category. Just like the countless of actors standing at the podium, I have a list that is too long, and yet I am bursting with joy, gratitude, and the need to honor all with a thank you. When will have the chance to publish a book again? And to immortalize my gratitude?

I could not have done this without the countless mentors, teachers, friends, family, and colleagues who stood by me. So, I am providing acknowledgment and, similar to a movie, a long list of credits. When each person should be remembered and thanked.

* * *

First and foremost, I want to thank David Meerman Scott. Thank you for the challenge you gave me. I always said I would write a book, but I was more like the 80 percent of Americans who harbored a lofty dream, not believing it would come true. But with your matter-of-fact outline of the possibility and challenge to me, I believed and took it on. Three years later, I have this book in hand. Thank you.

To my business partner and nephew-in-law, Zachary Lewis Houghton, thank you for keeping the roof over our heads as I spent countless hours writing. Also, I am grateful for your faith in the project and for being the consummate editor with a keen design eye, helping realize my dream of having a book cover that would remind the reader of Andy Warhol.

To Lisa Duncan, my voicewriter, I am grateful for your loyalty and support. When I was lost in the woods of words and handed over my messy second draft, somehow, you could make sense of my vision for the book.

To my honest critics, Sage Toomey, Neil Beam, Ingvil Gaasland, and Anne Blütecher Holter, thank you for your honesty and for chopping the book into a million pieces. At certain times, each of you turned my life upside down, yet the quality would not be as good without that. I am so grateful for your honesty. I cried tears of gratitude and feel blessed to have critics and friends like you by my side.

To my editors, Lisa Duncan, Zachary L. Taylor, and Richard Willett, I am honored to have had you edit my book, and I am truly grateful for your keen eyes finding the right words and cleaning up the book. A special thank you to our proofreader Lynda Rozell for ensuring all the I's are dotted and the T's are crossed.

To my designer, Olivier Darbonville, thank you for interpreting the ideas brought to you and bringing so many concepts to life. It has been a pleasure.

To my fellow communicators who have spent countless hours discussing and dialoguing the importance of strategic communications, particularly to Mike White, Ana Manrique, Marleen Laschet, Zontee Hou, Dennis Larsen, Anne Steenstrup-Duch, Cathrine Torp, Marc Cloosterman, Uzy Igweatu, Hege J. Tunstad, Sudipa Chakraborty, Professor Myrtle Jones, and Jesse Scinto. A special thank you to Ingrid Helsingen Warner for the monthly breakfasts, keeping us updated and inspired. And to Alison Cran. We spent many hours of travel and time dialoguing best practices, and here we are. Thank you for the journey.

To EACD (European Association of Communications Directors): I am deeply grateful for your strategic communication leadership. Your dynamic, innovative, and nurturing community has been instrumental in refining my understanding of industry best practices in this constantly changing business landscape.

To Professor Dragana Bozin: I am forever grateful for your feedback regarding my thesis on fame and the development of Diotima's Fame Ladder. You gave me the confidence to add these ideas to the book.

To Bjørn Richard Johansen and Loveleen Rihel Brenna: Thank you for the last-minute assistance enriching the book. Your contributions made a big difference.

To my clients: Thank you for sharing your stories. This book would not be as rich without your examples. It has been an honor to serve you and witness your growth and success.

Mentors and teachers

Professor Peggy Brønn, my mentor and collaborator: It is truly an honor to have worked with you on CCS and to have been allowed to conduct research with you and present our paper at the IEA GHGT-14. It was the seed that gave me confidence to write. Thank you.

Dr. Alexander Buhmann and Prof. Dr. Ansgar Zerfass: Thank you for your guidance and the time you dedicated to counseling me. Your insights on best practices have been decisive in shaping the direction of my professional journey. I also deeply appreciate your leadership in founding and expanding #NORA – The Nordic Alliance for Communication & Management, one of the leading spaces for research, dialogue, and development in strategic communication.

Pattie Pao: I met you on my flight to attend the Obama Inauguration and sat next to you in row 7. Well, you turned my life upside down for the better. Your councel on business branding was invaluable, and sharing a bed with us on our crazy journey brings a smile and a chuckle.

Borghild Eldøen: Thank you for believing in me and advising me to finish my master's degree at Columbia University. You convinced me, and I completed it. More importantly, you taught me the importance of seeing and honoring everyone, and I will never forget your story about Conoco Philips.

Trudi Baldwin: I extend my heartfelt gratitude for your pioneering efforts in founding the Strategic Communications program at Columbia University. Our serendipitous meeting at the strategy lecture was a pivotal moment that positively changed the trajectory of my career.

Jim Palos: Thank you for founding the Institute of Media and Entertainment (IME) and inviting me to be part of its beginning. Learning from the giants in the media and entertainment industry and leading professors on innovation, branding, and entertainment economics from IESE, Princeton, and Northwestern gave me a foundation that has been the bedrock of my career and this book.

Professor David Aikman: Thank you for the exciting adventure at the Ethics and Public Policy Center (EPPC) and the privilege of being part of bringing your ideas and vision to life and teaching me the importance of accuracy, ethics, and integrity in reporting.

A heartfelt thanks to my family and friends
To Mom, thank you for the late-night discussions around the Kitchen table that could last until 2:00 a.m. Your love of politics, media, and culture transferred to me, challenging my ideas and teaching me the importance of reading, researching, and always questioning the source.

To Dad, thank you for being the greatest investor in my education driving along the countryside and talking about life.

To my brothers, thank you for the lively debates and sharpening my ideas with your invaluable perspectives. But most of all, for giving me the incredible joy of being an aunt to my wonderful nieces and nephews. They are truly the brightest joy and blessings in my life.

Thank you to my friends who have lent me their listening ears, supported me with their friendship, and given me the confidence to move forward— Karin Lillehei Bakhtiar, Heidi Stangeland, Yamilca Rodriguez, Hege M. F. Wennes, Sylvi Saure Finsrud, Stephanie DeLeonardis, Ragni Hatlebakk, and Odd Vidar Osen. And to my musical Chess friends—Mette Wasland, Shaun Reid, and Eilert Vigebo—for celebrating music, life, and friendship. The memories are still with me.

Café's my second home

This book would not have been possible without the cafes where I wrote. If I had been in Norway, my first and only place would be Kaffebrenneriert. Since I wrote this in the Phoenix area, I would like to thank Fair Trade Café and its owner, Stephanie Vasquez, for establishing a place where I mornings and weekends, sipping the house specialty, "The Phoenix." Thank you for creating a friendly place with the loveliest guests.

To JoJo Coffeehouse and Nanci Harrington—Thank you for letting me have my corner to write and have the celebratory Coffee Fleet.

And when I needed a break, my go-to was Black Rock Coffee—thank you for a breath of fresh air and providing a fusion of strong coffee and a smile. It made my day and gave me the extra push to move forward.

Thanks.

"Coffee is a language itself."

—JACKIE CHAN

Thank you to my fellow entrepreneurs

I decided to "burn all boats" during COVID-19, to risk it all and jump off the ledge of comfort to become an entrepreneur. I am indebted to the entrepreneurs who paved the way, willingly looking back to coach, mentor, and consult, lifting me through the valleys with the sweet ointments of words to nudge me in the right direction and celebrate at the mountain top---via masterminds and retreats to multiple webinars, books, and podcasts with hundreds of hours of conversations. Thank you -- Michael Hyatt, Nicolay Lange-Nielsen, Donald Miller, Dr. Bradley Nelson, Becky Graff, Phoenix West Devereux, Scott A Martin, Rachael Handley, Katie Carlson, Dr. Joe Dispenza, Lewis Howes, Fusun Rynart, Tory Dunlap, Claudette Anderson, Sean & Sax Whalen, Tony Robbins, Astrid Nöbauer, Dean Graziosi, Bridger Pennington, Marie Forleo, Molly McPherson, Tony & Bri Lister, Keith Cunningham, Tim Ferris, Pat Flynn, Russell Brunson, Kiana Danial, Ray Edwards, John Meese, Gerald & Allison Mayah Rose Rogers, Gary Vaynerchuk, Rachel Pedersen, Stone Fredrikson, Amy Joy, Tiffany Carter, Danielle LaPorte, Grant Cardone, Brandon & Natalie Dawson, Leila & Alex Hormozi, Mandy Perry, Chandler Bolt, and Michelle Sorro.

Variety is the Spice of Life

I am grateful for the blessing of having landed the jobs or projects of my dreams over and over again. For me, the experience I gained in varied industries has made for a unique, fulfilling, and decades-long career. These significant experiences allowed me to build new skills and expertise in each position, learning powerful and humbling lessons about my capabilities, perceptions, misconceptions, and venturing way outside of my comfort zone. I have learned not to hide my interest or competency, and I understand that nobody knows it all. Today, I am thankful for each and every one of these positions, employers, and clients. I am a cocktail made up of all of the industries, supervisors, colleagues, associations, and committees with which I have been involved. All of this prepared me to be who and what I am today, and I am so grateful for what I can share because of it.

Many thanks to the many.

ABOUT THE AUTHOR

TORUND BRYHN, a Norwegian American, is on a mission to make people, organizations, and causes famous for their contributions to the world.

For the past two decades, she has expanded the influence and rehabilitated the reputation of brands across energy, climate, government, entertainment, and travel sectors. Her master's degree in strategic communication from Columbia University adds an academic edge to her practical expertise.

With a track record of securing media attention from prestigious outlets like BBC, *TIME*, and the *Telegraph*, she leads her team at Diotima Strategies to transform companies and leaders into pioneers in their respective industry sectors.

As the host of the "Become Famous" podcast, she delves into the intricacies of public influence and leadership. As a seasoned speaker, Torund has graced stages across three continents on the power of words to ignite action.

When not working, Torund hangs out with her nieces and nephews or at a café in Norway or Arizona, writing or engaging in debates and conversations with friends.

NOTES

Introduction

1   This quote was first printed in the program for a 1968 exhibition of Warhol's work at the Moderna Museet in Stockholm, Sweden.

2   Chris Hayes, "On the Internet, We're Always Famous," *The New Yorker*, September 24, 2021, https://www.newyorker.com/news/essay/on-the-internet-were-always-famous.

3   Fab 5 Freddy, "Smoke Signals," The Andy Warhol Diaries: The Inner Life of an Artist No One Really Knew, episode 1, aired March 9, 2022.

4   Merriam-Webster. Definition of Public Figure. November 7, 2023. Accessed December 6, 2023. https://www.merriam-webster.com/dictionary/public%20figure.

PART ONE: WHY Fame Revolution and Why You Are a Public Figure

5   Alex Barinka. "Meta's Instagram Users Reach 2 Billion, Closing In on Facebook." Bloomberg. October 26, 2022 .https://www.bloomberg.com/news/articles/2022-10-26/meta-s-instagram-users-reach-2-billion-closing-in-on-facebook.

6   Blake Droesch. "Is Everyone on Instagram an Influencer?" eMarketers. March 5, 2019. Accessed October 23, 2023. https://www.insiderintelligence.com/content/is-everyone-on-instagram-an-influencer.

7   Tubics. "How Many YouTube Channels Are There?" Accessed October 2023. https://www.tubics.com/blog/number-of-youtube-channels#:~:text=As%20of%202020%2C%20there%20are,hours%20of%20video%20every%20minute.

8   HubSpot "Instagram Marketing." Accessed October 2, 2023. https://www.hubspot.com/instagram-marketing.

9   "Tech Experts Talk About Internet's Impact on Daily Life," *Today at Elon*, Elon University, June 27, 2018, https://www.elon.edu/u/news/2018/06/27/tech-experts-talk-about-internets-impact-on-daily-life.

10   "How Many Smartphones Are in the World?," BankMyCell, Accessed October 2, 2023, https://www.bankmycell.com/blog/how-many-phones-are-in-the-world#:~:text=According%20to%20Statista%2C%20the%20current,world's%20population%20owns%20a%20smartphone, citing Statista.

11   ChatGPT, conversation with author, October 23, 2023.

12   Verified with ChatGPT. August 23, 2023.

13   Wikipedia contributors, 'Marie Forleo,' Wikipedia, The Free Encyclopedia, [access date: October 22, 2023], https://en.wikipedia.org/wiki?curid=38364467.

14   BER staff, "Paying Attention: The Attention Economy," *Berkley Economic Review,* March 31, 2020, Accessed October 2, 2023, https://econreview.berkeley.edu/paying-attention-the-attention-economy/.

15   Michael Wolf, *The Entertainment Economy: How Mega-Media Forces Are Transforming Our Lives* (New York: Crown Currency, 1999).

16   Philipp Kristian Diekhöner, *The Trust Economy: Building Strong Networks and Realising Exponential Value in the Digital Age* (Singapore: Marshall Cavendish International (Asia) Pte Ltd, 2017), Kindle edition.

17   B. Joseph Pine II and James H. Gilmore, "Welcome to the Experience Economy," *Harvard Business Review,* July–August 1998, https://hbr.org/1998/07/welcome-to-the-experience-economy.

18   Bruce Upbin. "The Web Is Much Bigger (And Smaller) Than You Think." *Forbes.* April 24, 2012. https://www.forbes.com/sites/ciocentral/2012/04/24/the-web-is-much-bigger-and-smaller-than-you-think/?sh=7fa129417619.

19   Kalev Leetaru. "Is Social Media's Self-Service Fame The Root Of Online Toxicity?" *Forbes.* Updated July 17, 2019. Accessed October 22, 2023. https://www.forbes.com/sites/kalevleetaru/2019/07/17/is-social-medias-self-service-fame-the-root-of-online-toxicity/?sh=2e4060ca63fd.

20   Belle Wong, J.D., "Top Social Media Statistics And Trends Of 2023," *Forbes,* May 18, 2023. Accessed October 2, 2023, https://www.forbes.com/advisor/business/social-media-statistics/#source.

21   Jessica DeMilt. "The Origins of Twitter," Pennington Creative. Accessed November 4, 2023. https://penningtoncreative.com/the-origins-of-twitter/#:~:text=On%20July%2015th%2C%202006%2C%20Twitter,South%20by%20Southwest%20Interactive%20conference.

22   The Guardian Advertising. Accessed November 4, 2023. https://advertising.theguardian.com/us/advertising/audience

23   Annabel Acton, "How To Stop Wasting 2.5 Hours On Email Every Day," *Forbes,* July 13, 2017. https://www.forbes.com/sites/annabelacton/2017/07/13/innovators-challenge-how-to-stop-wasting-time-on-emails/?sh=1e5aff5c9788.

24   Paula Peters, "Remote Work Is Rapidly Changing Business Writing," *Medium,* March 17, 2021, https://medium.com/@peterswriting/remote-work-is-rapidly-changing-business-writing-f8408f1205fc.

25   Ibid.

26   Josh Howarth. "27 New Online Shopping Statistics for 2023." *Exploding Topics,* January 6, 2023. Accessed September 13, 2023. https://explodingtopics.com/blog/online-shopping-stats.

27   Tyler Cowen, *What Price Fame?* (Boston: President and Fellows at Harvard College, 2000), 101.

28   "Jordan Peterson Comments on the Queen's Passing," *Jordan B. Peterson YouTube Channel*, September 9, 2022. Accessed September 10, 2022, https://www.youtube.com/watch?v=_5os9bT9zuo&t=373s.

29   Tyler Cowen, *What Price Fame?* (Boston: President and Fellows at Harvard College, 2000), 102.

30   Jamie L. Vernon, "Understanding the Butterfly Effect," *American Scientist,* May-June 2017, Volume 105, Number 3, 130, https://www.americanscientist.org/article/understanding-the-butterfly-effect.

31   Kathy O'Brien. *You Matter More Than You Think: Quantum Social Change for a Thriving World.* cCHANGE Press, 2021.

32   Ibid p. 110

33   Chris Hayes. "On the Internet, We're Always Famous." The New Yorker. September 24, 2021. https://www.newyorker.com/news/essay/on-the-internet-were-always-famous.

34   Emily Dickinson. "Fame is a bee." In The Poems of Emily Dickinson, edited by R. W. Franklin. Cambridge, MA: The Belknap Press of Harvard University Press, 1999. Accessed October 23, 2023. https://www.poetryfoundation.org/poems/52139/fame-is-a-bee-1788.

35   Eileen Shim. "The Science Behind Why You Look Weird In Your Selfies." Mic.com. Published March 28, 2014. Accessed October 23, 2023. https://www.mic.com/articles/86445/the-science-behind-why-you-look-weird-in-your-selfies."

36   Emily Hund. The Influencer Industry: The Quest for Authenticity on Social Media. Princeton, NJ: Princeton University Press, 2023. p. 20.

37   Ibid p. 7.

38   Ibid p. 7.

39   Carla A. Harris. "Expect to Win: 10 Proven Strategies for Thriving in the Workplace." New York, NY: Plume, 2010. 21.

40   Carla A. Harris. "Lead to Win: How to Be a Powerful, Impactful, Influential Leader in Any Environment." New York, NY: Avery Publishing, 2022. 124.

41   Michael Koenigs and Cameron Covell. "Is this the world's best bus driver?" ABC7 Eyewitness News KGO-TV (San Francisco, CA) and WABC-TV (New York, NY). January 18, 2023. Accessed September 4, 2023. https://abc7.com/norway-rob-bus-driver-tiktok-viral-dance/12712988/

42   Valerie Bonk. "A UPS driver started posting dog pictures in 2013. It's now a viral sensation with 1.6M likes." USAToday.com. Updated January 9, 2020. https://www.usatoday.com/story/news/nation/2020/01/08/ups-dogs-facebook-instagram-twitter-ups-driver-goes-viral/2842966001/.

43   Tom T. "Avskiltet Norway Rob." Buss Magasinet. April 11, 2023. https://bussmagasinet.no/avskiltet-norway-rob/.

44   Tara Coomans. "How to Skyrocket Your Business to the Top With Thought Leadership and Visibility," Entrepreneur. December 19, 2022. Accessed September 19, 2023. https://www.entrepreneur.com/leadership/the-most-successful-leaders-are-the-most-visible-heres/439421#:~:text=Being%20visible%20is%20about%20serving,speaking%20out%20on%20social%20issues.

45   Tonia E. Ries. "2023 Edelman Trust Barometer: Global Report" Edelman, January 15, 2023, https://www.edelman.com/sites/g/files/aatuss191/files/2023-03/2023%20Edelman%20Trust%20Barometer%20Global%20Report%20FINAL.pdf.

46   Ibid.

47   Stock Analysis. "Box, Inc. Revenue." Accessed October 13, 2023. https://stockanalysis.com/stocks/box/revenue/.

48   Tonia E. Ries. "2023 Edelman Trust Barometer: Global Report" Edelman, January 15, 2023, https://www.edelman.com/sites/g/files/aatuss191/files/2023-03/2023%20Edelman%20Trust%20Barometer%20Global%20Report%20FINAL.pdf.

49   Ibid.

50   Adam Bryant. "The Quality that Box CEO Aaron Levie Values Most in New Hires: Humility." LinkedIn, September 23, 2019. Accessed September 4, 2023. https://www.linkedin.com/pulse/quality-box-ceo-aaron-levie-values-most-new-hires-humility-bryant/.

51   Joe Kingsbury, David Bersoff, Tusar Barik, and Hannah Buzicky. "2021 B2B Thought Leadership Impact Study." Edelman LinkedIn. September 21, 2021. https://business.linkedin.com/marketing-solutions/b2b-thought-leadership-research.

52   Tumisang Bogwasi. "Brand Storytelling Statistics." The Brand Shop. Accessed August 25, 2023. https://www.blog.thebrandshopbw.com/brand-storytelling-statistics-and-trends/#:~:text=Here%20are%20some%20key%20brand,stories%20influence%20their%20purchasing%20decisions

53   Jen Dewar. "7 Learning and Development Statistics You Should Know." WorkRamp.com. March 20, 2022. https://www.workramp.com/blog/learning-and-development-statistics/#:~:text=94%25%20of%20workers%20said%20they,their%20onboarding%20process%20was%20exceptional.

54   Kelli Mason. "Over 4 in 5 Gen Z Adults Want Companies to Take a Stand." JobSage. May 16, 2022. Accessed December 3, 2023. https://www.jobsage.com/blog/companies-social-issues-survey/

55   Jim Stengel, *Grow: How Ideals Power Growth and Profit at the World's 50 Greatest Companies* (New York, NY: Currency, 2011), Kindle location 119.

56   Michael Wolf, *The Entertainment Economy: How Mega-Media Forces Are Transforming Our Lives* (New York: Crown Currency, 2010), Kindle location 1012 of 3874.

57   Sam Orches."Taco Bell stays fresh and innovative as it builds on a six-decade legacy." *Nation's Restaurant News*. Nov 14, 2023. https://www.nrn.com/quick-service/taco-bell-stays-fresh-and-innovative-it-builds-six-decade-legacy

58   Markham Heid. "Does Thinking Burn Calories? Here's What the Science Says." *TIME*. September19, 2018. https://time.com/5400025/does-thinking-burn-calories/

59   Mimi Montgomery. "Do You Have What It Takes to Be the Taylor Swift Reporter?" *Washingtonian*. September 13, 2023. https://www.washingtonian.com/2023/09/13/do-you-have-what-it-takes-to-be-the-taylor-swift-reporter/.

60   Mimi Montgomery. "Taylor Swift Reporting Job: Will a Legally Blonde-Inspired Video Win a Maryland Woman the Gig?" *Washingtonian*. September 29, 2023. https://www.washingtonian.com/2023/09/29/taylor-swift-reporting-job-will-a-legally-blonde-inspired-video-win-a-maryland-woman-the-gig/.

61   Chris Willman. "Gannett's Taylor Swift Reporter, Revealed: Meet Bryan West, the First Full-Time Swiftie Journalist (EXCLUSIVE)." *Variety*. https://variety.com/2023/music/news/taylor-swift-reporter-usa-today-gannett-hire-1235781178/.

62   Francesca Gino. "Research: It Pays to Be Yourself." *Harvard Business Review.* February 13, 2020. https://hbr.org/2020/02/research-it-pays-to-be-yourself.

63   Jori Finkel. "Art auctions on cruise ships lead to anger and lawsuits." *The New York Times,* July 16, 2008. https://www.nytimes.com/2008/07/16/arts/16iht-16crui.14537457.html.

PART TWO: *How to Become Famous: The Public Figure Strategy*

64   Taylor Swift Switzerland. "Secret Sessions." 2019. Accessed October 30, 2023. https://taylorswiftswitzerland.ch/index.php/wiki/secret-sessions/

65   Taylor Swift Switzerland. "13 Management." Accessed October 30, 2023. https://taylorswiftswitzerland.ch/index.php/wiki/13-management/

66   Seija Rankin. "Taylor Swift divulges the secrets to her album Easter eggs in *EW's* exclusive video." *Entertainment Weekly.* May 9, 2019. https://ew.com/music/2019/05/09/taylor-swift-secrets-album-easter-eggs/

67   The Editors. "40+ of Taylor Swift's Most Brilliant Easter Eggs, Decoded." *Cosmopolitan.* Accessed October 30, 2023. https://www.cosmopolitan.com/entertainment/celebs/g45551106/taylor-swift-easter-eggs/

68   Brendan Morrow. "All the records Taylor Swift has broken in 2023." *The WEEK.* Accessed October 30, 2023. https://theweek.com/culture/entertainment/1025810/taylor-swift-records-2023#

69   Buzz Feed. "21 Behind-The-Scenes Facts About Taylor Swift's Eras Tour That'll Make You Appreciate The Concert (And Movie) Even More." Yahoo! Entertainment. Accessed October 30, 2023. https://www.yahoo.com/entertainment/21-behind-scenes-facts-taylor-183638271.html#~:text=9.,Menu%2C%20Room%2C%20and%20more.

70   Rania Aniftos. "Taylor Swift's Eras Tour Truck Company Owner Speaks Out About 'Life-Changing' Bonuses." *Billboard.* Accessed October 30, 2023. https://www.billboard.com/music/music-news/taylor-swift-eras-tour-truck-company-owner-bonuses-1235384480/

71   "Mid-Year Top Tours: No. 1 Taylor Swift's 'Eras Tour.'" Pollstar. Accessed, November 18, 2023. https://news.pollstar.com/2023/06/26/mid-year-top-tours-no-1-taylor-swifts-eras-tour/

72   Jeannie Kopstein and Mariah Espada. "The Staggering Economic Impact of Taylor Swift's Eras Tour." https://time.com/6307420/taylor-swift-eras-tour-money-economy/

73   "Ben Sisario. How Taylor Swift's Eras Tour Conquered the World." *The New York Times.* Aug. 5, 2023. https://www.nytimes.com/2023/08/05/arts/music/taylor-swift-eras-tour.html.

74   Misbah Haque. "How much do the pros (like Alex Hormozi) spend on their content marketing strategies." Mizhq.com. Accessed August 25, 2023.. https://mizhq.com/how-much-do-the-pros-spend-on-their-content-marketing-strategies/.

75   David Patrick. "The Math Of Adele's Album Releases: Can A Hidden Pattern Help Predict When She'll Release Next?." AoPS. Accessed August 25, 2023.https://artofproblemsolving.com/blog/articles/the-math-of-adeles-album-releases.

76   Ameet Ranadive "Lessons from Pixar 1: The Braintrust." *Medium* January 11, 2016. https://medium.com/great-business-stories/lessons-from-pixar-1-the-braintrust-e306843a5153.

77   Ibid.

78   Ibid.

79   Elizabeth Isele. "When Starting A Business, You Need A Brain Trust." *Forbes.* Dec 23, 2014. https://www.forbes.com/sites/nextavenue/2014/12/23/when-starting-a-business-you-need-a-brain-trust/?sh=11a5a8501ce2.

80   Deena Prichep. "Like Moths To A Flame: Why Modern-Day Guests Always Gather In The Kitchen." NPR. December 22, 2018. https://www.npr.org/sections/thesalt/2018/12/22/678952170/like-moths-to-a-flame-why-modern-day-guests-always-gather-in-the-kitchen#:~:text=%22I%20think%20people%20want%20to,that%20glass%20of%20wine%20down.

81   Josh Dornbrack."The rise of the Chief of Staff." *Business Leader.* April 4, 2023. Accessed August 26, 2023. https://www.businessleader.co.uk/rise-of-the-chief-of-staff/

82   Dan Ciampa. "The Case for a Chief of Staff." *Harvard Business Review.* Issue: May–June 2020. Accessed August 13, 2023. https://hbr.org/2020/05/the-case-for-a-chief-of-staff

83   Christine Barton, Nicki Cave, Phillip Cook, and Martin Reeves. June 12, 2020. "The Heart of CEO Effectiveness." https://www.bcg.com/publications/2020/heart-ceo-effectiveness.

84   The Chief of Staff Association. Accessed August 27, 2023. https://www.csa.org/

85   Jessica Stillman. "Your Self-Promoting Is More Annoying Than You Think." *INC Magazine.* October 27, 2014. Accessed August 26, 2023. https://www.inc.com/jessica-stillman/your-self-promoting-is-more-annoying-than-you-think.html

86   Hugh McIntyre. "This 23-Year-Old Helped Make Kygo One Of The Biggest Names In Music." *Forbes.* November 25, 2016. Accessed August 27, 2023. https://www.forbes.com/sites/hughmcintyre/2016/11/25/x-this-23-year-old-helped-make-kygo-one-of-the-biggest-names-in-music/?sh=a8b093c17b53

87   Variety Staff. "Kygo and Manager Myles Shear Launch Label With Sony Music (EXCLUSIVE)." *Variety.* October 4, 2018. Accessed August 27, 2023. https://variety.com/2018/music/news/kygo-myles-shear-label-sony-1202967454/

88   Menios Constantinou, "Fame and Fortune Is No Fast Track to Happiness," *IMPACT,* Australian Catholic University. Accessed March 20, 2022. https://www.impact.acu.edu.au/lifestyle/fame-and-fortune-is-no-fast-track-to-happiness,

89   Conversation with ChapGPT and validated the list. November 23. 2023.

90   Link to (RED) Logo: https://www.red.org/.

91   Ron Nixon. "Bottom Line for (Red)" *The New York Times.* February 6, 2008. Accessed August 25, 2023. https://www.nytimes.com/2008/02/06/business/06red.html.

92   Gabriel Beltrone. "Bono is Superbrand." *AdWeek*. September 28, 2014. Accessed August 25, 2023. https://www.adweek.com/brand-marketing/bono-superbrand-who-makes-world-better-place-160395/.

93   Nikki Carlson. "Why Giving Back Increases Brand Loyalty." *Forbes*. Jun 10, 2019. https://www.forbes.com/sites/theyec/2019/06/10/why-giving-back-increases-brand-loyalty/?sh=c75cd1570d29.

94   Simon Evans. "Around the world in 22 carbon capture projects." CarbonBrief. October 7, 2014. Accessed October 28, 2022. https://www.carbonbrief.org/around-the-world-in-22-carbon-capture-projects/

95   "Global Status CCS 2021." Global CCS Institute, page 14. https://www.globalccsinstitute.com/wp-content/uploads/2021/11/Global-Status-of-CCS-2021-Global-CCS-Institute-1121.pdf

96   Lynn S. Paine. "What Does "Stakeholder Capitalism" Mean to You?" *Harvard Business Review*. September – October 2023. Accessed December 26, 2023. https://hbr.org/2023/09/what-does-stakeholder-capitalism-mean-to-you.

97   Rashad D. Grove. "11 Usher songs that changed the game forever," *Revolt*. October, 15, 2018. https://www.revolt.tv/article/2018-10-15/98901/11-usher-songs-that-changed-the-game-forever/#:~:text=After%20his%20first%20single%20failed,have%20success%20on%20the%20charts.

98   Robert Murray. "This is what makes brands stand out." LinkedIn. Accessed. November 23, 2023. https://www.linkedin.com/posts/robbiemurray_branding-brandingtips-brandbuilding-activity-7106184467504869376-Wbl-/

99   Russell Brunson. "Throwing Rocks At The Red Ocean." LinkedIn. May 17, 2019. https://www.linkedin.com/pulse/throwing-rocks-red-ocean-russell-brunson/

100 Jessica Hetherington. "If everyone likes you, you aren't being real enough" LinkedIn. February 10, 2017. https://www.linkedin.com/pulse/everyone-likes-you-arent-being-real-enough-jessica-hetherington/

101 Hans Christian Andersen, "The Emperor's New Clothes," trans. Jean Hersholt, last modified February 23, 2023, The Hans Christian Andersen Center, Department for the Study of Culture, Faculty of Humanities, University of Southern Denmark, https://andersen.sdu.dk/vaerk/hersholt/TheEmperorsNewClothes_e.html.

102 Ibid.

103 Ibid.

104 Ibid.

105 Based on materials from MIT course taken in 2013 and verified with ChatGPT. November 26, 2023.

106 Davia Temin "You Have 15 Minutes To Respond To A Crisis: A Checklist of Dos And Don'ts." *Forbes*. August .6, 2015, https://www.forbes.com/sites/daviatemin/2015/08/06/you-have-15-minutes-to-respond-to-a-crisis-a-checklist-of-dos-and-donts/?sh=705714fa50a8

107 "The Six Principles of CERC," The Centers for Disease Control's (CDC) Crisis and Emergency Risk Communication (CERC) manual, 2018, accessed November 27, 2023, https://emergency.cdc.gov/cerc/ppt/CERC_Introduction.pdf.

108 Legal Information Institute. Definition of Public Figure. Accessed December 7, 2023. https://www. law.cornell.edu/wex/public_figure

109 "Public Figures vs. Private Figures: Which one are you?" Lubin Austermuehle. Accessed, December 28, 2023 https://www.chicagobusinesslawfirm.com/public-figures-vs-private-figures-which-one-are-.

110 Melanie LoBue. "The Business Case for Reputation." REPTRAK Blog post. August 21, 2018. https://www.reptrak.com/blog/the-business-case-for-reputation/#:~:text=Yes%2C%20really.,an%20 average%20of%20%241%20billion.

111 Rory F. Knight and Deborah Pretty. "Reputation & Value." Oxford Metrica 2019. https://www. oxfordmetrica.com/public/CMS/Files/488/01RepComAIG.pdf

112 Sam Meredith. "*A financial banana republic:* UBS-Credit Suisse deal puts Switzerland's reputation on the line." CNBC. March 21, 2023. https://www.cnbc.com/2023/03/21/ubs-credit-suisse-deal-puts-switzerlands-reputation-on-the-line.html.

113 Ibid.

114 AON "Managing Risk: How To Maximize Performance In Volatile Times." https://www.aon. com/2019-top-global-risks-management-economics-geopolitics-brand-damage-insights/index.html

115 Rory F. Knight and Deborah Pretty. "Reputation & Value." Oxford Metrica 2019 https://www. oxfordmetrica.com/public/CMS/Files/488/01RepComAIG.pdf

PART THREE: *The Exploration of Fame*

116 Martini Fisher. "Diotima and the Philosophy of Love." MartiniFisher website. December 21, 2022. Accessed October 23, 2023. https://martinifisher.com/2022/12/21/diotima-and-the-origin-of-platonic-love/

117 Mark K. Setton. "Hidden Foundations of Western Philosophy: Diotima and the Ladder of Love." LinkedIn. February 11, 2022. Accessed October 28, 2023. https://www.linkedin.com/pulse/hidden-founder-western-philosophy-brdiotima-ladder-love-setton/

118 Joseph Epstein. "Think You Have a Book in You? Think Again." *The New York Times,* Published September 28, 2002. Accessed October 28, 2023. https://www.nytimes.com/2002/09/28/opinion/think-you-have-a-book-in-you-think-again.html

119 Jo Confino and Br Pháp Hữu. "Connecting to Our Roots: Ancestors, Continuation and Transformation." The Way Out Is In, Episode 5, Plum Village, September 10, 2021. https:// plumvillage.org/podcast/connecting-to-our-roots-ancestors-continuation-and-transformation.

120 BBC. "The Coronation of His Majesty the King and Her Majesty the Queen Consort on the BBC – Key Facts and Figures." BBC Media Centre. Accessed October 29, 2023. Updated: May 5, 2023. https://www.bbc.com/mediacentre/2023/coronation-on-the-bbc-key-facts-and-figures#:~:text=The%20Coronation%20Ceremony%20and%20Coronation,event%20ever%20on%20 BBC%20iPlayer.

121 Brené Brown. *Daring Greatly: How the Courage to Be Vulnerable Transforms the Way We Live, Love, Parent, and Lead.* 1st ed. Avery, 2012, p. 145.

122 "Interview with Adele – 'The bigger your career gets, the smaller your life gets,'" SVT/NRK/*Skavlan*, December 11, 2015, https://www.youtube.com/watch?v=16cH5a16Oig.

123 Russell Brunson, "Expert Secrets." Hay House Inc May 2020, 82–83.

124 Ibid. p. 82–83.

125 Sebastian Ocklenburg, Ph.D. "5 Reasons We Want to Be Remembered." *Psychology Today*, December 30, 2022 https://www.psychologytoday.com/us/blog/the-asymmetric-brain/202212/5-reasons-why-people-wish-to-be-remembered-after-death.

126 Sylvia Plath. "The Unabridged Journals of Sylvia Plath Quotes," Anchor Publishing. December 18, 2007. Accessed October 29, 2023. Goodreads: https://www.goodreads.com/quotes/1280815-there-is-still-time-to-veer-to-sally-forth-knapsack#:~:text=There%20is%20still%20time%20to%20veer%2C%20to%20sally%20forth%2C%20knapsack,Shall%20she%2C%20shall%20she%20veer%3F

Notes on the Usage of AI Tools:

With the emergence of ChatGPT and other AI tools, it is necessary to indicate when AI is used, yet the preferred method of doing so is still evolving. In this book, we followed the guidelines in the Chicago Manual of Style, which instructs me to log my conversations with AI as an author. Ironically, as an author, I am asked to log my conversations with AI, but not the countless conversations I have had with people while writing this book. In these murky times, without clear direction on what types of conversation, I have referenced in the text or the notes the conversations with individuals and AI that influenced the book's content, such as when I asked how many tasks a mobile phone replaced or my conversation with Ingvil Gaasland on the downside to fame. -

Other usages:

ChatGPT:

- Validation: As many of my ideas are new, along with testing my ideas with colleagues, mentors, and academic leaders, I tested how ChatGPT would respond to Fame Revolution, Public Figure = people + public, Diotima Fame Ladder. Both humans and AI approved my thesis and theories.
- Encyclopedia and dictionary: Since ChatGPT is user-friendly for locating dates, definitions, and synonyms, it became my go-to resource. From there, I validated the information with reliable sources such as the Merriam-Webster dictionary for definitions, books, and Britannica for key historical dates and references.

Grammarly:

- Editing: As grammar and punctuation are two of my weaknesses when it comes to writing, most of the text in the book would go through Grammarly before I engaged an editor.

Scribbr:

- Plagiarism: The book has gone through the AI tool for detecting plagiarism. This is to ensure that I have cited all sources.

BIBLIOGRAPHY

Acton, Annabel. "How To Stop Wasting 2.5 Hours On Email Every Day." *Forbes*. July 13, 2017. https://www.forbes.com/sites/annabelacton/2017/07/13/innovators-challenge-how-to-stop-wasting-time-on-emails/?sh=1e5aff5c9788.

Acemoglu, Daron, and Simon Johnson. *Power and Progress: Our 1000-Year Struggle Over Technology and Prosperity*. Public Affairs, Hachette Books, 2023.

Adair, Douglass. *Fame and the Founding Fathers*. Carmel, Indiana: Liberty Fund INC, 1974.

Agar, Michael. *Language Shock: Understanding the Culture of Conversation*. New York, NY: William Morrow and Company, 1994.

Ahmed, Ajaz and Stefan Olander. *Velocity: The Seven New Laws for a World Gone Digital*. Westminster, UK: Ebury Digital, 2012.

Ariely, Dan. *Predictably Irrational: The Hidden Forces That Shape Our Decisions*. New York, NY: HarperCollins, 2009.

BankMyCell. "How Many Smartphones Are in the World?" Accessed October 2, 2023. https://www.bankmycell.com/blog/how-many-phones-are-in-the-world. Citing Statista.

Barabasi, Albert-Laszlo, and Jennifer Frangos. *Linked: The New Science of Networks*. La Vergne, TN: Basic Books, 2014.

Battelle, John. *The Search: How Google and Its Rivals Rewrote the Rules of Business and Transformed Our Culture*. Edmonton, Alberta: Portfolio, 2006.

Benardete, Seth, and Allan David Bloom. *Plato's Symposium*. Chicago, IL: University of Chicago Press, 2001.

BER staff. "Paying Attention: The Attention Economy." *Berkley Economic Review*. March 31, 2020. Accessed October 2, 2023. https://econreview.berkeley.edu/paying-attention-the-attention-economy/.

Bell, Marcus and Carolyn Bell. *Bellringer Branding Bible: The 5 Musician Branding Principles for Singers, Rappers, DJs, Music Producers, Composers, Writers, and Recording Artists. (Artist Development Book 1)*. SheBell Publishing, 2018.

Berger, Jonah. *Contagious: Why Things Catch On*. New York, NY: Simon & Schuster, 2016.

Bernays, Edward. *Propaganda*. Brooklyn, NY: Ig Publishing, 2004.

Biesenbach, Rob. *Unleash the Power of Storytelling: Win Hearts, Change Minds, Get Results*. Chicago, IL: Eastlawn Media, 2018.

Blank, Steve. *The Four Steps to the Epiphany: Successful Strategies for Products That Win*. 5th ed. Hoboken, New Jersey: Wiley, 2013.

Bohns, Vanessa. *You Have More Influence than You Think: How We Underestimate Our Power of Persuasion, and Why It Matters*. New York, NY: WW Norton, 2021.

Borne, Ben, CMP. "What's the Diff? Marketing, Communications and PR." Marketing News Canada. March 10, 2023. https://marketingnewscanada.com/news/whats-the-diff-marketing-communications-and-pr.

Bouchot, Henry. *A Millennial's Guide to Running for Office: How to Get Elected without Kissing the Ring*. Boston, MA: John Henry Publishers, 2021.

Brady, Kathleen. *Ida Tarbell: Portrait of a Muckraker*. Pittsburgh, PA: University of PittsburghPress, 1989.

Bragman, Howard. *Where's My Fifteen Minutes?: Get Your Company, Your Cause, or Yourself the Recognition You Deserve*. New York, NY: Portfolio, 2008.

Braudy, Leo. *The Frenzy of Renown: Fame and Its History.* New York, NY: Vintage Books, 1997.

Braun, Randi. *Something Major: The New Playbook for Women at Work.* Potomac, MD: New Degree Press, 2023.

Brenna, Loveleen Rihel, *The Parable of the Dog and the Peackock.* Phoenix, AZ: st. john's press, 2022.

Brosseau, Denise. *Ready to Be a Thought Leader?: How to Increase Your Influence, Impact, and Success.* Nashville, TN: John Wiley & Sons, 2013.

Brown, Brené. *Power of Vulnerability: Teachings on Authenticity, Connection and Courage.* Louisville, CO: Sounds True, 2012.

Brunson, Russell. *Expert Secrets: The Underground Playbook for Converting Your Online Visitors into Lifelong Customer.* Carlsbad, California: Hay House Inc, 2017.

Burkus, David. *Friend of a Friend: Understanding the Hidden Networks That Can Transform Your Life and Your Career.* Boston, MA: Houghton Mifflin Harcourt Publishing Company, 2018.

Cardone, Grant. *The 10X Rule: The Only Difference between Success and Failure.* Chichester, England: John Wiley & Sons, 2011.

Carson, Mel. *Introduction to Personal Branding: Ten Steps toward a New Professional You.* Scotts Valley, CA: CreateSpace Independent Publishing, 2016.

Chernow, Ron. *Titan: The Life of John D. Rockefeller, Sr.* 2nd ed. New York, NY: Vintage Books, 2004.

Clark, Tim, in collaboration with Alexander Osterwalder and Yves Pigneur. *Business Model You: A One-Page Method for Reinventing Your Career.* Hoboken, New Jersey: John Wiley & Sons, 2012.

Chan Kim, W., and Renee A. Mauborgne. *Blue Ocean Strategy, Expanded Edition: How to Create Uncontested Market Space and Make the Competition Irrelevant.* Boston, MA: Harvard Business School Press, 2015.

Clark, Dorie. *Entrepreneurial You: Monetize Your Expertise, Create Multiple Income Streams, and Thrive.* Boston, MA: Harvard Business Review Press, 2017.

Cloud, Henry. *The Power of the Other: The Startling Effect Other People Have on You, from the Boardroom to the Bedroom and beyond—and What to Do about It.* New York, NY: HarperBusiness, 2016.

Conway, J. North. *American Literacy: Fifty Books that Define Our Culture and Ourselves.* New York, NY: William Morrow and Company, 1993.

Cowen, Tyler. *What Price Fame?* Boston: President and Fellows at Harvard College, 2000.

Cracknell, Andrew. *The Real Mad Men: The Renegades of Madison Avenue and the Golden Age of Advertising.* Boulder, CO: Perseus Books, 2011.

D'Angour, Armand. *Socrates in Love: The Making of a Philosopher.* London, England: Bloomsbury Publishing PLC, 2019.

Deutscher, Guy. *The Unfolding of Language: An Evolutionary Tour of Mankind's Greatest Invention.* New York, NY: Metropolitan Books, 2005.

Dichter, Ernest. *The Strategy of Desire.* Edited by Ernest Dichter. Somerset, NJ: Transaction, 2002.

Diekhöner, Philipp Kristian. *The Trust Economy: Building Strong Networks and Realising Exponential Value in the Digital Age.* Singapore: Marshall Cavendish International (Asia) Pte Ltd, 2017. Kindle edition.

Dispenza, Dr. Joe. *Becoming Supernatural: How Common People Are Doing the Uncommon.* Hay House Inc., 2017.

Doherty, Thomas. *Little Lindy Is Kidnapped: How the Media Covered the Crime of the Century.* New York, NY: Columbia University Press, 2020.

Duffy, James P. *Lindberg vs. Roosevelt.* New York, NY: MJF Books, 2010.

Earls, Mark. *Herd: How to Change Mass Behaviour by Harnessing Our True Nature*. Chichester, England: John Wiley & Sons, 2009.

Easter, Michael. *The Comfort Crisis: Embrace Discomfort to Reclaim Your Wild, Happy, Healthy Self*. Emmaus, PA: Rodale Books, 2021.

Edwards, Betty. *Drawing on the Right Side of the Brain: A Course in Enhancing Creativity and Artistic Confidence*. New York, NY: TarcherPerigee, 2012.

Emre, Merve. *The Personality Brokers: The Strange History of Myers-Briggs and the Birth of Personality Testing*. New York, NY: Doubleday Books, 2018.

Ewen Stuart. *PR! A Social History of Spin*. New York, NY: Basic Books, 1996.

Ferguson, Niall. *The Square and the Tower: Networks and Power, from the Freemasons to Facebook*. London, UK: Penguin Press, 2018.

Flynn, Pat. *Superfans: The Easy Way to Stand out, Grow Your Tribe, and Build a Successful Business*. Redding, CA: New Type Publishing, 2019.

Freeman, Joanne, B. *Affairs of Honor: National Politics in the New Republic*. New Haven, CT: Yale University Press, 2001.

Garcia, Samuel. *Political Campaigns Online and on Social Media*. Self-published, 2015. Amazon.

Gooden, Philip. *Chaucer and the House of Fame*. Book 1 of Geoffrey Chaucer Mysteries. Sharpe Books, 2020.

Grant, Adam. *Power Moves: Lessons from Davos. Austin, TX*. Audible Originals. 2019.

Greene Robert. *The Laws of Human Nature*. New York: Viking, 2018.

Grimsgaard, Wanda. *Deign og Strategi: Processer og Metoder for Strategisk Utvikling av Design* [Design and Strategy: A Step-by-Step Guide]. Oslo, Norge: Cappelen Damm Akademisk, 2018.

Gorton, Stephanie. *Citizen Reporters: S.S. McClure, Ida Tarbell, and the Magazine That Rewrote America*. Hopewell, VA: Ecco Press, 2020.

Gutsche, Jeremy. *Create the Future. Tactics for Disruptive Thinking*. New York, NY: Fast Compass Press, 2020.

Harris, Carla A. *Expect to Win: 10 Proven Strategies for Thriving in the Workplace*. New York, NY: Plume, 2010.

Harris, Carla A. *Lead to Win: How to Be a Powerful, Impactful, Influential Leader in Any Environment*. New York, NY: Avery Publishing, 2022.

Harrison, Scott. *Thirst: A Story of Redemption, Compassion, and a Mission to Bring Clean Water to the World. Crown*. New York, NY: Currency, 2020.

Hayes, Chris. "On the Internet, We're Always Famous." *The New Yorker*. September 24, 2021. https://www.newyorker.com/news/essay/on-the-internet-were-always-famous.

Hennessy, Brittany. *Influencer: Building Your Personal Brand in the Age of Social Media*. Citadel Press: New York, NY, 2018.

Hogshead, Sally. *Fascinate. How to Make Your Brand Impossible to Resist*. New York, NY: Harper Business, 2014.

Hogshead, Sally. *How the World Sees You: Discover Your Highest Value Through the Science of Fascination*. New York, NY: Harper Business, 2016.

Holiday, Ryan. *Trust Me, I'm Lying: Confessions of a Media Manipulator*. London, England: Portfolio Penguin, 2013.

Hoover, Herbert. *American Individualism*, Kindle Edition. Stanford, CA: Hoover Press, 2016.

Hopkins, Claude C. *Scientific Advertising*. North Charleston, SC: CreateSpace Independent Publishing Platform, 2010.

Howes, Lewis. *The School of Greatness: A Real-World Guide to Living Bigger, Loving Deeper, and Leaving a Legacy.* Emmaus, Pennsylvania: Rodale, 2015

Hund Emily. *The Influencer Industry: The Quest for Authenticity on Social Media.* Princeton, NJ: Princeton University Press, 2023, 20.

Jackson, Curtis. *Hustle Harder, Hustle Smarter.* New York, NY: Amistad Press, 2023.

Johnson, Cynthia. *Platform: How to Fast-Track Your Personal Platform.* Berkeley, CA: Ten Speed Press, 2019.

Johnson, Spencer. *Who Moved My Cheese?* New York, NY: G.P. Putnam's Sons, 1998, 2002.

Kang, Karen. *Branding Pays: The Five-Step System To Reinvent Your Personal Brand.* Palo Alto, CA: Branding Pays Media, 2013.

Kawasaki, Guy, and Peg Fitzpatrick. *The Art of Social Media: Power Tips for Power Users.* New York, NY: Portfolio, 2014.

Knight, Phil. *Shoe Dog: A Memoir by the Creator of Nike.* New York, NY: Scribner Book Company, 2016.

Kotter, John P., and Dan S. Cohen. *The Heart of Change: Real-Life Stories of How People Change Their Organizations.* Boston, MA: Harvard Business Review Press, 2012.

Kovarik, Bill. *Revolutions in Communication: Media History from Gutenberg to the Digital Age.* 2nd ed. New York, NY: Bloomsbury Academic, 2015.

Kurtzman, Joel. *Thought Leaders: Insights on the Future of Business.* San Francisco: Jossey-Bass Publishers, 1998.

LaBalme, Victoria. *Risk Forward. Embrace the Unknown and Unlock Your Hidden Genius.* Carlsbad, California: Hay House Inc, 2021.

Lakoff, George. *Don't Think of an Elephant!: Know Your Values and Frame the Debate.* White River Junction, VT: Chelsea Green Publishing, 1990.

Lakoff, George, and Elisabeth Wehling. *Your Brain's Politics: How the Science of Mind Explains the Political Divide.* Exeter, England: Societas, 2016.

Layden, Tim. *Blood, Sweat and Chalk: The Ultimate Football Playbook: How the Great Coaches Built Today's Game.* New York, NY: Time Inc Home Entertainment. 2011.

Le Bon, Gustave. *The Crowd: A Study of the Popular Mind.* Sunnyvale, CA: Loki's Publishing, 2016.

Lee, Shannon. *Be Water My Friend: Teachings of Bruce Lee.* New York, NY: Flatiron Books, 2020.

Lippmann, Walter. *Public Opinion.* Overland Park, KS: Digireads.com, 2020.

Longhurst, Jon. *1000 True Fans: Use Kevin Kelly's Simple Idea to Earn A Living Doing What You Love.* Amazon KDP, 2017.

Marcus, Sharon. *The Drama of Celebrity.* Princeton, New Jersey: Princeton University Press, 2019.

Mark, Margaret, and Carol S. Pearson. *The Hero and the Outlaw: Building Extraordinary Brands through the Power of Archetypes.* New York, NY: McGraw-Hill Professional, 2001.

Martin, Everett. *The Behavior of Crowds: A Psychological Study.* Andesite Press, 2015.

McPherson, Molly. *Indestructible: Reclaim Control and Respond with Confidence in a Media Crisis.* Austin, TX: Mandala Tree Press, 2021.

Miller, Donald. *Building A Story Brand: Clarify Your Message so Customers Will Listen.* Nashville, TN: Thomas Nelson, 2018.

Miller, Donald. *Hero on a Mission: A Path to a Meaningful Life.* Nashville, TN: HarperCollins Focus, 2022.

Miller, Donald, and J. J. Peterson. *Marketing Made Simple: A Step-by-Step StoryBrand Guide for Any Business.* Nashville, TN: HarperCollins Focus, 2020.

Millman, Debbie. *Brand Thinking and Other Noble Pursuits.* New York, NY: Allworth Press, 2013.

Moore, Geoffrey A. *Crossing the Chasm, 3rd Edition: Marketing and Selling Disruptive Products to Mainstream Customers.* New York, NY: HarperBusiness, 2014.

Navidi, Sandra. *Superhubs: How the Financial Elite & Their Networks Rule the World.* London, UK: Nicholas Brealey Publishing, 2017.

Nayeri, Dina. *Who Gets Believed? When the Truth is Not Enough.* New York, NY: Catapult, 2023.

Neuman, Johanna. *Gilded Suffragists: The New York Socialites Who Fought for Women's Right to Vote.* New York, NY: New York University Press, 2019.

Packard, Vance. *The Hidden Persuaders.* Brooklyn, NY: Ig Publishing, 2007.

Payne, Tom. *Fame: What the Classics Tell Us About Our Cult of Celebrity.* London, UK: Picador, 2012.

Peppernell, Courtney. *Pillow Thoughts.* Kansas City, Missouri: Andrews McMeel Publishing, 2017.

O'Brien, Karen. *You Matter More than You Think: Quantum Social Change for a Thriving World.* cCHANGE Press, 2021.

Pine II, B. Joseph, and James H. Gilmore. "Welcome to the Experience Economy." *Harvard Business Review,* July–August 1998. https://hbr.org/1998/07/welcome-to-the-experience-economy.

Pitron, Guillaume. *The Dark Cloud: The Hidden Costs of the Digital World.* London, UK: Scribe Publications, 2023.

Piazza, Jo. *Celebrity, Inc: How Famous People Make Money.* New York, NY: Open Road Media, 2011.

Pope, Alexander. *The Temple of Fame.* London, UK: Forgotten Books, 1715, 2018.

Postman, Neil. *Amusing Ourselves to Death: Public Discourse in the Age of Show Business.* New York, NY: Penguin, 2010.

Rahe, Paul A. "Fame, Founders, and the Idea of Founding in the Eighteenth Century." *The Noblest Minds: Fame, Honor, and the American Founding,* edited by Peter McNamara, Rowman & Littlefield, 1999.

Reynolds, Garr. *The Naked Presenter: Delivering Powerful Presentations with or without Slides.* Indianapolis, IN: New Riders Publishing, 2010.

Ries, Al, and Laura Ries. *The Fall of Advertising and the Rise of PR.* New York, NY: HarperBusiness, 2004.

Ripley, Amanda. *The Unthinkable: Who Survives When Disaster Strikes—and Why.* New York, NY: Random House, 2009.

Ronzio, Chris. *The Business Playbook: How to Document and Delegate What You Do so Your Company Can Grow beyond You.* Austin, TX: Lioncrest Publishing, 2021.

Rose, Chris. *How to Win Campaigns: 100 Steps to Success.* London, UK: Earthscan, 2005.

Rose, Chris. *How to Win Campaigns: Communications for Change.* 2nd ed. London, England: Earthscan, 2010.

Sachs, Jonah. *Winning the Story Wars: Why Those Who Tell (and Live) the Best Stories Will Rule the Future.* Boston, MA: Harvard Business Review Press, 2012.

Sander, Emily. *An Insider's Perspective on the Chief of Staff: Why You Need One and How to Be a Great One.* Independently published, 2023.

Sax, David. *The Future is Analog: How to Create a Human World.* New York, NY: Hachette Book Group, 2023.

Schaefer, Mark. *Known: The Handbook for Building and Unleashing Your Personal Brand in the Digital Age.* Louisville, TN: Schaefer Marketing Solutions, 2017.

Scheuer, Jeffrey. *The Sound Bite Society: Television and the American Mind.* New York, NY: Four Walls Eight Windows, 1999.

Scott, David Meerman and Scott, Reico. *Fanocracy: Turning Fans into Customers and Customers into Fans.* Portfolio, 2020.

Scott, David Meerman, and Richard Jurek. *Marketing the Moon: The Selling of the Apollo Lunar Program.* Cambridge, Massachusetts: The MIT Press, 2014.

Scott, David Meerman. *The New Rules of Marketing and PR: How to Use Content Marketing, Podcasting, Social Media, AI, Live Video, and Newsjacking to Reach Buyers Directly.* 8th ed. Nashville, TN: John Wiley & Sons, 2022.

Sennett, Richard. *The Fall of Public Man.* New York: Knopf, 1977.

Sipos, Dario. *Digital Personal Branding: The Essential Guide to Online Personal Branding in the Digital Age.* Johannesburg, South Africa: Dwr-Distribution Wholesale Representation D.O.O., 2021.

Smit, Irene, and Astrid Van Der Hulst. *A Book That Loves You.* Amsterdam, Netherlands: DPG Media B.V. 2022.

Smith, Sally Bedell. *Reflected Glory.* New York, NY: Simon & Schuster, 1997.

Stancik, Cat, and Tobin Slaven. *Experts Never Chase: The Hassle-Free Guide for Expert-Based Entrepreneurs.* Bangor, ME: Musttryit! Media, 2021.

Stengel, Jim. *Grow: How Ideals Power Growth and Profit at the World's 50 Greatest Companies.* New York, NY: Currency, 2011.

Sullivan, Dan with Dr. Benjamin Hardy. *10X Is Easier than 2X: How World-Class Entrepreneurs Achieve More by Doing Less.* Carlsbad, CA: Hay House Inc., 2023.

Sullivan, Terry. *The Nerve Center: Lessons in Governing from the White House Chiefs of Staff.* College Station, TX: Texas A&M University Press, 2004.

Switalski, Bryan. *Mxltiply.* Leverage Clarity Publishing, 2021.

Tarbell, Ida M. *All in the Day's Work: An Autobiography.* Baltimore, MD: University of Illinois Press, 2003.

Tarbell, Ida M. *The History of the Standard Oil Company.* New York, NY: WW Norton, 1969.

The Andy Warhol Diaries: The Inner Life of an Artist No One Really Knew. Episode 1, "Smoke Signals." Netflix, March 9, 2022.

Trent, Judith S., Robert V. Friedenberg, and Robert E. Denton Jr. *Political Campaign Communication: Principles and Practices.* 7th ed. Lanham, Maryland: Rowman & Littlefield Publishing Inc., 2011.

Trout, Jack, and Al Ries. *Positioning: The Battle for Your Mind.* New York, NY: McGraw-Hill Professional, 2001.

Unerman, Sue, Kathryn Jacob, and Mark Edwards. *Belonging: The Key to Transforming and Maintaining Diversity, Inclusion and Equality at Work.* London, England: Bloomsbury Business, 2020.

Vaynerchuk, Gary. *The Thank You Economy.* New York, NY: HarperBusiness, 2011.

Weber, Ozlem Ahiska. *Authenticity to Agility: 4 Powerful Tools to Transform Your Career.* Vienna, Austria: OAW Publishing, 2021.

Weinberg, Steve. *Taking on the Trust: How Ida Tarbell Brought Down John D. Rockefeller and Standard Oil.* New York, NY: WW Norton, 2009.

Weiner, Eric. *The Socrates Express: In Search of Life Lessons from Dead Philosophers.* New York, NY: Simon & Schuster, 2020.

Whipple, Chris. *The Gatekeepers: How the White House Chiefs of Staff Define Every Presidency,* New York City, New York, Crown Publishing Group. 2017

Wiseman, Richard. *Moonshot: What Landing a Man on the Moon Teaches Us About Collaboration, Creativity, and the Mind-Set for Success.* London: TarcherPerigee, 2019.

Wish, Peter A. *The Candidate's 7 Deadly Sins the Candidate's 7 Deadly Sins: Using Emotional Optics to Turn Political Vices into Virtues*. Austin, TX: Lioncrest Publishing, 2020.

Witty, Adam, and Rusty Shelton. *Authority Marketing: How to Leverage 7 Pillars of Thought Leadership to Make Competition Irrelevant*. Charleston, SC: ForbesBooks, 2018.

Wolf, Michael. *The Entertainment Economy: How Mega-Media Forces Are Transforming Our Lives*. New York, NY: Crown Business, 2003.

Wong, Belle. "Top Social Media Statistics And Trends Of 2023." *Forbes*. Updated: May 18, 2023. Accessed October 2, 2023. https://www.forbes.com/advisor/business/social-media-statistics/#source.

Wu, Tim. *The Attention Merchants: The Epic Scramble to Get inside Our Heads*. New York, NY: Knopf Publishing Group, 2016.

Young, A. *Brand Media Strategy: Integrated Communications Planning in the Digital Era*. Basingstoke, England: Palgrave Macmillan, 2016.

Zweig, Jessica. *Be: A No-Bullsh*t Guide to Increasing Your Self-Worth by Simply Being Yourself*. Boulder, Colorado: Sounds True, 2021